One Hundred and One Reasons Why We Are Baptized

The First Principles and Ordinances Series
Volume Three – Baptism

Philip M. Hudson

Copyright 2019 by Philip M. Hudson.
The book author retains sole copyright
to his contributions to this book.

Published 2019.
Printed in the United States of America.

All rights reserved.

No portion of this book may be reproduced, stored in a
retrieval system, or transmitted in any form or by any means
– electronic, mechanical, photocopy, recording, scanning, or
other – except for brief quotations in critical reviews or articles,
without the prior written permission of the author.

ISBN 978-1-950647-14-9

Illustrations – Google Images.

This book may be ordered from online bookstores.

Publishng assistance by BookCrafters
Parker, Colorado.
www.bookcrafters.net

Our
baptism compels
us to consider the
possibility that we might
one day be like the Savior.
We believe that His grace consists
of the gifts and power by which we
may be brought to His perfection
and stature, so that we may
enjoy not only what
He has, but also
what He
is.

Those who
demand outward
evidence of the power
of God as a condition of
their belief seek to circumvent
the process by which both faith and
knowledge are developed. They want
the proof, but without having first paid
the price. As with adulterers, who expect
immediate gratification, they want to be
theologically titillated by experiencing
the result, but without having first
accepted the responsibilities
that come with baptism.

Table of Contents

- Acknowledgements..i
- Preface..v
- Introduction...ix
- One Through One Hundred and One...1
- One Hundred and Two Through One Hundred and Thirty Eight.................................203
- Appendix 1: One Hundred and One Reasons Why We Are Baptized..........................279
- Appendix 2: An Additional Three Dozen Reasons..285
- Appendix 3: Discussion Questions..291
- Appendix 4: Baptismal Prayers in The Standard Works..361
- Appendix 4: The Fourth Article of Faith..363
- Appendix 5: Bible Dictionary (Baptism)..365
- Appendix 6: Topical Guide (Baptism)...369
- Appendix 7: Brigham Young's Testimony Relating to His Baptism.............................373
- Appendix 8: Lorenzo Snow's Testimony Relating to His Baptism...............................375
- Appendix 9: Phil Hudson's Testimony of Baptism..377
- About The Author..381
- By The Author...383
- What More Can I Say?...387

The key
to liberation
from our bondage
to sin, to our freedom
to become, is an adjustment
in attitude that is reflected in
our desire to be born again. To
paraphrase Helen Keller, the real
tragedy is not those of us who
are born without sight, but
those of us who do
not have vision.

Acknowledgements

In this volume, I have attributed quotations to original authors whenever possible, as well as when I have editorialized their ideas. In many cases, however, my language will naturally reflect the teachings of leaders and lay members of The Church of Jesus Christ of Latter-day Saints.

The list of those who have contributed to this book is endless. As I have organized my own thoughts, I have realized how heavily I have borrowed from the towering examples of those who, over the years, have been my mystical mentors, my sensible chaperones, my spiritual guides, my surrogate saviors, my compassionate critics, and everything in between.

They are my avatars, manifestations of deity in bodily forms, my na'vi, the visionaries, who communicate with God on a level to which I can only aspire, and my tsaddik, whom I esteem as intuitive interpreters of biblical law and scripture. They are my divine teachers incarnate. They have offered listening ears, extended open arms, lifted my spirits, shown me the way, emboldened me with words of encouragement, cheered me on with wise counsel, stretched my mind, reinforced my faith, strengthened my testimony, vitalized my conversion, helped me to discover my wings, given immaterial support, provided of their means, taught me humility, been there to steady me, soothed my troubled soul, stepped in to nurture me, led me to fountains of living water, wet my parched lips with inspired counsel, and bound up my wounds.

Every family member, teacher, student, classmate, business associate, mentor, friend, priesthood brother, relief society sister, ordinance worker, and temple patron with whom I have come in contact has influenced me. Every author, poet, journalist, essayist, thespian, satirist, and lyricist, has moved me in some positive way. They have taught me to find the silk purse in every sow's ear and the silver lining in every cloud. When I have been given a lemon, they have shown me where to find the recipe for lemonade.

With their positive influence, I have learned to keep tempests in teapots where they belong, and to put them in perspective. I have tried to retain the joyful anticipation of the optimistic little boy, who, when faced with the daunting task of shoveling up an enormous pile of manure in a horse stall near his home, enthusiastically set about his task with the exclamation: "There's got to be a pony in there, somewhere!"

Well did the poet teach: "No man is an island, entire of itself. Every man is a piece of the continent, a part of the main. If a clod be washed away by the sea, Europe is the less, as well as if a promontory were, as well as if a manor of thy friends or of thine own were. Any man's death diminishes me, because I am involved in mankind, and therefore never send to know for whom the bell tolls. It tolls for thee." (John Donne).

When I think of the influence of a multitude of angels thinly disguised as my family, friends, and peers, I remember the words of Sir Isaac Newton, who, when pressed to reveal the great secret behind his accomplishments, simply replied: "I stood on the shoulders of giants." Of course, at the end of the day, I alone am responsible for the contents of this volume. But I hope my interpretation of principles and doctrine will cultivate your interest to dig deeper into the themes woven into this tapestry, by turning to the scriptures and seeking inspiration from the Spirit. My only goal is to help you to expand your insights into the telestial mile markers, the terrestrial truths, and the celestial guidelines that accompany each of us during our quest for enlightenment.

We
are baptized to
evenly distribute the
weight of our temporal
baggage, that it might
be easier for us to
enter in at the
strait gate.

We are baptized
that we might have
hope in our Savior. It
invites us to consider the
possibility that we might one
day be like Him. We believe that
His grace consists of the gifts and
power by which we may be brought
to His perfection and stature, so
that we may enjoy not only
what He has, but also
what He is.

Preface

"Behold, he changed their hearts; yea, he awakened them out of a deep sleep, and they awoke unto God. Behold, they were in the midst of darkness; nevertheless, their souls were illuminated by the light of the everlasting word."
(Alma 5:7).

This book was inspired by the capacity of baptism to change our hearts. Those who have come up out of the world to join the Church in our day via the portal of baptism know how the people of Zarahemla felt, when they exclaimed to their prophet Benjamin: "We believe all the words which thou hast spoken unto us; and also, we know of their surety and truth, because of the Spirit of the Lord Omnipotent, which has wrought a mighty change in us, or in our hearts, that we have no more disposition to do evil, but to do good continually." (Mosiah 5:2).

Alma posed a rhetorical question to those who had been rejuvenated in the refreshing waters of baptism: "Have ye spiritually been born of God?" he asked. "Have ye received his image in your countenances? Have ye experienced this mighty change in your hearts?" (Alma 5:14). Then, by extension, he continued: "If ye have experienced a change of heart, and if ye have felt to sing the song of redeeming love, I would ask, can ye feel so now?" (Alma 5:26). This book has been written not only to prepare our friends and neighbors, and our little children for baptism, but also to help those of us who have long since entered the healing waters to sustain the feelings we then experienced.

In the physical world, although we may have previously enjoyed active lifestyles, our hearts sometimes begin to falter. They may skip a beat or two now and then, or we may suffer from arrhythmia (an abnormal heart rhythm), tachycardia (an abnormally rapid heart rate), or bradycardia (an abnormally slow heart rate). We may experience shortness of breath, or suffer from angina, the chest pain that is related to insufficient oxygenated blood reaching the heart muscle. When we exhibit the symptoms of heart disease, we are quick to initiate protocols designed to restore function. We make dietary changes, go to a gym, take the stairs instead of the elevator, and modify other habit patterns. We read everything we can about the subject, and follow the counsel of experts in the fields of medicine, physical therapy, and biofeedback. We seek inspiration from lifestyle coaches and self-help gurus. We learn how to monitor our cardiovascular health, and we establish benchmarks to more easily gauge our progress toward the achievement of our goals. When we re-establish sustainable levels of fitness, we eschew the poor lifestyle choices that had aforetime compromised our health, and now would threaten to abrogate our gains.

There is a spiritual equivalent to the healthy lifestyle protocols that are initiated to address heart disease. Baptism is a doctrinal digitalis that has the capacity to "lift up (and strengthen our) hearts (that we might) be glad." (D&C 29:5). Those who decline the invitation to be baptized, however, risk being left with heavy hearts that bear the weight of wickedness. When their lives are in commotion, surely their hearts shall fail them. (See D&C 88:91).

Before the foundation of the world, Heavenly Father knew that His children would need a powerful antidote to the physical and spiritual assaults on the integrity of their hearts that would be a part of the opposition in all things required by the principle of free will that is integral to the Plan of Salvation. Because "they that be whole need not a physician, but they that are sick," baptism was instituted in the lone and dreary world as the spiritual equivalent of powerful heart medication, surgical implants, and even organ transplants, that are required to address the cardiomyopathy of compromised hearts. (Luke 5:31).

When the children of God have forsaken the world and have embraced the lifestyle of saints, they experience in baptism a figurative organ transplant procedure. Those who have literally had heart transplants find it necessary to adhere to a cocktail of immuno-suppressant medication, following a strict regimen, for the rest of their lives. The same prescription must be taken, in a specific dose, at the same time every day. The routine must be followed without variation, in order to maintain a homeostatic balance that minimizes the risk of failure of the surgical procedure. All doctor's appointments must be kept, every recommended laboratory test must be performed, medication side effects must be monitored, and drug interactions and the signs and symptoms of organ rejection must be managed.

The same anti-rejection protocols must be followed after we have spiritually changed our hearts and have been born again through baptism. As the prophet Ezekiel declared: "A new heart also will I give you, and a new spirit will I put within you: and I will take away the stony heart out of your flesh, and I will give you an heart of flesh." (Ezekiel 36:26).

If we are not vigilant, however, our new hearts will surely fail us. Our heaven-sent immuno-suppressant medication comes in the form of prayer, service, and temple attendance. Our strict regimen takes the shape of regular church attendance. Our diligence with medication is manifest in the ordinances of the Gospel, and our determination to maintain heart-healthy lifestyle choices includes the bread and water that is offered on a weekly basis during our ward Sacrament services.

We are meticulous to keep our appointments with our spiritual physicians, and we look forward to the house calls represented in visits by ministering brothers and sisters. We take advantage of accountability interviews with our ward and stake leaders. We are alert to our need for regularly recurring repentance and are sensitive to the spiritual promptings that assure us that we have received forgiveness of our sins and are on the path of progress. If we sense that our organ transplant has begun to fail, or if we feel that it is being rejected because of the insidious effects of carnality, sensuality, or devilishness, we hasten to the temple, for we know to Whom we must turn for guidance and direction, so that we might be able to once again sing the song of redeeming love that comes with spiritual heart health.

We put our shoulders to the wheel, and push along. We tailor ministering messages to the changing needs of our brothers and sisters. We cycle through the Standard Works in Sunday School class every four years, even if for no other reason than that we need to maintain a high level of fitness on the stationary bicycle of belief. If our efforts seem repetitive, it may just be that the Choreographer of the universe is interested in theatrical encore.

Baptism is not pedestrian, but is spectacular; it is not dreary, but is dramatic; and it is not uninteresting, but is stimulating. It quietly establishes a habit pattern of obedience designed to last a lifetime. Baptism is of such magnitude, and has such an outward and upward thrust, that it can reap rewards that reach all the way into eternity.

Following our baptism, critics who focus only on physical fitness, while neglecting spiritual strength, might see only frivolous repetition in the efforts of baptized members of the Church to maintain spiritually aerobic health. They confuse the philosophies of men mingled with scripture, for the Doctrine of Christ. In fact, those of us who have undergone the spiritual heart transplant of baptism, enjoy an indescribable moment in the sun, when the light of understanding illuminates our minds and confirms the divine potential of the new organ beating steadily in our chest.

By remembering our covenant of baptism, we enjoy a gift that keeps on giving, as our new hearts beat 80 times per minute, 4,800 times per hour, and 115,200 times per day. To the Lord, all things are spiritual, and not at any time has He given us laws that are temporal. (See D&C 29:324). We remember this, as, over the course of a year, our new hearts beat over 42 million times. In 70 years, that's almost 3 billion beats. Baptism has the capacity to pump the spiritual element through 100,000 miles of blood vessels in our circulatory systems, 2,000 gallons of it daily, 730,000 gallons per year, or up to 51,000,000 gallons in 70 years.

Every day of our lives, as the sunrise breaks over the eastern sky, the self-evident question is unequivocally answered with our baptism and in the subsequent conduct of our lives: "What think ye of Christ? Whose son is he?" (Matthew 22:42).

Our discipline weaves a tapestry that testifies we have been born again to enjoy one more day on earth. We are fortified in baptism to meet our most daunting challenges. Our new hearts almost burst with the spiritual element that sustains our forward momentum, as we push on toward the unexplored reaches of eternity. We realize that our baptism has not only the capacity to improve our lifestyle, but also that it taps into God's power to sustain our very lives. He has provided a marvelous opportunity for us to probe the limits of our potential and to enjoy spiritual stability. Our baptism casts us off into a stream of revelation, that we might be carried along in the quickening currents of direct experience with the Infinite.

"All saints who remember to keep and do these sayings, walking in obedience to the commandments, shall receive health in their navel and marrow to their bones; and shall find wisdom and great treasures of knowledge, even hidden treasures; and shall run and not be weary, and shall walk and not faint."
(D&C 89:18).

Introduction

Gospel principles are the foundation truths that are embedded in doctrine. They are eternally valid, while values are beliefs that are culturally or personally determined, and that may change with circumstances. Baptism is an excellent example of an ordinance that is the expression of a Gospel principle.

Baptism amplifies the quiet spiritual stirrings that underlie our experience, and is a portal opening up into the matchless vistas of spiritual experience. There are no social, economic, cultural, environmental, or genealogical prerequisites that limit who may receive its blessings. The only real condition for receiving the priesthood ordinance of baptism is bringing "forth fruit meet for repentance." (Alma 13:13).

The repentant, Joseph Smith said, are "baptized after the manner of his burial, being buried in the water in his name, and this according to the commandment which he has given – That by keeping the commandments they might be washed and cleansed from all their sins." (D&C 76:51-52). "Consequently, the baptismal font was instituted as a similitude of the grave." (D&C 128:13).

Paul taught that being immersed in water and coming out again is symbolic of both death and resurrection. He wrote: "Therefore, we are buried with him by baptism into death: that like as Christ was raised up from the dead by the glory of the Father, even so we also should walk in newness of life. For if we have been planted together in the likeness of his death, we shall be also in the likeness of his resurrection." (Romans 6:4).

He also taught that there is "one Lord, one faith, (and) one baptism." (Ephesians 4:5). There was no disputation regarding the correct administration of the ordinance of baptism as long as the Apostles walked the earth. When they were martyred, however, and their priesthood authority died with them, confusion arose concerning the simplest policies, procedures, and doctrines of the kingdom, and there was no enlightened solution to the problem. Apostasy resulted, that only ended with the direct latter day intervention in the Sacred Grove by Heavenly Father and His Son Jesus Christ. (See J.S.H. 1:16-20).

Paul had prophesied of the coming apostasy from the faith. He wrote to the saints: "Be not soon shaken in mind, or be troubled, neither by spirit, nor by word, nor by letter as from us, as that the day of Christ is at hand. Let no man deceive you by any means: for that day shall not come, except there come a falling away first." (2 Thessalonians 2:2-3).

In the third century A.D., the Church historian Eusebius provided a glimpse of that falling away. He wrote: "A change came over us. We yielded to pride, sloth, mutual envy, and abuse. We warred upon ourselves as occasion offered, and we used the weapons of words. Leaders fought and laity formed factions. Unspeakable hypocrisy and dissimulation traveled to the farthest limits of evil." ("The Essential Eusebius," p. 177).

Later, during the Age of Chivalry, Charlemagne urged churchmen to faithful Gospel scholarship. "In a letter to abbots and bishops, he complained of illiterate monks: 'What pious devotion had faithfully prompted in their A leader of the Reformation in America, Roger Williams, wrote: "There is no regularly constituted church on earth, nor any person authorized to administer any church ordinance (such as baptism); nor can there be until new apostles are sent by the Great Head of the Church, for Whose coming I am seeking." ("Picturesque America," p. 502, see also the 5th Article of Faith).

Finally, Thomas Jefferson fumed that "the religion builders have so distorted and deformed the doctrines of Jesus, so muffled them in mysticisms, fancies, and falsehoods, have caricatured them into forms so inconceivable, as to shock reasonable thinkers. Happy in the prospect of a restoration of primitive Christianity, I must leave to younger persons to encounter and lop off the false branches that have been engrafted into it by the mythologists of the middle and modern ages." ("Jefferson's Complete Works," 7:210 & 257).

The Restoration reestablished the necessity of the ordinance of baptism and reinstated the authority to act in the name of God. Anciently, Christ gave the Nephite Twelve the specific words that they were to employ in the baptismal prayer, so that there might be no misunderstanding. Because this prayer authorizes the officiant to invoke the Holy Names of all three members of the Godhead, its words convey unmatched power, and suggest, without reservation, the sanction and approval of God Himself.

We must be baptized for the remission of sins because the principle upon which the ordinance is anchored is based on a commandment found throughout the canon of scripture: "Repent, and be baptized every one of you in the name of Jesus Christ for the remission of sins." (Acts 2:38). In the scriptures, Jesus Himself, and little children, are the only perfect examples. He said: "Ye must repent, and be baptized in my name, and become as a little child, or ye can in nowise inherit the kingdom of God." (3 Nephi 11:38).

We must be baptized to become members of the Church of Jesus Christ. "All those who humble themselves before God, and desire to be baptized (that) have truly repented of all their sins...shall be received by baptism into his church." (D&C 20:37). In a beautiful admonition, Alma described 14 key qualities that Latter-day Saints should have as they come out of the waters of baptism. "Be humble," he said, "and be submissive and gentle; easy to be entreated; full of patience and long-suffering; being temperate in all things; being diligent in keeping the commandments of God at all times; asking for whatsoever things ye stand in need, both spiritual and temporal, always returning thanks unto God for whatsoever things ye do receive. And see that ye have faith, hope, and charity, and then will ye always abound in good works." (Alma 7:23-24). The characteristics of the Zion society he envisioned are simply the result of a spiritual transformation that takes place as the saints live the Celestial Law of the Lord.

We must be baptized that we might walk in the Light of the Spirit, and not just of the Light of Christ. "If thou wilt turn unto me, and (be baptized) ye shall receive the gift of the Holy Ghost." (Moses 6:52). As we participate in the ordinance of the Sacrament in renewal of the baptismal covenant, and so live that the Holy Ghost may be our Companion, we will be guided unerringly.

Brigham Young declared: "Every individual that lives according to the laws that the Lord has given to His people, and has received the blessings that He has in store for the faithful, should be able to know the things of God from the things which are not of God, the light from the darkness, that which comes from heaven and that which comes from somewhere else. This is the satisfaction and the consolation that the Latter-day Saints enjoy by living their religion. This is the knowledge which every one who thus lives possesses." (D.B.Y., p. 35).

Following his own baptism, Joseph Smith wrote: "Our minds being now enlightened, we began to have the scriptures laid open to our understandings, and the true meaning and intention of their more mysterious passages revealed unto us in a manner which we never could attain to previously, nor ever before had thought of." (J.S.H. 1:74).

We are baptized that we might follow in the footsteps of the Savior. Obedience frees us from the uncertainties of mortality. Joseph F. Smith taught that we need not fear in our hearts when we have lived up to the principles of truth and righteousness, according to our knowledge and understanding.

The Savior, Who was our Exemplar, both physically and symbolically descended beneath us all, when He was baptized in Jordan, which is the lowest body of fresh water upon the face of the earth. In our own day, "persecutions may rage, mobs may combine, armies may assemble, calumny may defame, but the truth of God will go forth boldly, nobly, and independent," proclaimed by baptized members of the Lord's missionary army, "until it has penetrated every continent, visited every clime, swept every country, and sounded in every ear, till the purposes of God shall be accomplished and the Great Jehovah shall say 'The work is done.'" (Joseph Smith, H.C. 4:540).

Although telestial turf is Satan's home ground, and the quicksand of secular humanism and other false ideologies lies ready to suck the unwary into the underworld of the adversary, "no power on earth or hell can overthrow or defeat that which God has decreed. Every plan of the adversary will fail, for the Lord knows our secret thoughts and sees the future with a vision clear and perfect, even as though it were in the past." (Joseph Fielding Smith, Jr.).

Baptism is the gateway through which we enter as we embark on the path of eternal progress leading to the Celestial Kingdom. The Savior promised: "Whoso believeth in me, and is baptized...shall inherit the kingdom of God." (3 Nephi 11:33). Those who are baptized "have come out of the world, have left the loneliness and estrangement of a fallen creation, and have entered the realm of divine experience. They have forsaken the orphanage of spiritual alienation, and have been received into the family and household of the Lord Jesus Christ. They have left the ranks of the nameless, and have taken upon them the blessed name of Jesus Christ. They are Christians. Through their Master, they become, in time, joint heirs to all that the Father has." (Doctrinal Commentary on The Book of Mormon," 4:202). Referring to those who lived following the post-mortal ministry of the Savior among the Nephites, Mormon simply exclaimed: "How blessed were they!" (4 Nephi 1:18).

In contrast, those who do not believe in the power of God unto salvation, and are not baptized, will not be able to continue their progression, and will therefore be damned. This is not an arbitrary man-made judgment with corollaries, footnotes, and exceptions to the rule. God's laws are not subject to appeal, amendment, or interpretation. Baptism is the key element of a perfect Plan that is all the more beautiful because of its simplicity. The ordinance is clearly established in the Bible and is clarified in companion scriptures. It's administration is carefully articulated in The Book of Mormon to silence doctrinal disputations among the people. It is the ordinance that is central to The Plan of Salvation, and is the hinge upon which swings the gate leading to eternal life with Heavenly Father.

As King Benjamin so clearly taught: "Under this head ye are made free, and there is no other head whereby ye can be made free. There is no other name given whereby salvation cometh; therefore, I would that ye should take upon you the name of Christ, all you that have entered into the covenant with God that ye should be obedient unto the end of your lives. And it shall come to pass that whosoever doeth this shall be found at the right hand of God, for he shall know the name by which he is called; for he shall be called by the name of Christ. And now it shall come to pass, that whosoever shall not take upon him the name of Christ must be called by some other name; therefore, he findeth himself on the left hand of God." (Mosiah 5:8-10).

Benjamin's discourse expressed a divine perspective. It echoed the prophets, who from the foundation of the world have clarified again and again the first principles and ordinances of the Gospel Plan. When we hear the Lord's anointed repeating themselves, we need to perk up our ears and listen carefully, for "surely the Lord God will do nothing, but he revealeth his secret unto his servants the prophets." (Amos 2:7).

All who have reached the age of accountability are invited to be baptized. At that age, we are old enough to comprehend covenants with our Creator. Almost a year before the formal organization of the Church, the Lord taught Joseph Smith that we must repent "if we have arrived at the years of accountability," (D&C 18:42), that elsewhere is specified as the age of eight. (See D&C 68:27).

All those who have reached the age of accountability have been guided by the light of Christ to establish the foundation of an understanding of what is good and what is evil. (See 2 Nephi 9:25-26). Because of the Atonement, all have equal opportunity before the Lord, and baptism becomes the powerful ordinance it was meant to be. Ultimately, we may all "have the privilege, living or dead, of accepting the conditions of the great Plan of Redemption provided by the Father, through the Son, before the world was." (John Taylor, "Mediation and Atonement," p. 181).

Baptism helps to make our lives a time of testing, or of putting to the proof our declared values. It gives us a new beginning, which is why it is called a rebirth. If we are baptized after we have reached the age of accountability, we are freed from the stain of sin that has been accumulating since that time. "Inasmuch as ye were born into the world by water, and blood, and the spirit, which I have made, and so became of dust a living soul, even so ye must be born again into the kingdom of heaven, of water, and of the Spirit, and be cleansed by blood, even the blood of mine Only Begotten." (Moses 6:59).

The covenant of baptism is a two-way promise. We make a covenant with the Lord to come into the fold of God, to bear each other's burdens, to stand as His witnesses at all times and in all places, and to serve Him and keep His commandments. In turn, the Lord promises to forgive our sins, to pour out His Spirit more abundantly upon us, to give us daily guidance and help, with a promise that we will come forth in the First Resurrection, and be rewarded with eternal life.

The intensity of the ordinance allows us to discover for ourselves the very personal levels of the experiences of the Savior. When He speaks of "knowing Him," the Savior is referring to a special sense of the word. It is not enough that we know about Him, by reading the Gospels, or by listening to others speak of Him. We must know Him through the bonds of common experience and common feeling. Our baptism was meant to be an immersion in the tangible element of Spirit.

We can feel as did the Dead Sea Covenanters, who wrote of their baptismal experience: "His sin is forgiven him and in the humility of his soul he is for all the Laws of God; his flesh is cleansed shining bright in the waters of purification, even in the waters of baptism, and he shall be given a new name in due time to walk perfect in all the ways of God." ("The Manual of Discipline" or "The Serek Scroll" from The Dead Sea Scrolls).

Melvin J. Ballard was one who, following his baptism, was able to walk perfectly in all the ways of God. He said: "I found myself one evening in the dreams of the night in the sacred building, the temple. After a season of prayer and rejoicing, I was informed that I should have the privilege of entering into one of those rooms, to meet a glorious Personage, and, as I entered the door, I saw, seated on a raised platform, the most glorious Being my eyes have ever beheld or that I ever conceived existed in all the eternal worlds. As I approached to be introduced, he arose and stepped towards me with extended arms and he smiled as he softly spoke my name. If I shall live to be a million years old, I shall never forget that smile. He took me in his arms and kissed me, pressed me to his bosom and blessed me, until the marrow of my bones seemed to melt. When he had finished, I fell at his feet, and as I bathed them with my tears and kisses, I saw the prints of the nails in the feet of the Redeemer of the world. The feeling that I had in the presence of Him who hath all things in His hands, to have His love, His affection and His blessing was such that if I ever can receive that of which I had but a foretaste, I would give all I am, all that I ever hope to be, to feel what I then felt." ("Sermons and Missionary Experiences of Melvin Joseph Ballard," p. 156). Mormon desired that his brethren might have similar cherished relationships with the Lord, and so he found it necessary to speak to his son about a practice that had crept into the Church that grieved him tremendously. He had learned that there had been disputations among his people concerning the baptism of their little children. (See Moroni 8:5).

There have always been such disputes. The practice of infant baptism in the various sects in the Last Days, and the differences of opinion regarding the correct method of the administration of baptism in Joseph Smith's day, made the Restoration of the Gospel necessary. The Atonement made the correct administration of the ordinance of baptism possible. It is critically important that the sacred ordinance admitting an applicant into the fold of Christ be carried out according to His instruction, for, as noted above, there is ultimately "one Lord, one faith, (and only) one baptism." (Ephesiahs 4:5). "Except a man be born of water and of the Spirit," declared the Savior, "he cannot enter into the kingdom of God." (John 3:5).

Even in the days of the patriarchs, there was confusion concerning the proper administration of the ordinance of baptism. "And it came to pass, that Abram fell on his face, and called upon the name of the Lord. And God talked with him, saying, my people have gone astray from my precepts, and have not kept mine ordinances, which I gave unto their fathers. And they have not observed mine anointing, and the burial, or baptism wherewith I commanded them; but have turned from the commandment, and taken unto themselves the washing of children, and the blood of sprinkling; And have said that the blood of the righteous Abel was shed for sins; and have not known wherein they are accountable before me." (J.S.T. Genesis 17:3-7).

Mormon considered the dispute to be of such magnitude that immediately upon learning of it, he sought the advice of the Lord concerning the matter. The ecclesiastical counsel that he then gave came by direct revelation by the power of the Spirit, just as it has in the Last Days. The reason that a correct understanding of baptism is essential is that the ordinance lies at the very heart of the Gospel of Jesus Christ.

As the Savior taught the Nephites: "This is the gospel which I have given unto you – that I came into the world to do the will of my Father, because my Father sent me. And my Father sent me that I might be lifted up upon the cross; and after that I had been lifted up upon the cross, that I might draw all men unto me. ...And it shall come to pass, that whoso repenteth and is baptized in my name shall be filled. ...And he that endureth not unto the end, the same is he that is also hewn down and cast into the fire, from whence they can no more return, because of the justice of the Father." (3 Nephi 27:13-21).

Mormon had a correct understanding of the mission of the Redeemer, and knew that He had come "into the world not to call the righteous but sinners to repentance; the whole need no physician, but they that are sick; wherefore little children are whole, for they are not capable of committing sin. (Moroni 8:8). Therefore, he said, "It is solemn mockery before God, that ye should baptize little children," because to do so denies the far-reaching power of the Atonement. (Moroni 8:9).

The doctrine of infant baptism denies that Jesus Christ atoned for the "original sin" of Adam, and ignores the concept of individual accountability. It demands that little children who die without baptism cannot enter heaven. But the Atonement did redeem them from the Fall. They are capable of actions that are inconsistent with obedience to Gospel principles, but they are not counted against them as sins, for they are not culpable.

Rather, Mormon wrote: "This thing shall ye teach – repentance and baptism unto those who are accountable and capable of committing sin; yea, teach parents that they must repent and be baptized, and humble themselves as their little children, and they shall all be saved with their little children." (Moroni 8:10). Then, for added emphasis, he declared: "Little children need no repentance, neither baptism. Behold, baptism is unto repentance to the fulfilling the commandments unto the remission of sins. But little children are alive in Christ, even from the foundation of the world." (Moroni 8:11-12).

It was an integral part of The Plan of Salvation, ordained in the Grand Council in Heaven before the world was, that little children who died before the age of accountability would be saved in the Celestial Kingdom by the power of the Infinite Atonement. "If not so, God is a partial God, and also a changeable God, and a respecter of persons; for how many little children have died without baptism!" Moroni 8:22).

Those who labor under the burden of a belief in infant baptism are "in the gall of bitterness," for how could a just and loving Father in Heaven consign so many of His innocent children to an eternal fate which, on their own merits, they did not deserve?" (Moroni 8:14). These ignorant individuals are "in the bonds of iniquity" in the sense that they must experience despair or hopelessness regarding their little ones who have died without baptism. (Moroni 8:14).

"Despair cometh because of iniquity" because sin clouds vision, and unrepentant sinners can see no way out of their miserable situation. (Moroni 10:22). Apostate teaching leaves no alternative but to suggest, "if little children could not be saved without baptism, these must have gone to an endless hell." (Moroni 8:13).

It is those who persist in the practice of infant baptism, however, who "must go down to hell," wrote Mormon. (Moroni 8:14). While those who teach the doctrine of infant baptism believe that children who die without the ordinance will go to hell, the truth is that it is the professors of that doctrine who are themselves "in danger of death, hell, and an endless torment." (Moroni 8:21).

"For awful is the wickedness to suppose that God saveth one child because of baptism, and the other must perish because he hath no baptism. Wo be unto them that shall pervert the ways of the Lord after this manner, for (after they have been taught about the role of accountability following the fall of Adam, and the necessity of the Savior's redemption) they shall perish except they repent." (Moroni 8:15-16).

The scriptures are specific because our eternal welfare depends upon our correct understanding of this doctrine. All else hangs in the balance. At the end of the day, in the absence of sin, there is no need for repentance, or for baptism. This doctrine was established before the foundation of the world. "For the power of redemption cometh on all those that have no law; wherefore, he that is...under no condemnation cannot repent; and unto such baptism availeth nothing." (Mormon 8:22).

In a grand summary statement, Mormon concluded: "The first fruits of repentance is baptism; and baptism cometh by faith unto the fulfilling the commandments; and the fulfilling the commandments bringeth remission of sins; and the remission of sins bringeth meekness, and lowliness of heart; and because of meekness and lowliness of heart cometh the visitation of the Holy Ghost, which Comforter filleth with hope and perfect love, which love endureth by diligence unto prayer, until the end shall come, when all the saints shall dwell with God." (Moroni 8:25-26).

1000 years earlier, Nephi had written extensively regarding the doctrine of baptism. 2 Nephi Chapters 31-33 represent the culmination of his desire to persuade those living in the Last Days "to come unto the God of Abraham, and the God of Isaac, and the God of Jacob, and be saved." (1 Nephi 6:4). These chapters comprise Nephi's last recorded sermon, and address what he called "the doctrine of Christ." (2 Nephi 31:2). Simply stated, this doctrine is that if we have faith in Jesus Christ, repent of our sins, and enter into a baptismal covenant with the Lord, we will receive the Holy Ghost, Who will then guide us, showing us the things we must do to achieve salvation and exaltation.

Nephi emphasized that the Lord would be baptized "to fulfil all righteousness," which is to obey every commandment and to perform every ordinance necessary to attain eternal life. (2 Nephi 31:5). The doctrine of Christ speaks to our spirits, for every Gospel principle carries a witness that it is true. The language of the Spirit is universal, and when the Holy Ghost illuminates our minds, we enjoy spiritual fluency. Such familiarity, such ease with the doctrines, and such comfort with the revealed word of God, open up vistas of eternal proportion.

The Book of Mormon does not make any special mention of the manner of baptism among Nephi's contemporaries, for baptism had always been the standard for the Children of the Covenant. Five hundred years later in the Old World, when John the Baptist went into the wilderness of Judea preaching repentance and baptism by immersion, his actions didn't arouse any curiosity among the people, as if he were introducing some new and strange doctrine. The Jews of that day understood it as an essential Gospel ordinance, and so it was. Even the Jewish Encyclopedia states: "John stood forth in the spirit of the prophets of old to preach his baptism of repentance symbolized by cleansing with water." (Volume 2, p. 499).

"The fact that baptism was practiced in ancient Israel might (also) help to explain why the Savior was not criticized by the orthodox Jews who were quick to rebuke Him whenever He did anything contrary to their law. However, not a single word of criticism concerning the baptism of Jesus Christ is found in the entire New Testament." ("Commentary on The Book of Mormon," p. 155).

It is obvious that baptism is an ordinance of great antiquity, and one requiring humility and obedience before God the Father. The Lamb of God was indeed baptized, for Elder Howard W. Hunter declared: "Jesus entered into all the saving ordinances of the Melchizedek Priesthood," and baptism qualifies one to participate in these. (Los Angeles Area Conference Address, 1980).

The Savior's example demonstrated that entrance into the Church and Kingdom is strait; that is to say, it is narrowly defined. There should be no variance of opinion regarding the prescribed way. He set the pattern when He said: "Follow thou me." (2 Nephi 31:10). The ecclesiastical responsibility of the Lord's anointed has always been to teach correct principles. Witness the Latter-day prophets who pointedly invite less active members of the Church to return to the fold in full fellowship.

To a later Nephite society, the Savior Himself taught with unmistakable clarity. "And he said unto them: On this wise shall ye baptize; and there shall be no disputations among you." (3 Nephi 11:22). "Neither shall there be disputations among you concerning the points of my doctrine." (3 Nephi 11:28). There followed explicit instruction to the priesthood leaders of the Nephite Church regarding the manner of baptism. The history of post-apostolic Christianity bears witness that it is vitally important that the members of His Church be taught the Doctrine of Christ. As Nephi asked: "Wherefore, my beloved brethren, can we follow Jesus save we shall be willing to keep the commandments of the Father? And the Father said: Repent ye, repent ye, and be baptized in the name of my Beloved Son." (2 Nephi 31:10-11).

Baptism, then, serves many purposes. Among these, 1) It illustrates our desire to follow the righteous example of the Savior, 2) It is an expression of our obedience, 3) It allows us to receive a remission of sins, if we are baptized after the age of accountability, 4) It enables us to gain admission to the Church, through an ordinance performed by His legal administrators, 5) It provides us with access to personal sanctification through the Holy Ghost, and 6) It is outwardly symbolic as the gateway to the Celestial Kingdom of God. As this book illustrates, there are dozens of additional reasons why we are baptized.

Nephi taught: "I know that if ye shall follow the Son, with full purpose of heart, acting no hypocrisy and no deception before God, but with real intent, repenting of your sins, witnessing unto the Father that ye are willing to take upon you the name of Christ, by baptism – yea, by following your Lord and your Savior down into the water, according to his word, behold, then shall ye receive the Holy Ghost; yea, then cometh the baptism of fire and of the Holy Ghost; and then can ye speak with the tongue of angels, and shout praises unto the Holy One of Israel." (2 Nephi 31:13).

He added the testimony of the Father to his own words: "And I heard a voice from the Father, saying: Yea, the words of my Beloved are true and faithful. He that endureth to the end, the same shall be saved." (2 Nephi 31:15). It is not often in the scriptures that the solemn testimony of God the Father is recorded, but baptism is such an important ordinance of the Gospel and is so central to the Doctrine of Christ that it merits such attention. Just so, the same holy witness attended the baptism of Jesus at Jordan. (See Matthew 3:17).

The atoning blood of Jesus Christ cleanses, while the Holy Ghost purges the effects of sin. (See Moses 6:60). "For the gate by which ye should enter is repentance and baptism by water; and then cometh a remission of your sins by fire and by the Holy Ghost." This puts us on the "strait and narrow path that leads to eternal life." (2 Nephi 31:17-18).

Then, we must "press forward" with complete dedication and "steadfastness," or confidence and a firm determination in Christ, "having a perfect brightness of hope," or perfect faith, and charity, or "a love of God and of all men." If we do this, "feasting upon the word of Christ," or receiving strength and nourishment from the scriptures, and endure to the end in righteousness, we "shall have eternal life," which is the greatest gift that God can bestow. (2 Nephi 31:20). This is our on-going opportunity and responsibility.

Nephi stated this doctrine in simple language that is difficult to misinterpret. "This is the way," he said, "and there is none other way nor name given under heaven whereby (we) can be saved in the kingdom of God. And now, behold, this is the Doctrine of Christ, and the only and true doctrine of the Father, and of the Son, and of the Holy Ghost, which is one God, without end." (2 Nephi 31:21).

This doctrine becomes the Gospel of the Father as well as of the Son and the Holy Ghost, because these three distinct members of the Godhead are One, in complete unity, love, and purpose. As we focus on the ordinance of baptism, we can see how our Father, His Son, and the Holy Ghost work together to provide the opportunity for us to have immortality and eternal life. "For by the water ye keep the commandment; by the Spirit ye are justified, and by the blood ye are sanctified." (Moses 6:60).

Christ is the Author of Salvation (Hebrews 5:9), and the Finisher of our Faith, (Hebrews 12:2), but The Plan was introduced to His spirit children by Heavenly Father. (See 2 Nephi 9:13), By the spirit of revelation, the Holy Ghost testifies of Christ and of the Father's Plan. (D&C 8:2-3). Working in perfect harmony, They promote the doctrine of Christ with one shared goal: to bring us to the waters of baptism, to the very Portal of the Celestial Kingdom.

We are baptized
that the Spirit of the
Lord Omnipotent might
work "a mighty change in
us, or in our hearts, that we
have no more disposition to do
evil, but to do good continually."
(Mosiah 5:2).

It is our baptism that knits our hearts together in unity and in love. It is the first of several steps that give those who are living on both sides of the veil the tools they need to successfully confront eternity.

One Hundred and One Reasons Why We Are Baptized

With our baptism comes
the dawn of recognition that the
blessing of happiness is a gift that
Heavenly Father weaves into every Gospel
principle. When we accept the invitation to
"try the virtue of the word of God" and are
exposed to the fruit of the Tree of Life,
we open our senses to the matchless
realm of joy that can be ours
only through obedience.
(See Alma 31:5).

1.

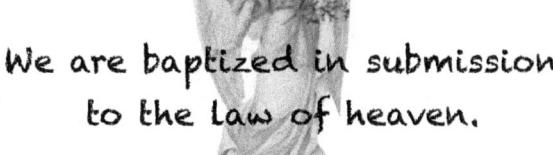

We are baptized in submission to the law of heaven.

Has baptism always been performed in the Lord's own way?

Anciently, there was confusion concerning the proper administration of the ordinance. "And it came to pass, that Abram fell on his face, and called upon the name of the Lord. And God talked with him, saying, My people have gone astray from my precepts, and have not kept mine ordinances, which I gave unto their fathers. And they have not observed mine anointing, and the burial, or baptism wherewith I commanded them." (J.S.T. Genesis 17:3-5).

How do some people "wrest the scriptures" that relate to baptism?" (D&C 10:63).

They "have turned from the commandment, and taken unto themselves the washing of children, and the blood of sprinkling, and have said that the blood of the righteous Abel was shed for sins, and have not known wherein they are accountable before me." (J.S.T. Genesis 17:6-7).

Do you think the Savior's Apostles administered baptism correctly?

As long as the Apostles walked the earth, there was no disputation regarding the ordinance of baptism. When they were martyred, however, and their priesthood authority died with them, commotion arose concerning the simplest policies, procedures, and doctrines of the kingdom, and there was no enlightened solution to the problem.

What happened when the priesthood authority of the Apostles was lost?

Apostasy resulted, requiring the direct latter-day intervention of Heavenly Father and His Son Jesus Christ. (See J.S.H. 1:16-20).

Bathed in the stunning clarity of Light, those who have been baptized often stare in wide-eyed wonder at the beautiful simplicity of the interwoven threads within the pattern of Gospel principles that make up the tapestry of The Plan of Salvation.

2.

We are baptized as a witness that we are willing
to follow in the footsteps of the Savior.

What does it mean to follow the Savior with full purpose of heart?

It means to act without hypocrisy or deception before God, and "with real intent, repenting of (our) sins, witnessing unto the Father that (we) are willing to take upon (ourselves) the name of Christ, by baptism - yea, by following (our) Lord and (our) Savior down into the water." (2 Nephi 31:13).

Do the scriptures make any special mention of the manner of baptism?

They do not, although baptism by immersion was the standard. For example, when John the Baptist went into the wilderness of Judea preaching repentance and baptism, his actions didn't arouse any curiosity among the people, as if he were introducing some new and strange doctrine. The Jews of that day understood it as an essential Gospel ordinance, and so it was. Even the "Jewish Encyclopedia" states: "John stood forth in the spirit of the prophets of old to preach his baptism of repentance, symbolized by cleansing with water."

When was the ordinance of baptism first administered?

Baptism is an ordinance of great antiquity, requiring humility and obedience before God the Father. In fact, "the Lamb of God ... fulfil(ed) all righteousness in being baptized by water." (2 Nephi 31:6). As Elder Howard W. Hunter declared: "Jesus entered into all the saving ordinances of the Melchizedek Priesthood," and it is baptism that qualifies us to participate in these rites.

What about Adam? Where in the scriptures do we learn about his baptism?

"Adam cried unto the Lord, and he was caught away by the Spirit of the Lord, and was carried down into the water, and was laid under the water, and was brought forth out of the water. And thus he was baptized, and the Spirit of God descended upon him, and thus he was born of the Spirit, and became quickened in the inner man." (Moses 6:65-66).

With baptism, we
choose liberty and eternal
life, instead of captivity and spiritual
death. We choose to live our lives within the
context of the Gospel and its laws; without it,
unbridled freedom would lead to tyranny. We are
free to choose whether or not we wish to
be baptized, but we cannot choose
to escape the consequences,
if we choose unwisely.

3.

We are baptized to demonstrate our obedience to the will of the Savior.

How did the voice of the Lord teach Nephi about the ordinance of baptism?

"Follow me," it urged, "and do the things which ye have seen me do ... with full purpose of heart, acting no hypocrisy and no deception before God, but with real intent, repenting of your sins, witnessing unto the Father that ye are willing to take upon you the name of Christ by baptism." (2 Nephi 3:12-13).

How difficult is it to follow the commandment to be baptized?

When we are obedient, we will not recoil from the uncertainties of mortality. Joseph F. Smith declared: "We need not fear in our hearts when we are conscious of having lived up to the principles of truth and righteousness as God has required it at our hands, according to our best knowledge and understanding."

What happens when we surrender our will to the guidance of our Heavenly Father?

We tingle with a consciousness of our communion with the infinite. As Parley P. Pratt declared: "I have received the Holy Anointing, and I can never rest until the last enemy is conquered, death destroyed, and truth reigns triumphant."

How can baptism influence our attitude about obedience?

After our baptism, we discover that obedience is no longer inconvenient, but has become our quest. In that moment, said Ezra Taft Benson, God endows us with power. When we are diligent in our obedience, our agency enjoys its greatest expression. This is one of the hardest things for the unconverted to understand.

Baptism opens
a portal to principles,
ordinances, and covenants that
enable us to be sanctified, to be worthy
to live again in a state of holiness in the
presence of our Heavenly Father. Because
of baptism, we may all "continue in the
supplicating of his grace," to one day
stand blameless before Him
at His Pleasing Bar.
(See Alma 7:3).

4.

We are baptized in similitude of the supreme act of humility by the Savior.

Why do you think the Savior chose to be baptized in the Jordan River?

He Who was our Exemplar descended beneath us all, both physically and symbolically, when He was baptized in Jordan, the lowest body of fresh water upon the face of the earth. In our own day, the meek shall inherit the earth, though "persecutions may rage, mobs may combine, armies may assemble, (and) calumny may defame." (Joseph Smith, in "The Wentworth Letter," H.C. 4:540).

How can our baptism help us to feel good about ourselves?

The principles of true conversion point us in the direction of humility. We have a conscious and unmistakable recognition of our iniquities, and a deep godly sorrow. Next comes inescapable suffering that stimulates an appeal to the Savior, together with our awakening understanding of the power of the Atonement. From Him, comes forgiveness, spiritual enlightenment, and great joy. This motivates us to commit ourselves to a lifestyle of righteousness and service.

How is baptism related to the Atonement of Jesus Christ?

Because of the Atonement, we all have equal opportunity before the Lord. With free will comes the power to accept or reject the principles of The Plan that was created for our benefit before the world was made.

Why do you think the age of eight is described as the age of accountability? (See D&C 29:47).

Baptism at the age of eight captures the heart of a little child before it has been exposed to the cankering influences and corrosive elements of the world, before their hearts are set upon temporal things, and their spirituality has been so weakened that interaction with Heavenly Father God is longer part of their daily experience. Better than the rest of us, little children have a capacity to "lay aside the things of this world, and seek for the things of a better." (D&C 25:10).

At our baptism, if we listen
very carefully, we can hear the
gentle rustling of the wings of angels
coming from behind a slightly-parted veil.
The company of beings from the unseen
world sweeps the cobwebs from our
minds and opens up to our view
undreamed vistas of otherwise
inaccessible experience.

5.

We are baptized to "fulfill all righteousness." (Matthew 3:15).

How can envisioning our own baptism make us feel so good inside?

Baptism speaks to our spirits, for every Gospel principle carries within itself a witness that it is true. Its language is universal, and when the Holy Ghost illuminates our minds, we enjoy fluency, familiarity, and ease with the doctrines, and a comfortable association with the revealed word of God that opens up vistas of eternal proportion before our eyes. "For God speaketh once, yea twice, yet man perceiveth it not. In a dream, in a vision of the night, when deep sleep falleth upon men, in slumberings upon the bed; Then he openeth the ears of men, and sealeth their instruction." (Job 33:14-16).

Why do you think the Savior, Who was without sin, submitted to baptism?

The Lord was baptized as an example to us that we must obey every commandment and participate in every ordinance that God has decreed is necessary to attain eternal life. (See 2 Nephi 31:5).

How can parents help their children to "fulfill all righteousness?" (2 Nephi 31:5).

The baptism of children is the culmination of a process begun much earlier, as their caregivers introduce them to the concepts pertaining to The Plan of Salvation, by preaching, teaching, and expounding upon the principles, and by bringing them into focus with meaningful illustrations. Then, their charges are introduced to instruction that exhorts them to obedience, leading to a dramatic expansion of understanding. (See D&C 20:46-52).

What else can parents do to prepare their children for baptism?

The worth of principles is validated through personal witness. Our desire to be baptized becomes the outward expression of our personal dedication to obedience. It is the public manifestation of our desire to have a private covenant relationship with God. It is the voluntary surrender of our agency to a higher power, the subjugation of our will, to His will. Our testimonies represent promises and covenants that young and impressionable minds can easily grasp.

Our
baptism compels
us to consider the
possibility that we might
one day be like the Savior.
We believe that His grace consists
of the gifts and power by which we
may be brought to His perfection
and stature, so that we may
enjoy not only what
He has, but also
what He
is.

6.

We are baptized to receive a remission of our sins, if we have reached the age of accountability.

What has the Atonement of Jesus Christ got to do with baptism?

The atoning blood of Jesus Christ cleanses, while the Holy Ghost purges the effects of sin. (See Moses 6:60). "For the gate by which (we) should enter is repentance and baptism by water, and then cometh a remission of (our) sins by fire and by the Holy Ghost." This puts us on the "strait and narrow path that leads to eternal life." (2 Nephi 31:17-18).

Why do you think God has given us the commandment to be baptized?

We must be baptized for the remission of sins. The foundation principle upon which the ordinance is anchored is based upon an injunction found throughout the canon of scripture: "Repent, and be baptized every one of you in the name of Jesus Christ for the remission of sins." (Acts 2:38).

Who among us is free from the stain of sin?

Jesus, together with little children, are cited in the scriptures as the only perfect examples. He said: "Ye must repent, and be baptized in my name, and become as a little child, or ye can in nowise inherit the kingdom of God." (3 Nephi 11:38).

What happens to the innocence of children if they are not baptized at the age of eight?

As William Wordsworth observed: "Heaven lies about us in our infancy. Shades of the prison house begin to close upon the growing boy. But he beholds the light and whence it flows. He sees it in his joy. The youth, who daily farther from the east must travel, still is nature's priest. And by the vision splendid, is on his way attended. At length, the man perceives it die away, and fade into the light of common day." ("Ode: Intimations of Immortality").

Baptism is the
great equalizer
for Heavenly Father's
children. The ordinances
that are part of The Plan will
always stand ready to save our
souls, but in the meantime, we
may worship Almighty God
according to the dictates
of our conscience.

7.

We are baptized to gain admission to the Lord's church, which is "the only true and living church upon the face of the whole earth" with which He is pleased. (D&C 1:31).

How is baptism Heavenly Father's formal invitation to come into the Savior's fold and to be called His people? (See Mosiah 18:8).

"All those who humble themselves before God, and desire to be baptized (who) have truly repented of all their sins ... shall be received by baptism into his church." (D&C 20:37).

What other qualities must we have, before we are baptized?

In a beautiful admonition, Alma described the qualities that we strive for as we enter the waters of baptism. "Be humble," he said, "and be submissive and gentle; easy to be entreated; full of patience and long-suffering; being temperate in all things; being diligent in keeping the commandments of God at all times; asking for whatsoever things ye stand in need, both spiritual and temporal, always returning thanks unto God for whatsoever things ye do receive. And see that ye have faith, hope, and charity, and then will ye always abound in good works." (Alma 7:23-24).

What can we do to help to create a Zion society?

Its characteristics are simply the result of a spiritual transformation in the lives of those who have been baptized and confirmed as members of the Church of Jesus Christ.

To whom is admission to the Lord's Church reserved?

Peter said: "Of a truth, I perceive that God is no respecter of persons. But in every nation, he that feareth him, and worketh righteousness, is accepted with him." (Acts 10:34-35). In particular, when the Gentile nations of the earth receive the Gospel, the elect among them will be converted by the power of the Holy Ghost, and be carried along the path leading to eternal life.

The differences
between us matter very little.
Saints and sinners are not so very
different, after all. Baptism
is the great equalizer.
(See Acts 10:34).

8.

We are baptized that we might experience sanctification through fire and the Holy Ghost.
(See Mosiah 5:7).

What is one of the special responsibilities of the Holy Ghost?

It is to bear a sacred witness of the validity of every Gospel ordinance. Because there can be no greater witness, the Atonement is only complete with the baptism of fire and the unimpeachable witness of the Holy Ghost. Thus, Mercy satisfies Justice, and the penitent faithful receive a remission of sins in a symbolic rite of purification. (See 2 Nephi 31:17).

How does it make you feel to know that Heavenly Father is a party to your baptism?

Those who make sacred promises with Him at the waters of baptism will be visited "with fire and with the Holy Ghost." (3 Nephi 11:36). Fire and smoke have always been symbolic of the presence of the Lord and of the glory of celestial realms. His Spirit is like a burning fire. In the language of Joseph Smith: "God Almighty Himself dwells in eternal fire. Our God is a consuming fire." (See Deuteronomy 4:24, & Hebrews 12:24).

Why must we be baptized before we can receive the gift of the Holy Ghost?

"Every individual who lives according to the laws that the Lord has given to His people, and has received the blessings that He has in store for the faithful, will be able to know the things of God from the things which are not of God, the light from the darkness, that which comes from heaven, and that which comes from somewhere else. This is the satisfaction and the consolation that the Latter-day Saints enjoy by living their religion. This is the knowledge which every one who thus lives possesses." (Brigham Young).

What kinds of worldly influences are constantly at work to drive away the Spirit?

In order to bring revelation into harmony with their myopic view, the worldly disparage its delivery. But their feeble efforts ring hollow when compared to the thunder, lightning, and burning bushes of Sinai. Their determination to synchronize their expectations with their narrow perception of reality attempts to marginalize the importance of communication with God. Their attempts to meddle with its manifestation in order to satisfy prurient interest cannot amend His unalterable decrees. Though they tamper with holy things to indulge their adulterous cravings, the signs and tokens remain unblemished.

A life-long
learning laboratory gives
each of us the opportunity to mold
our nature to more closely resemble
that of our Father in Heaven. He
initiated baptism to make
that metamorphosis
possible.

9.

We are baptized that we might be
spiritually begotten of Christ.
(See Mosiah 5:7).

What was the experience of Joseph Smith following his own baptism?

He wrote: "Our minds being now enlightened, we began to have the scriptures laid open to our understandings, and the true meaning and intention of their more mysterious passages revealed unto us in a manner which we never could attain to previously, nor ever before had thought of." (J.S.H. 1:74).

What did Jesus teach Nicodemus about being "born again," (John 3:3) and about being "spiritually begotten?" (Mosiah 5:7).

We are taught that as we are immersed in the healing waters, we are born again. "Nicodemus saith unto him, How can a man be born when he is old? Can he enter the second time into his mother's womb, and be born? Jesus answered, Verily, verily, I say unto thee, Except a man be born of water and of the Spirit, he cannot enter into the kingdom of God." (John 3:4-4).

How does The Plan of Salvation make it easier for us to be more sensitive to the whisperings of the Spirit?

During the Creation, God made "the greater light to rule the day, and the lesser light to rule the night." (Genesis 1:16). It is illuminating to think of the greater light as the Holy Ghost, and the lesser light as the Light of Christ. The purpose of the lesser light is to lead Heavenly Father's children to His doorstep, where the greater light of the Holy Ghost is waiting to invite them to enjoy His grace through the portal of baptism.

How can baptism help us to edit the story of our lives?

When we are spiritually begotten of Christ, we are given the invitation to re-write the record of our lives. We cannot go back and create a new beginning, but we can begin now to make a new ending. Our lives become fairytales that are waiting to be written.

Baptism is the
catalyst that propels us upward
toward discovery of the personal
levels of experience with the Savior, for
when He speaks of "knowing Him," He must be
referring to a special sense of the word. It is not
enough that we know about Him by reading the
Gospels, or by listening to others speak of
Him. We must know Him through the
bonds of common experience
and common feeling.

10.

We are baptized that our hearts might be changed through faith on the name of Jesus Christ.
(See Mosiah 5:7).

How is our desire to be baptized linked to faith?

Faith requires effort. It is a gift that must be earned. We are taught: "Behold, you have not understood; you have supposed that I would give it unto you, when you took no thought save it was to ask me. But, behold, I say unto you, that you must study it out in your mind." (D&C 9:7-8). In fact, "it is impossible to advance in the principles of truth, to increase in heavenly knowledge, except we exercise our reasoning faculties and exert ourselves." (Lorenzo Snow). To increase in faith, we exercise our agency, but it is not free. It is purchased at a substantial price.

What blessings do we receive as our hearts are changed through faith?

"All saints who remember to keep and do these sayings, walking in obedience to the commandments, shall receive health in their navel and marrow to their bones, and shall find wisdom and great treasures of knowledge, even hidden treasures, and shall run and not be weary, and shall walk and not faint. And I, the Lord, give unto them a promise, that the destroying angel shall pass them by, as the children of Israel, and not slay them." (D&C 89:18-21).

How would you describe faith in Christ?

It is not naiveté or gullibility, nor is it wishful thinking. It is more than confidence and greater than optimism. Faith and positive thinking go hand in hand, but faith is more than an attitude. Faith precedes the miracle. We have faith to believe what we do not see, but the reward of faith is to see what we believe.

How do we develop our faith?

During its genesis, it is necessary to take a few steps into the darkness. Then faith, the spiritual strong searchlight, will illuminate the way. Ultimately, our faith is confirmed by direct experience with the Spirit, that validates Heavenly Father as its Author and Finisher.

Baptism represents more than
the making of resolutions, that can be
nothing more than promises to ourselves that
are generally kept for a few days or weeks at
best, before they are abandoned and we return to
our previously held lifestyles. The ordinance of
baptism has staying power. Baptism has no
bias; its basis is belief, nurtured
by the rich culture medium
of faith, repentance and
the companionship
of the Spirit.

11.

We are baptized that we might be born of Jesus Christ.
(See Mosiah 5:7).

Why would the prophets teach that it is necessary to be born again? (See Mosiah 5:7).

Birth is not a question of development or of maturation, but rather of generation. It is one of the most emotional, miraculous, and awe-inspiring events of mortality. Just so, the process of kindling our divine spark, of igniting the spirit lying dormant within us, of awakening our divine potential, and of nurturing the God in embryo that is present within each of us, is described as being "born again."

How can baptism help us to internalize eternal principles? (See Jeremiah 31:33).

The ordinance of baptism is of such power that it drives the law into our inward parts, so that it is written upon our hearts. A mighty change takes place as we experience the process of sanctification. When we are born again, the desired result of all Gospel-oriented teaching has been achieved, and we have no more disposition to do evil, but to do good continually. (See Mosiah 5:2).

For what purpose is the law driven into our inward parts? (See Jeremiah 31:33).

When the law is woven into the sinews of our souls, that it becomes an essential element of the tapestry of our lives and becomes central to the very pattern upon which we trace our progress along the path of progression, our "minds become single to God, and the days will come that (we) shall see him, for he will unveil his face unto (us)." (D&C 88:68).

How can baptism heal our spiritual blindness? (See John 9:39-41).

The key to our liberation from bondage to sin, to our freedom to become, is an attitude adjustment that is reflected in our desire to be born again. To paraphrase Helen Keller, the real tragedy is not that some of us are born without sight, but that many of us see but do not have vision.

Those who demand outward
evidence of the power of God
as a condition for their belief seek to
circumvent the process by which both faith and
knowledge are developed. They want proof without
price. As with the adulterer, they seek
the result without accepting
the responsibility.

12.

We are baptized in a symbolic re-birth, as we pass through a tangible portal in the similitude of the grave.

What is the "similitude of the grave?" (D&C 128:13).

"Know ye not that, so many of us as were baptized into Jesus Christ were baptized into his death? Therefore, we are buried with him by baptism into death, that like as Christ was raised up from the dead by the glory of the Father, even so we also should walk in newness of life" through the symbolism of being born again, with baptism by immersion. (Romans 6:3).

To what end are we re-born?

"For if we have been planted together in the likeness of his death, we shall be also in the likeness of his resurrection. Knowing this, that our old man is crucified with him, that the body of sin might be destroyed, that henceforth we should not serve sin." (Romans 6:5-6).

What are we taught about the symbolism of baptism?

Immersion in water is symbolic of the burial of Christ. (See 3 Nephi 11:23). Joseph Smith said the repentant are "baptized after the manner of his burial, being buried in the water in his name, and this according to the commandment which he has given - That by keeping the commandments they might be washed and cleansed from all their sins." (D&C 76:51-52). "Consequently, the baptismal font was instituted as a similitude of the grave." (D&C 128:13).

What was the Apostle Paul's instruction that related to baptism?

He taught that being immersed in water and coming out again is symbolic of death and resurrection. From Rome, he wrote: "For if we have been planted together in the likeness of his death, we shall be also in the likeness of his resurrection." (Romans 6:4).

Baptism was not
conceived to follow the
receipt of signs from heaven.
Our faith precedes the miracle.
We must take a few steps into the
darkness, and then faith, that spiritual
strong searchlight, will illuminate
the way. Spiritual confirmation
always flows along the
pathway created
by faith.

13.

We are baptized in order to qualify for the blessings that are found in the other ordinances of the Gospel.

What has the Savior promised to give us when we are baptized?

He declared: "Whoso believeth in me, and is baptized ... shall inherit the kingdom of God." (3 Nephi 11:33).

What blessings may we receive when we are baptized?

We "come out of the world, leaving the loneliness and estrangement of a fallen creation to enter the realm of divine experience. We forsake the orphanage of spiritual alienation, to be received into the family and household of the Lord Jesus Christ." (Doctrinal Commentary on The Book of Mormon," 4:202).

How does our baptism qualify us to call ourselves Christians? (See Acts 26:28).

"We leave the ranks of the nameless, and take upon ourselves the blessed name of Jesus Christ. We become Christians. Through our Master, we become, in time, joint heirs to all that the Father has." (Doctrinal Commentary on The Book of Mormon," 4:202).

Are the guidelines for baptism subject to private interpretation? (See 2 Peter 1:20).

The ordinance of baptism has no corollaries, footnotes, or exceptions to the rule. The commandment to be baptized is not subject to appeal, amendment, or interpretation. The principle has a doctrinal foundation that is central to the Plan of Salvation, for it is the hinge upon which swings the gate leading to eternal life with Heavenly Father.

We have no
proof until we act on
the basis of belief. Then comes the
ratification of the reality, manifest as a
spiritual confirmation, but only after we
act in faith. That is the essence of
why James taught that "faith,
if it hath not works, is
dead, being alone."
(James 2:17).

14.

We are baptized that we might be better prepared to travel the established path that leads to the Celestial Kingdom of God.

Whose Plan makes it possible for us to return to our heavenly home?

Christ is the Author of Salvation, (Hebrews 5:9) and the Finisher of our Faith, (Hebrews 12:2), but The Plan was introduced by Heavenly Father to His spirit children. (2 Nephi 9:13). The Holy Ghost testifies of Christ and of our Father's Plan. (See D&C 8:2-3). In perfect harmony, the Godhead promotes the doctrine of Christ with one shared goal: To bring us to the waters of baptism, and thereafter to the portal of the Celestial Kingdom.

After our baptism, how does the path that leads back Home open up before us?

We await the further light and knowledge the Lord has promised to send to us. "For God, who commanded the light to shine out of darkness, hath shined in our hearts, to give the light of the knowledge of the glory of God in the face of Jesus Christ." (2 Corinthians 4:6).

How does The Plan hold "the key to the mysteries of the kingdom?" D&C 84:19).

Baptism opens up windows of opportunity, that we might better understand the principles of the Gospel. These are mysteries to those who have not spiritually prepared themselves for personal revelation from God. The Lord has assured us that we "shall know of a surety that these things are true, for from heaven will (He) declare it unto (us)." (D&C 5:12). When we are asked, as Antionah asked of Alma: "What does the scripture mean?" because of our baptism, we will know when and how to teach the principles that relate to doctrine. (Alma 12:21).

In what ways is baptism our R.S.V.P. to the invitation that has been sent out across the heavens from our Father?

Baptism surely delights God, for it emancipates us from the self-limiting conditions that had heretofore blinded us to a larger view of life. It frees us to pay closer attention to celestial guideposts and principles. It invites us to experience more intense and reflective self-awareness, deeper and more abiding humility, reinvigorated confidence, and incomprehensively more profound and enduring faith.

Baptism is the evidence
of our exercise of faith. We gain
spiritual maturity until our faith becomes
perfect knowledge. Initially, faith is to believe
what we do not see, and the reward of faith is
to see what we believe. The process by which
faith is developed is one of testing. The
Lord gives certain principles, and by
obedience to them, blessings
and power follow.

15.

We are baptized in the temporal expression of a spiritual reality.

How is baptism a "type?"

Baptism is symbolic. It has not only a present meaning, but also points to a future blessing or reality. Those who have moved beyond the age of accountability are buried in the cleansing water, to come forth in a newness of life, to be born again, that they might not suffer the second, or spiritual, death.

How are Gospel principles different from the shifting values of the world?

Gospel principles are truths that are eternally valid. Values are beliefs that are culturally or personally determined, and that may change with circumstances. Baptism is an ordinance that is the expression of a Gospel principle. A correct understanding of its administration is essential because it is a foundation ordinance that lies at the very heart of the doctrine of the Gospel of Jesus Christ.

Why do you think Heavenly Father chose water as the medium to convey spiritual truth?

There is irony in the fact that water may be the most abundant compound in the universe. As those who wrote the Serek Scroll described it, the penitent are "for all the laws of God, and their flesh is cleansed, shining bright in the waters of purification, even in the waters of baptism. They shall be given a new name in due time to walk perfect in all the ways of God." ("The Serek Scroll," or "Manual of Discipline," was discovered in 1947, in caves high above Qumran. It dates from around 400 B.C.).

How is baptism related to our adoption into the House of Israel?

Adoption grants us access to the privileges associated with the rights and responsibilities of the priesthood. We are continually learning about The New and Everlasting Covenant that relates to the covenant made anciently with our father Abraham, including the covenants made at our baptism and in the temple. All are expressions that are related to both present and anticipated temporal and spiritual blessings.

Temporal
baggage can create imbalance
that leads to confusion. Baptism jars
us out of our collective complacency by
upsetting the stagnation of the status
quo. It invites us to enjoy a settled
conviction in our minds by getting
our juices flowing, prodding
us to constructively expend
our energy, and putting
our agency to work.

16.

We are baptized that we might overcome spiritual death, and come into the presence of the Father, the Son, and the Holy Ghost.

Why do you think the baptismal prayer addresses Heavenly Father, as well as Jesus Christ, and the Holy Ghost?

As the officiant invokes their sacred names, all three members of the Godhead are invited to attend the baptismal service. The right arm is raised to the square in a symbolic gesture, as if it were reaching out to the delicious fruit of the tree of life. The sweet sensations of its taste are indelibly imprinted upon the minds of all who are present to witness the spiritual transformation of a child of God, even a god in embryo.

Why do you think Heavenly Father bore His testimony at the baptism of His Son?

It is not often in the scriptures that the solemn testimony of God the Father has been recorded. Baptism is such an important ordinance of the Gospel and is so central to the doctrine of Christ that it merits the attention of God's Holy Witness that attended and sanctioned the baptism of Jesus at Jordan. (See Matthew 3:17).

How does the Light of Christ influence us to come to the waters of baptism?

Until we are baptized, we abide by the Light of Christ, and only receive a taste of the limitless power and intrinsic illumination that rests within the Godhead itself. Following our baptism, however, we are blessed with an awakening comprehension, and we begin to understand that our "Father, and the Son, and the Holy Ghost are one," Who share divine power and authority. (3 Nephi 11:27).

Have you ever wondered how the Holy Ghost completes the "Holy Trinity?"

The Holy Ghost dazzles us with an endless reserve of revelation that provides illumination to every corner of our minds and our spirits. The promises proffered by the combined capacity of the intrinsic light possessed by the Holy Trinity, then, is beyond our comprehension.

Baptism encourages us
to step back, inhale deeply,
take a moment, and focus on the
things of importance in our busy lives.
The covenant gently guides us into
the warm embrace of daily
spiritual experiences.

17.

We are baptized in a palpable expression of the Doctrine of Christ.

Where in the scriptures has the doctrine of Christ been most clearly articulated?

In The Book of Mormon, Nephi clearly explained this doctrine; it is that all who have faith in Jesus Christ and truly repent of their sins, entering into a baptismal covenant with Him, will receive the Holy Ghost, Who will then direct their way, showing them the things they must do to merit the grace of God and inherit salvation. (See 2 Nephi Chapter 31).

Whose doctrine is it that finds expression in the Gospel?

This doctrine is properly the Gospel of the Father as well as of the Son and the Holy Ghost, because these three distinct members of the Godhead are One, in complete unity, love, and purpose.

How does the Holy Ghost help us to recognize the doctrine of Christ?

The ordinances of baptism and the receipt of the Holy Ghost, are the "fruit of the Spirit," (Galatians 5:22), that we receive when we have been taught the doctrine of Christ. As Nephi explained: "If ye will enter in by the way … it will show unto you all things what ye should do. Behold, this is the doctrine of Christ." (2 Nephi 32:5-6).

How does baptism help us to maintain our focus on the doctrine of Christ?

The ordinance of baptism helps us to appreciate how our Father, Jesus Christ, and the Holy Ghost unite to provide the blessing of immortality and eternal life. "For by the water (we) keep the commandment, by the Spirit (we) are justified, and by the blood (we) are sanctified." (Moses 6:60).

Baptism is
the first definitive step
on our journey to Christ. The path
that lies beyond the font leads to the
tree of life. It is not a freeway, but a
toll road. Until we have paid the price,
we cannot hope to comprehend with
fluency the language of the Spirit
that clearly explains how to
make our way to the tree,
that we might harvest
its delicious fruit.

18.

We are baptized to facilitate the temporal implementation of The Plan of Salvation.
(See D&C 3:1).

Have you ever thought about how brilliantly The Plan of Salvation has been scripted, that it might prepare us to be reunited with our Heavenly Father?

The Plan of Salvation allows us to monitor our relationship with God during our engagement with our mortal mission. The Plan is founded upon the points of doctrine that focus on salvation, and upon these elements hinges its correct understanding. The "Plan of Salvation," as it turns out, is a very good choice of words when describing the intimacy that our Heavenly Father has with each of us.

For what purpose was The Plan of Salvation conceived?

It is a practical model that allows us to reconcile our place in the cosmos with eternity, by giving us down to earth instruction relating to our heavenly potential. It gives us the tools to work out our salvation before the Lord, even as we toil with telestial trivialities. (See Philippians 2:12).

How does The Plan of Salvation help us to bridge the gap between mortality and eternity?

The Plan creates a link between the realities of our physical world and the promises of eternity, and seamlessly harmonizes the two in ways that provide us with practical tools we can use to hash out the details of our progression toward that "undiscovered country from whose bourn no traveler returns." (Shakespeare, "Hamlet").

How do the 7 "Rs" prepare us to meet our Heavenly Father?

Because of the principle of opposition, the Atonement is the only reasonable alternative to an otherwise overwhelmingly negative influence competing for dominance in our lives. Its only stipulation is that we go through the process of repentance wherein we Recognize our transgression, experience Remorse, Renounce the self-defeating behavior, Resolve to do better, make Restitution where possible, and then do our part to establish a Reconciliation with the Spirit, and ultimately Receive a remission of sin through the grace of God our Redeemer.

Baptism coherently
stitches foundation principles
together into an understandable
pattern, so that the power of the word
and the witness of truth may be
conveyed without the need
for external warrant.

19.

We are baptized that we might have opportunities to bear each other's burdens. (See Mosiah 18:8).

How can we help to bear each other's burdens?

Since Cain first made the inquiry, we have grappled with the question: "Am I my brother's keeper?" (Genesis 4:9). As true disciples, however, we answer with acts of quiet Christianity. "There are some people in this world," John Taylor declared, "who, if a man were poor or hungry, would say, let us pray for him. I would suggest a little different regimen. Rather, take him a bag of flour and a little beef or pork. A few such comforts will do him more good than your prayers." (C.R., 10/1877).

How can we give more freely of ourselves?

When a child of God is down and out, an ounce of help is better than a pound of preaching. Socrates said, "Know thyself." Cicero urged, "Control Thyself." But the Gospel teaches that we must give of ourselves. (See 1 Timothy 4:15). We establish our commitment to actively embrace the demands of discipleship by following the example of the Savior. After all, "are we not all beggars? Do we not all depend upon the same Being, even God, for all the substance which we have?" (Mosiah 4:19).

How can we provide help to those in need without enabling them?

Helping hands are not synonymous with handouts and the sooner we recognize that we are on the "dole," the faster we can get off it. We may not be standing in line at soup kitchens, and we may not be receiving free turkey dinners at the Union Gospel Mission, but in whatever circumstances we find ourselves, we need the tools that have been provided "to stand independent above all other creatures." (D&C 78:14).

What should we do if we feel someone is not deserving of our help?

We cannot allow our prejudices to determine the depth of our compassion, or debate the merits of the petitions of the impoverished before providing aid. We can learn from the example of the Sons of Mosiah, who ignored the outcries of those who characterized the Lamanites to whom they desired to minister as "a stiffnecked people, whose hearts delight in the shedding of blood, whose days have been spent in the grossest iniquity, whose ways have been the ways of a transgressor from the beginning." (Alma 26:23-25).

"For this end was the law given," that we might be "made alive in Christ because of our faith." (2 Nephi 25:25).

20.

> We are baptized that we
> might be given the privilege to
> "mourn with those that mourn."
> (Mosiah 18:9).

How can our covenant of baptism help us to put smiles on the faces of those who mourn?

When we mourn with those who mourn, we smile with all our heart and with all our might. If we do nothing else, we can be the smile on the faces of those who mourn, or stand in need of comfort.

How can baptism help those who mourn to look at life with new eyes?

"If we looked at mortality as the whole of existence, then pain, sorrow, failure, and short life would be calamity. But if we look upon life as an eternal thing stretching far into the pre-mortal past and on into the eternal post-death future, then all that happens may be put in proper perspective." (Spencer W. Kimball, "Faith Precedes The Miracle," p. 103).

How difficult would it be to face life's hardships without the support of the Gospel?

Without the influence of the Savior, "we wait for light, but behold obscurity; for brightness, but we walk in darkness. We grope for the wall like the blind ... as if we had no eyes. We stumble at noonday as in the night. We are in desolate places as dead men. We roar like bears, and mourn sore like doves. We look for judgment, but there is none; for salvation, but it is far off from us. For our transgressions are multiplied before (God), and our sins testify against us." (Isaiah 59:9-12).

How does knowing that we are the children of God help us to face the adversity that is a part of life?

The light that blazes from our Creator to illuminate the work of His hands shows us the way we must go in order to dwell within the secure envelope of the word of God. He is "a lamp unto (our) feet, and a light unto (our) path." (Psalms 119:105). And by extension: "All things bright and beautiful, all creatures great and small. All things wise and wonderful. The Lord God made them all." (Cecil Francis Alexander).

Raw and
ugly sores that
have been inflicted by worldly
influences are healed in the waters
of baptism. The Balm of Gilead
prevails over even the most
powerful onslaughts
that Babylon can
muster.

21.

We are baptized that we might comfort those that stand in need of comfort."
(Mosiah 18:9).

Why is "Comforter" an appropriate name for the Holy Ghost?

With our baptism comes "the remission of sins (which) bringeth meekness, and lowliness of heart, and because of meekness and lowliness of heart cometh the visitation of the Holy Ghost, which Comforter filleth with hope and perfect love, which love endureth by diligence unto prayer, until the end shall come, when all the saints shall dwell with God." (Moroni 8:26).

Why do you think we are asked to provide comfort to the downtrodden?

Baptism pushes us out of our comfort zones that can be suffocating to our spirits. Our covenant of baptism is designed to make saints of sinners as it works on us to hate our former lives in the world, and to strive to be better than we have ever been before, by finding ways to minister to the needs of others. (See John 12:25).

How does baptism help us to choose the harder right, instead of the easier wrong?

We must guard ourselves against languishing at the aid stations that have been providentially scattered throughout Babylon, as well as at the cafés conveniently located along the broad boulevards of Idumea.

How does baptism empower us to choose wisely?

We are free to choose how we will respond in any given situation. "Between stimulus and response, there is a space. Therein is our power to choose, and therein lies our growth and our freedom. Forces beyond our control can take away everything we possess except one thing, and that is our freedom to choose how we will respond to the situation." (Victor Frankel). It is within that space that we choose to "comfort those that stand in need of comfort." (Mosiah 18:9).

Our
covenants, beginning
with baptism, bring the riches of
eternity within our grasp, by expanding
our vision beyond physical laws that pertain
only to the temporal world, toward an
appreciation of Gospel principles that
relate to the eternities. Baptism
invites us to reach out and
touch the face
of God.

22.

> We are baptized that we might have the courage "to stand as witnesses of God at all times and in all things, and in all places that (we) may be in." (Mosiah 18:9).

How can we bear witness of the truth?

The mission of the Holy Ghost, after bestowing all of the other blessings and gifts of which He is capable of providing, is ultimately to bear witness of the Father and the Son. "Wherefore I give you to understand," wrote Paul, "that no man speaking by the Spirit of God … can say that Jesus is the Lord, but by the Holy Ghost." (1 Corinthians 12:3).

How seriously must we take our witness of Christ?

Our witness must be genuine. It must come from our hearts, as well as our heads. It cannot ring hollow. Taking it lightly betrays an inner emptiness. It cannot be satisfied with the poor imitations of the inner peace that could have been ours. Anything less than complete obedience to our baptismal covenant to witness for Christ will surely estrange us from the Spirit, until we are left with neither root nor branch.

How is our witness of Christ quickened, after our baptism?

We witness for Christ by actions that often speak louder than words. Our righteous example may be the only "pamphlet" one who is not a member of the Church will ever "read." Nephi asked: "Wherefore, my beloved brethren, can we follow Jesus save we shall be willing to keep the commandments of the Father?" (2 Nephi 31:10). This involves being doers, and not just hearers, of the word. (See James 1:22).

How far-reaching in the world does the witness of the Holy Ghost extend?

The Holy Ghost is the author of acumen, the avatar of agency, the architect of aptitude, the benefactor of blessings, the champion of committed Christians, the craftsman of comfort, the designer of our discipleship, the engineer of erudition, the guarantor of gifts, the initiator of insight, the inventor of intelligence, the patron of perception, the provider of praise, the sponsor of scholarship, and the ultimate source of understanding.

We
may live in the
world as long as our feet
are firmly planted on Gospel
sod so that we recognize sounding
brass and tinkling cymbals for what they
really are. Baptism catalyzes a mystical and
metaphysical transformation wherein we
are figuratively born of God,
so that, with new eyes, we
can see more clearly.
(See Mosiah 5:7).

23.

> We are baptized that we might "be redeemed of God, and be numbered with those of the first resurrection, that (we might) have eternal life."
> (Mosiah 18:9).

Why do you think that so many people ignorantly worship an "unknown" God?

Paul observed of the Athenians, who were not so very different from many in our day, that they were inclined to bow down before unknown gods, whom therefore they ignorantly worshipped. (See Acts 17:23). It is in the hope that we might stand independently in our witness of Jesus Christ, the true and living God, that we are baptized.

How can baptism show the way to those who have adopted a lifestyle that falls short of obedience to true principles?

Baptism is the gold standard for those who have previously identified with the Pharisees or the Sadducees, with Buddha, Confucius, Guru Nanak, Zoroaster, or with gods of wood and stone. It supplants the monotheism of Islam and the Bahá'i, the pantheistic theology of Hinduism, Shintoism, and Taoism, secular humanism, irreligion, Catholicism and Eastern Orthodoxy. It trumps evangelical Christianity, fundamentalism, Protestantism, as well as the existential nihilism of the postmodern world.

After baptism, what takes places within our hearts as we consecrate our lives to the Savior?

At our baptism, we consecrate our lives to the Savior. We are cast us upon an altar of faith whose foundation is buttressed by a supernal display of divine direction. We are driven relentlessly forward with an unwavering confidence that His power to save might be unleashed in our behalf and flow over our wounds as a healing balm, that we might unflinchingly meet His penetrating gaze with clear eyes.

How can the desire for the world's goods be traumatizing?

The Devil uses subtlety, pacifying and lulling us into a false sense of worldly security, making us believe that we are gaining something when we are really losing. He does this to quietly avoid awakening our faculties to a harsh reality. He distorts our perspective and twists our very blessings into vehicles that amplify our feelings of self-sufficiency. Such emancipation from God comes at the cost of an ironclad compact with the devil.

At
our baptism, we
turn our thoughts to the
Savior without distraction,
that we might feel His energy
building within us, until it lifts us
to the zenith of experience where
the lines distinguishing mortality
from eternity blur, and we find
ourselves consumed in a fire
of everlasting burnings.

24.

We are baptized as a witness that we have made a covenant to serve God "and keep his commandments, that he (might) pour out his Spirit more abundantly" upon us. (Mosiah 18:10).

How does baptism encourage us to listen to the spiritual promptings that nudge us in the direction of our dreams?

"Answers to prayer come most often by a still voice and are discerned by our deepest, innermost feelings. We can know the will of God if we will take the time to pray, and to listen." (Ezra Taft Benson). We will be guided to Christ-like service if we put God first, and listen to the whisperings of the Holy Ghost.

As we make covenants with God, how are we transformed?

We experience the thrill of being spiritually begotten of Him, and of having our hearts changed through faith on His name. He is ever before us, and we want to turn our thoughts to Him without distraction, that we might feel His energy building within us, until it lifts us to the zenith of experience where the lines distinguishing mortality from eternity blur, and we find ourselves consumed in a fire of everlasting burnings. as we come face to face with eternity.

How do the whisperings of the Spirit encourage us to follow the Savior?

After the appearance of the resurrected Lord to His Apostles, Peter resumed his former occupation, and announced to the others, "I go a fishing." (John 21:3). But when the Savior appeared on the shore, and after He had instructed the Apostles, he said to Peter: "Follow me." (John 21:19). When the Savior figuratively appears beside the waters of baptism, we likewise hear His voice, and enthusiastically join Peter in the work of the ministry.

What does it mean to be "elect according to the foreknowledge of God?" (1 Peter 1:2).

Following our baptism, a dawn of recognition comes to us, as we realize that we are the "elect according to the foreknowledge of God the Father, through sanctification of the Spirit, unto obedience and sprinkling of the blood of Jesus Christ." (1 Peter 1:2). We obtain "precious faith," and become partakers "of the divine nature." (2 Peter 1:1 & 4).

In the
invigorating waters of
baptism, we catch a religious fever
that elevates our testimony temperature
enough to get our juices flowing with an
appreciation of Who the Savior really is.
Only then, will we experience the earth
shaking and mind bending theophany
that we are His spiritual offspring,
that we might recognize the
potential of our position.

25.

We are baptized that we might be given the tools we need to lengthen our stride.

After baptism, how can lengthening our stride sometimes cause discomfort?

In a violent confrontation of principles with values, that tears at the fabric of the natural world, exertion may stretch the limits of our stability. But in the process, we find new spiritual strength. When we go the second mile while lengthening our stride, we burst free of the shackles that had limited the expression of our potential. We receive the "gift of spiritual independence that removes the veil of insensitivity to our destiny." (Richard L. Gunn, "A Search for Sensitivity and Spirit," p. 197).

Why would the Savior urge us to go the second mile? (See Matthew 5:41).

He knows that by doing so, we will capture an independence that can be exhilarating, because it is accompanied by the recognition of new-found and soul-expanding opportunities. It crystalizes within us the realization that we are spiritual beings having mortal experiences, ennobling us with the sure knowledge that only the powers of heaven can countermand the dizzying inequities of life.

How are we fortified as we lengthen our stride?

As the process unfolds and we learn to balance our lives, our capacity to grow expands. We seize opportunities to be anxiously engaged in good causes. We think clearly, so that, on our own initiative, we can generate the power to avoid the conceptual cul-de-sacs, and doctrinal dead-ends that cause so many to lose their way.

How does lengthening our stride push us out of our comfort zones?

Each of us has 168 hours each week, much of it discretionary time to do with as we please. As few as two of these hours are spent in church. We need to ask ourselves: How many hours are wasted "hanging out" or are squandered watching television, playing video games, or on our computers or our mobile devices? How many hours do we devote to social media?

All
who enter the
waters of baptism
have a divine destiny
and are the nobility of
heaven. They are counted
among those of a choice
and chosen generation.
(See 1 Peter 2:9).

26.

We are baptized that we might no more be "strangers and foreigners," but instead, "fellow citizens with the saints, and of the household of God."
(Ephesians 2:19).

How can we enjoy the companionship of the Saints.

The waters of baptism temper our trials and tribulations within the fiery hot crucible of experience. Baptism amplifies the quiet spiritual stirrings that underlie our engagement with the community of the Saints. There are no social or genealogical prerequisites that limit membership in the Church, or determine who may be the recipients of the blessings of the Gospel. Bringing "forth fruit meet for repentance" is really the only condition for receiving the priesthood ordinance of baptism. (Alma 13:13).

What concern did Brigham Young express, relating to the temporal welfare of the Saints?

He declared: "The worst fear that I have about this people is that they will get rich in this country, forget God and his people, wax fat, and kick themselves out of the church and go to hell. This people will stand mobbing, robbing, poverty, and all manner of persecution, and be true. But my greater fear for them is that they cannot stand wealth; and yet they have to be tried with riches, for they will become the richest people on this earth." ("Brigham Young: The Man and His Work," p. 128).

Why is it important to maintain associations with the Saints?

Although he may not have been thinking globally, he did declare that Utah would become the crossroads of the west. "This will become the great highway of the nations. Kings and emperors and the noble and wise of the earth will visit us here, while the wicked and ungodly will envy us our comfortable homes and possessions."

How does fellowship with the Saints positively influence our ability to live in obedience to the principles of the Gospel?

As we adopt the life-style of the Latter-day Saints, our proper prior priesthood preparation will prevent poor performance. It will nudge us off our complacency plateaus, away from the trendy cafés situated along the broad avenues of Idumea, and transport us, as on the wings of eagles, beyond the threshold of our self-imposed limitations, out to the edge of eternity, where "forever" will breathtakingly stand revealed before us.

We are baptized because
none of us would choose to become
spiritually depleted, or to perish because
we neglect the things that matter most. We
understand the consequences of spiritual
starvation, doctrinal dehydration,
and intellectual inhibition.

27.

We are baptized that we might join the ranks of member missionaries.

Why should we be proud to be disciples of Jesus Christ?

The Lord uses His disciples, to "show unto the children of men that (He is) able to do (His) own work." (2 Nephi 27:21). That work is to perfect our brothers and sisters. As Paul wrote: "He hath chosen us in him before the foundation of the world, that we should be holy and without blame before him in love." (Ephesians 1:4).

Who are the "elect according to the foreknowledge of God?" (1 Peter 1:2).

The elect among the Gentile nations of the earth are those who are to be converted by the power of the Holy Ghost. Peter, who first brought the Gospel to the Gentiles, wrote: On them "also was poured out the gift of the Holy Ghost." (Acts 10:45). These gifts of the Spirit are sufficient to propel us, along with our fellow travelers, down the path leading to eternal life.

Who, among all of Heavenly Father's children, are candidates for baptism?

Mormon taught: "The first fruits of repentance is baptism" (Moroni 8:25). It is in the baptismal interview that priesthood leaders determine if a candidate meets the Lord's standard for baptism and is prepared to receive the gift of the Holy Ghost. This process fulfils the requirement that is established in the scriptures that candidates witness that they have "truly repented of all their sins." (D&C 20:37).

After we are baptized, how can we be good missionaries? (See D&C 13:1).

We can be valiant in the testimony of Jesus, and continue to make our offerings on the altar of faith. We can "take the Lord's side on every issue. We can think what He thinks, believe what He believes, say what He would say, and do what He would do." (Bruce R. McConkie).

As we think about our
baptism, we intuitively respond
to President Gordon B. Hinckley's
invitation to do a little better, to be a
little more kind, to be a little more merciful,
and a little more forgiving; "to put behind us our
weaknesses of the past, and go forth with new
energy and increased resolution to improve
the world about us, in our homes, in
our places of employment," and
"in our social activities."

28.

We are baptized that we might continue "steadfastly in the apostles' doctrine and fellowship, and in breaking of bread, and in prayers."
(Acts 2:41-42).

What does it mean to be "firm and steadfast in the faith?" (Helaman 15:8).

As we journey through "this vale of tears" (see Wycliffe's Bible, Psalms 84:6), the real journey to Christ has only just begun. Having been born again through baptism, we "press forward" with complete dedication and with "steadfastness," or with confidence and a firm determination in Christ, "having a perfect brightness of hope," or perfect faith, and charity, or "a love of God and of all men." If we do this, "feasting upon the word of Christ," by receiving strength and nourishment from the scriptures, and if we endure to the end, not in wickedness, but in righteousness, we "shall have eternal life," which is the greatest gift that God can bestow. (2 Nephi 31:20).

What qualities must we develop if we are to provide Gospel instruction to others?

We must have hearts that have become the receptacles of true and virtuous principles upon which we may draw in times of need, bowels that are moved to compassion for those who are struggling with misfortune, hands that have been taught to lift those who are in need of support, and feet that have been conditioned to carry us to those who are imprisoned by poor choices, bad habits, or unfortunate circumstances.

Who are "ministering angels?"

These are heavenly messengers who are nursemaids to those with tender testimonies. They reach out and caress those among us who are poor in spirit. From time to time, we all feel their influence, for we have been assisted by acts of providence, are the beneficiaries of divine intervention, have been touched by angels, moved to compassion, or have been otherwise blessed to "walk in the light of the Lord." (Isaiah 2:5).

After baptism, how are we prompted by the Spirit?

Guidance in the form of spiritual promptings and impressions are more common that many would suspect. Powerful intuitive communicators strongly influence nearly all of us to move in the direction of our dreams, toward a greater appreciation of the majesty and power of our Creator. Truly, He "is no respecter of persons" Who causes the sun to shine on the wicked, as well as on the just. (Acts 10:34).

God's
Plan prepares
those on both sides
of the veil to confront
eternity. Its doctrine identifies
the steps we must take to reach our
goals. We work within time lines that
are flexible enough to allow us to
make progress through trial and
error until we have achieved
successful outcomes.

29.

We are baptized that we might be clothed with
spiritual chain-mail, as protection against
the fiery darts of the adversary.
(See 1 Nephi 15:24).

How can Heavenly Father help us to resist Satan's temptations?

Baptism can replenish the power cells that fuel our actions, giving our sight infinite perspective in the flow of a pulsing stream of inspiration that has no temporal or spatial boundary. As we are swept up by quickening currents into the direct experience of a holy communion with God, Satan's enticements fade in their appeal, in the brilliant light of day.

How can immersion in the waters of baptism extinguish the fiery darts of the adversary?

Although telestial turf is Satan's home ground, and the quicksand of secular humanism and other false ideologies lies ready to suck the unwary into the underworld of Beelzebub, "no power on earth or hell can overthrow or defeat that which God has decreed. Every plan of the adversary will fail, for the Lord knows the secret thoughts of men, and sees the future with a vision clear and perfect, even as though it were in the past." (Joseph Fielding Smith, Jr.).

How can keeping our eyes focused on the Savior help us to look past the temptations of the world?

Baptism encourages us to turn our thoughts to heaven, and although they will always be higher than ours, His thoughts will have somehow become our thoughts, and His ways our ways. (See Isaiah 55:8-9). We will be mesmerized by His work and His glory, and will bed nudged ever closer to the mind-bending realization that "the universe is a machine for the making of gods." (Henri Bergson, "Two Sources of Religion and Morality").

How are free will, opposition, and baptism related?

Our baptism make a resounding statement that we have been born of God, have received His image in our countenances, and that we have experienced a mighty change in our hearts. (See Alma 5:14 & 26). Only then, through saving faith, will we be prepared to appropriately exercise our agency to decisively deal with the opposition that is integral to the successful execution of the Plan of Salvation.

The Gentile
nations of the earth
are to receive the Gospel,
and the elect among them are
to be converted by the power of
the Holy Ghost, to be carried
along the path leading
to eternal life.

30.

We are baptized that we might be
released from bondage to sin.
(See D&C 84:49).

What are the key points of King Benjamin's counsel that explain how to free ourselves from the stain of sin? (See Alma 5:21).

As he so clearly taught: "Under this head ye are made free, and there is no other head whereby ye can be made free. There is no other name given whereby salvation cometh. Therefore, I would that ye should take upon you the name of Christ, all you that have entered into the covenant with God that ye should be obedient unto the end of your lives." (Mosiah 5:8).

How do you feel about having prophets to whom we can turn for counsel and guidance?

From the foundation of the world, the prophets have clarified again and again the first principles and ordinances of the Gospel Plan. "Surely the Lord God will do nothing, but he revealeth his secret unto his servants the prophets." (Amos 2:7).

When we are baptized, Whose name do we take upon ourselves?

"And it shall come to pass that whosoever doeth this shall be found at the right hand of God, for he shall know the name by which he is called; for he shall be called by the name of Christ. And now it shall come to pass, that whosoever shall not take upon him the name of Christ must be called by some other name. Therefore, he findeth himself on the left hand of God." (Mosiah 5:9-10).

Without the guidance of our Heavenly Father, how can we hope to deal with opposition in our lives?

Opposition is necessary for The Plan to function, which makes baptism essential. Without it, we must remain in bondage to sin, for we all lack the spiritual horsepower to save ourselves. Truly, we need God every hour of our lives.

Living water is so crucial to our well-being that the Lord has provided the means to penetrate solid limestone, as it were, so that it may freely flow into our lives. Baptism creates a conduit that is chiseled through our rough exterior and stony nature with the tools of faith, obedience, study, prayer, good works, and other healthy lifestyle choices.

31.

We are baptized that we might participate in the foundation ordinance of The Plan of Salvation.

How can our lives become "days of probation?"

Baptism helps to make our mission in mortality a time of testing, or of putting to the proof our declared values.

How has baptism been likened to being reborn? (See John 3:3).

C.S. Lewis famously observed: "We can't go back and change the beginning, but we can start where we are and change the ending." Our re-birth frees us from the stain of sin that has been accumulating since the age of accountability. "Inasmuch as ye were born into the world by water, and blood, and the Spirit, which I have made, and so became of dust a living soul, even so ye must be born again into the kingdom of heaven, of water, and of the Spirit, and be cleansed by blood, even the blood of mine Only Begotten." (Moses 6:59).

Why is baptism an essential element in the formula that is found in the learning laboratory of life?

Experience is the active ingredient of a fertile matrix meticulously prepared by our Heavenly Father as the personalized petri dish that is best suited to our individual circumstances. This rich culture medium becomes just the agar we need in order to nurture our metamorphosis, to be transformed not by maturation but by generation into the full stature of our spirits. The infusion of a heavenly element readies us to receive with equanimity whatever might come during an incubation process that was initiated by divine design to be equally challenging and rewarding.

How can focusing our thoughts on the Savior make our baptismal covenant more meaningful?

The basic objectives of The Plan of Happiness are to keep the Savior in our thoughts, to encourage a daily atmosphere of reflection, to harmonize our behavior with His charitable example, to initiate positive change, and to maintain an eternal perspective.

The Lord Jehovah
said: "Thou shalt bring Aaron
and his sons unto the door of the
tabernacle of the congregation, and
wash them with water. And thou
shalt put upon Aaron the holy
garments, and anoint him,
and sanctify him."
(Exodus 40:12-13).

32.

We are baptized by immersion in water, that we might feel not only the spiritual significance, but also the physical intensity, of the covenant we make with our Heavenly Father.

How can we join heavenly choirs to give glory to God in the highest? (See Luke 2:14).

We can sing the songs of Zion that inspire, motivate, comfort, and strengthen us, while calming our troubled souls. Music and worship are elements of a unified whole. The instruments utilized, the way they are played, the volume and tempo, the lyrics if a vocal, the accompaniment, the attire and attitude of the performers, and the atmosphere in which the music is presented significantly influence our capacity for worship.

How can baptism help us to discover the personal levels of experience with the Savior?

At our baptism, we feel a tangible and palpable "covenant of peace" that moves in concentric waves, touching everything in its path. (Numbers 25:12). Isaiah exclaimed: "How beautiful upon the mountains are the feet of him that bringeth good tidings, that publisheth peace;" that embraceth the teachings of Jesus Christ, "that publisheth salvation; that saith unto" our spirits, "thy God reigneth!" (Isaiah 52:7).

What might we record in our journals about how we felt at our baptisms?

Perhaps we can record that "all the petty trials, sorrows, and sufferings of this life have faded away as temporary, harmless visions seen in a dream." (David O. McKay). Our reverence for the Savior must be in a category all by itself. It can never legitimately fall under the scrutiny of a critical eye, be subjected to unrighteous judgment, or find itself compromised by association with the profane. Our standard of reverence will be set so high that, when the line is crossed by those who find fault with the Author of Salvation, their guilt will be immediately and incontrovertibly established, and the consequences of their actions sealed.

How can we tingle with the consciousness of our kinship with the infinite?

We can feel as did the Dead Sea Covenanters, who wrote of their baptismal experience: "Our sins are forgiven and in the humility of our souls we are for all the Laws of God. Our flesh is cleansed shining bright in the waters of purification, even in the waters of baptism, and we shall be given new names in due time to walk perfect in all the ways of God." ("The Manual of Discipline" or "The Serek Scroll" from The Dead Sea Scrolls).

A
conduit
to living water
is created when we not
only believe, but also act on
our belief, by being honest, true,
chaste, benevolent, virtuous, kind,
and in doing good to others.

33.

We are baptized as Jesus Christ invites us, by name, to become His disciples.

Is it possible that the Godhead knows each of us by our name?

The ordinance confirms that They know each of us by name, and are willing to pause in Their busy schedules to witness our baptism, that we might be welcomed into the fold.

How is the covenant of baptism a two-way promise?

When we are baptized, we make covenants with our Heavenly Father to come into the fold of the Good Shepherd, to bear each other's burdens, to stand as witnesses of Jesus Christ at all times and in all places, and to serve Him and keep His commandments.

What does our Heavenly Father promise, in return?

In turn, He promises to forgive our sins, pour out His Spirit more abundantly upon us, give us daily guidance and help, bless us to come forth in the First Resurrection, and reward us with eternal life.

What does it mean to have His Spirit to be with us?

It means that we might feel the gentle caress of the hands of the Master Potter, as He turn our lives with the hand of time. It means that we have given Him permission, as the Artisan of our destiny, to mold us and shape us. (See Jeremiah 18:6). It means that we are the clay, He is our potter, and we are the work of His hand. (See Isaiah 64:8). It means that as our thoughts turn to the Savior, we remain impressionable and pliable to the things of the Holy Spirit.

Baptism
can give us the
perspective to see adversity
as a diamond dust that polishes
us to a high luster, rather than as an
abrasive that wears us down
and grinds
us up.

34.

We are baptized in a dramatic validation of the influence of the Light of Christ, and of the power of the Holy Ghost.

What does it feel like, when Heavenly Father inspires us by the "unspeakable gift of the Holy Ghost?" (D&C 121:26).

The Holy Ghost works on our conscience, gently guiding us past the first principles and ordinances of the Gospel, upward and onward to covenants relating to the priesthood and the temple. "For behold, thus saith the Lord God: I will give unto the children of men line upon line, precept upon precept, here a little and there a little, and blessed are those who hearken unto my precepts, and lend an ear unto my counsel, for they shall learn wisdom, for unto him that receiveth I will give more." (2 Nephi 28:30).

For how long will the Holy Ghost strive with us?

He will do so "till we all come in the unity of the faith, and of the knowledge of the Son of God, unto a perfect man, unto the measure of the stature of the fulness of Christ." (Ephesians 4:13).

How does the Light of Christ lead us to the Holy Ghost?

To animate our lives with energy, we have been given the Light of Christ. It proceeds from His throne as a powerful influence for good that grooms us to receive the Holy Ghost. It is a gift that miraculously multiplies even as it divides, influencing countless souls whose actions are governed by free will. It is given that we "may act in doctrine and principle pertaining to futurity, according to the moral agency" with which we have been amply endowed. (D&C 101:78).

How can the Light of Christ protect us from the influence of the adversary?

The Light of Christ has been benevolently bestowed upon all of us by One Whom we can be sure "denieth none that come unto him, black and white, bond and free, male and female; and he remembereth the heathen; and all are alike unto (Him), both Jew and Gentile." (2 Nephi 26:33). It stimulates soul-sweat as it works on our conscience, our sense of duty, and our scruples in the face of relentless opposition in all things. (See 2 Nephi 2:11).

Our covenant
of baptism quickens us, that we
might use opposition as the key it
was intended to be, to open up a portal
to the Spirit. We thereby internalize Gospel
principles, and in our obedience to
priesthood covenants, we may
do all things.

35.

We are baptized to affirm the innocence of little children.

How can it be, that from the foundation of the world, little children have been saved without baptism? (See D&C 137:10).

It was an integral element of The Plan of Salvation, ordained in the Grand Council in Heaven before the world was, that little children who died before the age of accountability would be saved in the Celestial Kingdom by the power of the Atonement. "If not so, God is a partial God, and also a changeable God, and a respecter of persons, for how many little children have died without baptism!" (Moroni 8:12).

Why is infant baptism a heretical practice?

It denies that Jesus Christ atoned for the "original sin" of Adam, and refutes the concept of individual accountability. It demands that little children who die without baptism cannot enter heaven. But the Atonement did redeem them from the Fall. They are capable of actions that are inconsistent with obedience to Gospel principles, but they are not counted against them as sins. Little children are not culpable.

What did Moroni have to say about baptism and accountability?

He wrote: "This thing shall ye teach - repentance and baptism unto those who are accountable and capable of committing sin. Yea, teach parents that they must repent and be baptized, and humble themselves as their little children, and they shall all be saved with their little children." (Moroni 8:10).

How did Moroni link accountability to the baptism of little children?

He declared: "Little children need no repentance, neither baptism. Behold, baptism is unto repentance to the fulfilling the commandments unto the remission of sins. But little children are alive in Christ, even from the foundation of the world." (Moroni 8:11-12).

As our circle of knowledge grows,
so do the borders of darkness that encroach
upon the edge of the light. The more we know,
the more we need to learn, in order to deal
with the opposition that is a part of all of
our undertakings. Baptism centers us,
and orients us toward the light
so that the shadows will
always be behind us.

36.

We are baptized that we might experience spiritual delight, without the rush of sensory overstimulation that is prevalent in our technological world.

How does baptism date back to an earlier time, when the pace of life was less hectic?

Baptism teaches us how to "caress the tender chords of associations, of gratitude, loyalty, and appreciation, of selflessness, helpfulness and forgiveness, of friendship, love, and compassion." It moves us, with "truth discovered and accepted, of beauty created and enjoyed, of goodness deepened and made manifest in life."

How does baptism invite us to stay in touch with our five physical senses, while enhancing contact with our spiritual sixth sense?

It invites us to sense the world about us, "to smell its fragrance, hear its sounds, glimpse its form and colors, and warm our souls in the glow of relationships; to feel an upward reach when made suddenly aware of a truth, a beauty, a goodness above and beyond our own attainment." (P.A. Anderson).

How is baptism the physical confirmation of a spiritual reality?

Progress to perfection is a process, and not a point. We do not need to be the stars of the show. Rather than becoming the objects of attention of an adoring paparazzi, we foresee ourselves being enveloped instead in dazzling clouds of divinely directed diamond dust that glitters with thousands of points of light. We are participants in daily dramas that far surpass the pomp and circumstance of any "American Idol" production.

How do the Light of Christ and the Holy Ghost provide unmatched sensory stimulation?

As fire in the sky, the air in the theater of life is charged with an electricity that represents the inevitable merger of the universal encouragement of the Light of Christ with the pointed and providential guidance provided by the Holy Ghost. Streaking in tandem across the heavens, their trajectories coalesce to trace a flaming trail that sparkles over a vast cosmic ocean that is alive with energy. Over the ebb and flow of its tide, an effectual bridge of understanding is created, that is buttressed by the cohesive influence of the mighty foundation of faith.

Because
of our baptismal
covenant, one day in the not too
distant future, the atmosphere will
be pungent with a heavenly aether that
is punctuated by the melodious strains of
our native language. Every detail will be
just as we had imagined it would be,
including the reassuring radiant
heat of a celestial fire
kindled beforehand
by Father.

37.

We are baptized "for the perfecting of the saints, for the work of the ministry, (and) for the edifying of the body of Christ."
(Ephesians 4:12).

What is the three-fold mission of the Church?

Paul would be in complete agreement with the mission statement of The Church of Jesus Christ of Latter-day Saints: To preach the Gospel, to perfect the Saints, and to redeem the dead.

What did Paul mean by the term: "the body of Christ?"

There is strength in numbers. Therefore, in the wisdom of God, His covenant children gather together in wards and stakes, that they might be mutually edified. They are a lot like snowflakes, that are one of nature's most fragile creations. Although delicate in structure, look at what they can do when they stick together.

What does it mean to edify the body of Christ?

The sturdiest plants that bear the best fruit are those that have deep roots in good, rich, nurturing soil. So, to edify the body of Christ, we must surround ourselves with the best that can be provided in music and art, conversation, example, decency, virtue, and honor. Then, with the members of the Church, we will grow freely, even as we send down taproots into Gospel soil to secure our solid footing.

Who is needed to edify the body of Christ?

That the whole may be kept in perfect working order, and so that all those within the fold may expand their capabilities to the level of their potential, the Church "hath need of every member." (D&C 84:110).

To whom
but God can we
turn for the assurance that
liberates us from fear, doubt, the
apprehension of danger, the turmoil
of the world, and from the vagaries of
men? Only when we have cast off the self-
limiting conditions and self-defeating
behaviors that blind us to a larger
view of life, will we enjoy a
settled conviction of the
truth in our
minds.

38.

We are baptized that we might "all come in the unity
of the faith, and of the knowledge of the Son
of God...unto the measure of the stature
of the fulness of Christ."
(Ephesians 4:13).

Why is it important for members of the Church to be unified in their faith?

When we begin to approach the fulness of the stature of Christ, we are akin to coast redwood trees, that are among the largest living things. The tallest tree reaches a height of over 360 feet, weighs hundreds of tons, and has been living for well over 2,000 years.

Why is unity in the faith critical to our survival?

Curiously, while most other trees of massive size have deep roots to support their great weight, the root system of the redwood is very shallow. The key to its survival is the intertwining of the roots of one tree with those of several of its neighbors. Redwoods live in groves; they cannot stand alone. Interdependence is critical to the stability and longevity of each individual tree.

How can baptism help us to become perfect in Christ? (See Moroni 10:32).

Baptism helps us to get off religious roundabouts. We "come unto Christ, and (are) perfected in him, and deny (ourselves) of all ungodliness; and if (we) shall deny (our)selves of all ungodliness, and love God with all (our) might, mind and strength, then is his grace sufficient for (us), that by his grace (we) may be perfect in Christ." (Moroni 10:32).

What happens to us as we mature in the Gospel?

We realize the potential of our position, as we become the sons and daughters of God. We are one in our Savior Jesus Christ, as He is one in the Father, and the Father one in Him, that we may be one. (See D&C 35:2). We retain our distinct individuality, but become unified in every other way.

When
we are baptized,
we very quickly recognize the
pathway that leads to a Christ-centered
life. The Sacrament allows us to regularly
recommit ourselves to internalize every
truth relating to eternal progression,
and endows us with the power
to endure to the end in
righteousness.

39.

We are baptized "that we henceforth be no more children, tossed to and fro." (Ephesians 4:14).

How does our baptism help us to face the adversity that pops up in even our well-balanced mortal lives?

Baptism helps us to be patient in our afflictions. Knowing that the Lord is with us until the end of our days helps us to endure our trials and tribulations, even when they are undeserved, or we do not understand why we have them. (See D&C 24:8).

How does our baptism help us to strengthen our relationship with Jesus Christ?

Because of our baptismal covenant, we will never again be left to fight our battles alone. Baptism establishes a covenant relationship with the Lord that invites Him to stand with us, to weigh-in on our side of the balance, even as the counterfeit coin of Satan's spurious currency clatters down in a cacophony of confusion on the other side of the scale.

How should we interact with those who are as children because they do not understand the principles of the Gospel?

As we interact with those who are struggling to feel even the influence of the Light of Christ, we must not pretend to know everything. We need to recognize when we are "speed listening," or formulating retorts in our mind, when we should instead be listening carefully. We need to resist the temptation to treat every conversation as a debate. As Isaiah counseled: "Come now, and let us reason together." (Isaiah 1:18).

How can we nurture understanding when our friends express confusion about the principle of baptism?

We should pose questions that lead to understanding, by frequently rehearsing the three magic words: "Tell me more." We should attentively listen for emotion, and always ask respectful questions. We need to discipline ourselves and ask ourselves: "How are our views similar?" and "Where is our common ground?" before offering responses.

At our baptismal services in particular, we feel the Spirit through the medium of music. We are reminded that even before the foundations of the earth were laid, music filled the celestial air, when "the morning stars sang together, and all the sons of God shouted for joy." (Job 38:7).

40.

We are baptized that we might speak
"the truth in love, (and) grow up
into him in all things, which
is the head, even Christ."
(Ephesians 4:15).

How is it easier to "speak the truth in love" after our baptism?

Robert D. Hales said: "For the most part, conversion happens over a period of time as study, prayer, experience, and faith help us to grow in our testimony and conversion." (C.R., 4/1997). The fruits of faith come more easily to the prepared mind, and nothing prepares us as does baptism!

How can baptism help us to "grow up into him in all things?"

Our baptism gives us the capacity to squarely face even our most stubborn challenges. It helps us to be unified with the Saints, even as we celebrate our individuality and diversity. It nurtures us to move from dependence, through independence, and finally to the mature state of interdependence. It gives us the tools to enjoy unity and conformity without at the same time sacrificing what makes each of us unique.

How can the Savior be our head, if we are unwilling to submit to baptism?

The truth be told, many of our friends are very close to becoming members of the Church. If they would just change one or two behaviors or beliefs, they would be spot-on. Here's a radical thought, though. What if, instead, we changed just one or two of our behaviors, or viewed our neighbors' beliefs in a more tolerant light? Might that not become a powerful tool of conversion?

How can speaking the truth in love cleanse our inner vessel? (See Alma 60:23).

Thinking about the Savior should be more than a repetitive exercise to be performed only by the numbers. It helps us to communicate feeling, capture emotion, contour attitude, crystallize thought, compartmentalize action, congeal passion, and convey sentiments that creates spiritual revitalization.

"Little children need no repentance, neither baptism. Behold, baptism is unto repentance to the fulfilling the commandments unto the remission of sins. But little children are alive in Christ, even from the foundation of the world."
(Moroni 8:11-12).

41.

We are baptized "unto the confounding
of false doctrines and laying
down of contentions."
(2 Nephi 3:12).

How does baptism prepare us to confound false doctrines?

Baptism blesses us with a hope in Christ. It calibrates our internal attitude control to an eternal perspective, and quickens our desire to be righteous in the face of obstacles, to resist opposition, and ultimately to rely upon the grace of God and the power of the Atonement.

In what ways are members of the Church particularly well-prepared to deal with the laying down of contentions?

Baptism gives our spiritual muscles pliancy and flexibility, that there might be room for the companionship of the Holy Ghost, "which maketh manifest unto the children of men, according to their faith." (Jarom 1:4). We will always be subject to the effects of adversity and opposition, but without the therapeutic benefits of baptism, we may needlessly suffer from a stiff neck that prevents us from looking up to Heavenly Father for guidance, over to priesthood leaders for counsel, around to seek out those in need, and down in an attitude of humility.

How does baptism gently guide us toward an appreciation of the peaceable things of the kingdom? (See D&C 39:6).

The principles of The Plan carry us from baptism to the covenants of the temple. "For behold, thus saith the Lord God: I will give unto the children of men line upon line, precept upon precept, here a little and there a little, and blessed are those who hearken unto my precepts, and lend an ear unto my counsel, for they shall learn wisdom, for unto him that receiveth I will give more." (2 Nephi 28:30).

Why is baptism as important a principle today as it has ever been in the past?

The Last Days mirror those of Mormon, who wrote that "there were sorceries, and witchcrafts, and magics, and the power of the evil one was wrought upon all the face of the land" because of the lack of faith of the people. (Mormon 1:19). Baptism is the spiritual equivalent of the boost we receive after consuming a power bar or energy drink 30 minutes before engaging in physical activity.

Whenever our priorities
are out of order, we lose the
power to bring about positive change.
Baptism, however, sharpens our perspective,
enabling us to comprehend and build
upon principles of perfection that
are validated by the Spirit and
emulated by the example
of the Savior.

42.

We are baptized that the light of our lives might grow "brighter and brighter until the perfect day."
(D&C 50:24).

What is the light of our lives? (See Mosiah 27:29).

"The spirit of man is the candle of the Lord." (Proverbs 20:27). When they come into the world, every child of God has a full measure of light, that represents the purity of the Spirit. Too often, life becomes a process of detraction in the sense that intrinsic light is lost, as the children of men succumb to worldly cares. The judgment may simply be a measurement of the numbers of foot-candles of light remaining, that we bring to the bar of justice.

When we came to earth from our heavenly home, do you think we were full of light?

"Our birth" may be only "a sleep and a forgetting." Perhaps "the soul that rises with us, our life's star, hath had elsewhere its setting, and cometh from afar." If so, then "not in entire forgetfulness, and not in utter nakedness, but trailing clouds of glory do we come, from God, who is our Home." (William Wordsworth, "Ode on Intimations of Immortality").

How can we protect our light from encroachment by the darkness that is all around us?

Politically correct tolerance embraces all sorts of deviant behavior. Flim-flam artists adroitly fleece us of our very identity as children of God, and most of the time, we are not even aware that the theft has taken place. "Vice is a monster of such frightful mien, as to be hated needs but to be seen. Yet seen too oft, familiar with her face, we first endure, then pity, then embrace." (Alexander Pope). We have come full circle from Eve's temptation in the Garden. Once again, we are beguiled by tinkling cymbals and sounding brass.

How can our baptism help us to be drawn to the light?

With baptism, there comes a familiarity with principles that stands in sharp contrast to the values of society that are continually morphed by the shifting sands of cultural expediency. The covenants we make at baptism protect us from these mutating tenets, and provide a stable moral basis that shapes us as we develop into the full stature of our spirits.

With our
baptism, we feel the word
enlarge our souls and enlighten
our understanding. As Brigham Young
said: "Every Gospel principle carries within
it a witness that it is true." In the economy of
the Gospel, "we often catch a spark from the
awakened memories of the immortal soul,
which lights up our whole being as with
the glory of our former home."
(Joseph F. Smith).

43.

We are baptized that the earth might "be full
of the knowledge of the Lord, as
the waters cover the sea."
(Isaiah 11:9).

Why is our participation in The Plan of Happiness important?

Our baptism leaves the world a better place than when we found it. When we pass beyond the veil, our loved ones will be left with legacies of both tangible and intangible remembrances. We will leave them with our testimonies. We will leave them with gratitude for the privilege and blessing to have been knit together in a family, that is the basic building block of Heavenly Father's great Plan of Happiness.

How can the baptism of our children make a positive difference in the world?

Our little ones are the nobility of heaven, a chosen generation with a divine destiny. We make whatever sacrifices are necessary to insure their continuing success. They come to us from their heavenly home "like gentle rain through darkened skies, with glory trailing from their feet as they go, and endless promise in their eyes." While under our care, they grow tall and strong, "like silver trees against the storm; who will not bend with the wind or the change, but stand to fight the world alone." (Doug Stewart).

How does baptism help us to trace our royal lineage, and teach us who we really are?

We "are the few, the warriors saved for Saturday, to come the last day of the world. We are they, of Saturday. We are the strong, the warriors rising in our might to win the battle raging in the hearts of men, on Saturday. We are strangers from a realm of light, who have forgotten all - the memory of our former life and the purpose of our call. And so, we must learn why we're here, and who we really are." (Doug Stewart).

How can the knowledge of the Lord increase in the earth when we are true to our baptismal covenant?

If we want the knowledge of the Lord to cover the earth, we need to plan our work and work our plan. We need to define our dreams as a sequence of steps that must be taken, and identify activities that must be performed well for our strategies to succeed. We need to identify and allocate available resources, so that we may understand beforehand the costs required to meet our goals. We need to identify specific tasks that must be performed and by whom, and find the time to follow through to successful conclusions.

Baptism can give us the
perspective to see adversity
as a diamond dust that polishes
us to a high luster, rather than as an
abrasive that wears us down
and grinds us up.

44.

We are baptized to capture the promise
of "the peace of God, which
passeth all understanding."
(Philippians 4:7).

How can baptism define the pathway to peace?

Those who are eight years of age are so recently removed from the stability and certainty of the eternal world, that they are often impatient to recapture the peaceful security and quiet serenity of the more relaxed, familiar, and predictable environment to which they had become accustomed. Their baptism gives them the opportunity to literally have the best of both worlds; to live on earth, but still enjoy a heavenly peace that surpasses understanding.

How can we find peace in the world today?

The innocence of children who are about to be baptized makes us optimistic that peace is within our reach. When we become as little children, "submissive, meek, humble, patient, (and) full of love," the enticings of the Holy Spirit help us to put off the natural man and to become saints through the Atonement of Jesus Christ. (Mosiah 3:19).

How does the world's concept of peace differ from that to which baptism invites us?

The world's definition of peace is remarkably superficial: often-times peace is only equated with the lack of bloodshed or active combatants. The Lord's definition is quite different. "His peace is not the peace of the world of ease, of luxury, idleness, absence of turmoil and strife, but the peace born of the righteous life, the peace that lifts the soul, that day by day brings us closer to the home of Eternal Peace, the dwelling place of our Father." (J. Reuben Clark, Jr.).

Without baptism, can we ever be at peace?

Until we acknowledge God's power, and have cast off the self-limiting conditions and self-defeating behaviors that blind us to a larger view of life, will we enjoy a settled conviction of the truth in our minds. The peace that follows obedience to celestial principles brings a greater reality within our reach. When we realize that we are not alone, we have begun a journey that will carry us to a higher state of being where we will find ourselves covered in star dust, as we mingle with the Gods.

Baptism creates
a groundswell of emotion that
generates the energy to lift us heavenward.
Worship is elevated to something that is more
dynamic than the simple mechanical observance
of a multiplicity of ceremonial rules. It helps
us to communicate feeling, capture emotion,
contour attitude, crystalize thought, congeal
passion, compartmentalize action, and
convey sentiments that creates
spiritual revitalization.

45.

*We are baptized that we might pause,
and reflect upon the things that
are really important
in our lives.*

Whose reflection do we see when we look down into the quiet waters of baptism?

Reflection is a good thing, especially when the light of Christ shines on our countenances. As Alma asked the people of Zarahemla, "And now, behold, I ask of you, my brethren of the church, have ye spiritually been born of God? Have ye received His image in your countenances? Have ye experienced this mighty change in your heart?" (Alma 5:14).

What kind of change comes over us at our baptism?

When we receive the image of the Lord in our countenance, our faces will reflect the light of Christ. When we experience a mighty change in our hearts, we will be transformed, not by maturation, but by generation. We will have become new creatures in Christ.

How does the world seek change?

The world attempts to make changes from the outside, and fails miserably. The Gospel changes us from the inside, and succeeds brilliantly. We are thus created to reach our potential in both the image and likeness of God, our Father.

Why is the worship of idols of any kind so destructive?

Idol worship is the epitome of taking the name of God in vain. One of the terrible consequences of the fascination of Babylon with idols is spiritual insensitivity. Isaiah foresaw the Last Days, when he wrote: "Stay yourselves, and wonder; cry ye out, and cry: they are drunken, but not with wine. They stagger, but not with strong drink. For the Lord hath poured out upon you the spirit of deep sleep, and hath closed your eyes: the prophets, and your rulers, and seers hath he covered." (Isaiah 29:9-11).

As we live in
harmony with the principles of
the Gospel, we begin to understand
how our covenants with God help us to
overcome adversity and gain self-mastery.
We learn how our covenants can help us
to focus our efforts to become as He is.
With a quickening pulse, we begin to
understand that our covenants
prepare us to become
as God is.

46.

We are baptized that we might affirm our faith in the immortality of our souls, because we feel, within ourselves, immortal longings.

How does it change our outlook on life, to know that we are spiritual beings having mortal experiences?

With Enos, we "rejoice in the day when (our) mortal shall put on immortality, and shall stand before him; then shall (we) see his face with pleasure, and he will say unto (us): Come unto me, ye blessed, there is a place prepared for you in the mansions of my Father." (Enos 1:27).

What does it feel like when the veil seems to be very thin?

Sometimes, when we brush against the veil, we feel inner stirrings that are the harmonic vibrations of the music of a heavenly choir, and we hear the indistinct murmurings of the voices of angelic messengers. This is one of the reasons that we are baptized; that while we yet dwell on the earth, we might nevertheless be blessed to be "partakers of the divine nature." (2 Peter 1:4).

What is magical about putting our lives in harmony with the principles of The Plan of Salvation?

There are rhythms in nature that we feel only when we are in harmony with eternal principles. The veil can be almost transparent in our lives when we are spiritually sensitive. As our powers expand, we experience the glittering facets of the life of the Spirit, until we feel that we have been cast off into a stream of revelation and carried along in the quickening currents of direct experience with God.

Why was the commandment to be baptized given, in the first place?

"For this end was the law given," to prepare us to be Christ-like, until "we are made alive in Christ because of our faith." (2 Nephi 25:25).

In moments of
deep reflection, as at the
waters of baptism, we envision
"stepping on shore, and finding it
heaven! We visualize taking hold of
a hand, and finding it God's hand.
We dream of passing from storm
and tempest to an unbroken
calm, and of waking up,
and finding it home."
(Anonymous).

47.

We are baptized that we might learn to abide by the laws of
the Celestial Kingdom, even as we dwell upon the
earth, that our hearts might burn within us, as
the Spirit speaks to us and opens the
scriptures to our understanding.
(See Luke 24:32).

What can happen to us if we wait another day to take advantage of repentance?

We must not wait to develop saving faith, or procrastinate the day of our repentance until we are spiritually dead to the Light of Christ. When we no longer are able to make the vital distinction between good and evil, or between light and darkness, we become subject to the wiles of the Devil. (See Alma 34:35).

What happens if we no longer honor our baptismal covenant to rely upon the Atonement of Christ by continually repenting of our sins?

The Spirit of the Lord withdraws and the Devil has power over the children of men, when they voluntarily surrender to him their freedom to act independently. This is the state of the unrepentant wicked, from which there may be no recovery. When the sword of Justice falls, it will be for them as if there had been no redemption made, and the Atonement will be of no effect. (See Alma 34:35).

When the wicked have no intention of repenting, what do you think will happen when "critical mass" is reached?

When depravity drives away the Spirit, and the lives of the wicked are thrown into imbalance, chaos and ruin are the inevitable result. The tragedy is not what becomes of them, but what they themselves have become.

Do you think angels take notice of our efforts to be obedient to the laws of heaven?

As the battle rages in the hearts of men, those who have been baptized will live their lives in crescendo. The deafening roar of their righteousness will command the attention of the very angels who wield the sword of Justice and who only await God's command to let it fall on an unrepentant world.

Our perfect
obedience to the laws and
ordinances of the Gospel qualifies us
to enter into the Rest of the Lord. Our
covenants have the power to move us along
the path of progression to the point that
we reflect God's divine nature and
feel comfortable in His presence.
This is one of the reasons why
we repetitively rehearse
the veil experience.

48.

We are baptized that we might think less in terms of self-sufficiency, and more about our Christ dependency.

What do you think it means to "come unto Christ?" (Moroni 10:32).

We realize that His message was intended to change not only behavior, but also nature. Perfect obedience to the laws and ordinances of the Gospel qualifies us to enter into the Rest of the Lord. Our covenants have the power to move us along the path of progression to the point that we reflect God's divine nature and feel comfortable in His presence. This is one of the reasons why we repetitively rehearse the veil experience in the temple.

What are some of the divine attributes that we can all work on after our baptisms?

We can be chaste in our behavior and love others. We can discipline our nature, and be righteous stewards. We can love our less fortunate brethren. We can take proper care of our bodies, and try to be in touch with the Spirit so that we better comprehend omniscience. We can pray to understand the gift of His Son, and we can ponder the power of His priesthood by participating in the ordinances of the Gospel.

How does baptism prepare us deal with the challenges of life?

By living in accordance with the principles of the Gospel, we begin to understand how our covenants with God help us to overcome adversity and gain self-mastery. We learn how our covenants can help us to focus our efforts to become as He is. As we do so, it begins to dawn on us that this is the purpose of the covenants we make with Him. With a quickening pulse, we begin to understand that our covenants prepare us to become as God is, and to feel comfortable in His presence.

How is our baptism an expression of our conviction that the Savior is the sole source of our protection?

He has promised us: "There is no weapon that is formed against you shall prosper." (D&C 71:9). If we keep our covenants, He will cause the heavens to shake for our good, "and Satan shall tremble and Zion shall rejoice upon the hills and flourish." (D&C 35:24).

Baptism empowers
us to follow through to
successful conclusions. The
Church is the vehicle
that makes this
possible.

49.

We are baptized that we might be given the tools to burst free of our self-imposed limitations.

What happens to us when we keep the Savior in our thoughts?

When the Savior is the focus of our lives, the clarity of our vision gives us the ability to overcome our weaknesses. Stumbling blocks become stepping stones, and through experience, we learn that "all things which are good cometh of Christ." (Moroni 7:24).

What happens to us when we lose the guidance of the Holy Ghost?

If we mistakenly trivialize celestial sureties, we become susceptible to the enticements of the Devil. Without the protective influence and guidance of the Holy Ghost, we are vulnerable to the lethal storms sweeping the face of the earth, which have been initiated by the destroyer. Then, we lose the power to resist telestial tempests, and the suffocating storms of Satan will suck the very life-sustaining marrow from our bones.

What happens to us when we are attuned to the whisperings of the Spirit?

The powers of heaven and earth amplify each other, and carry us along on waves of the Spirit. With baptism, all our trappings and pretenses are shorn away, outward observance and phylacteries are stripped from the ritual of our worship, and only our true feelings remain.

Why do we use the expression: "The healing waters of baptism?

Raw and ugly sores that have been inflicted by worldly influences are healed in the waters of baptism. The Balm of Gilead prevails over even the most powerful onslaughts that Babylon can muster.

With our
baptism, our attention
is focused on our testimonies, and
the covenant encourages us to nurture
them. Every day thereafter, we take
our testimony temperature, and
hope to regularly detect
its feverish pitch.

50.

We are baptized in white clothing, to symbolically express the purity of the ordinance and the proximity of the Spirit.

How does baptism invite the protection of heaven?

Angels will attend us after we have entered the Fold. "For I will go before your face," promised the Lord. "I will be on your right hand, and on your left, and my Spirit shall be in your hearts, and mine angels round about you, to bear you up." (D&C 84:88).

How can our baptism help us to maintain adequate reserves of the Spirit?

We are all faced with times when withdrawals must be made from our spiritual bank accounts. Because of our covenant consciousness, however, we do not write checks that cannot be cashed. We faithfully and consistently make deposits over a period of time, so that we can count upon the cornucopia of comfort created by the cushion of confidence that courses from consistently conforming our conduct to covenants contracted with our Creator.

How can something as simple as baptism protect us against something so comprehensive as the organized forces of evil?

Simply put, baptism exposes us to the process by which we progress. Heavenly Father designed baptism to test our mettle. This is why having the courage to be true to our convictions is so intimately tied to righteousness. Only when we act on the basis of faith will we receive a confirmation of the power behind the ordinance of baptism, as feelings of self-confidence grow and purposeful action replaces tentative overtures.

What is our best defense against evil?

The relevancy of King Benjamin's counsel is almost self-evident: "This much I can tell you," he said. "If ye do not watch yourselves, and your thoughts, and your words, and your deeds, and observe the commandments of God, and continue in the faith ... even unto the end of your lives, ye must perish." (Mosiah 4:30).

If we
want the knowledge
of the Lord to cover
the earth, we need to plan
our work, and work The Plan,
and to define our dreams so
that we may understand
beforehand the costs
required to meet
our goals.

51.

We are baptized that we might publish peace and tidings of great joy, endure to the end, and be lifted up at the last day, to inherit eternal life.
(See 1 Nephi 13:37).

How does the Gospel bring the world news of great joy and peace?

Aaron taught King Lamoni's father: "Since man had fallen, he could not merit anything of himself. But the sufferings and death of Christ atone for their sins, through faith and repentance, (and) he breaketh the bands of death, that the grave shall have no victory … that the sting of death should be swallowed up in the hopes of glory." (Alma 22:14).

What happens to us as we publish peace and glad tidings?

A groundswell of emotion generates the energy to lift us heavenward. Worship is elevated to something more dynamic than the simple mechanical observance of a multiplicity of ceremonial rules. Publishing peace is the daily antidote to our tendency toward pride, selfishness, and self-reliance.

What happens when we cannot generate the spiritual horsepower to express our feelings about the Savior?

Such was the case when Jesus asked the Pharisees: "What think ye of Christ? Whose son is he?" (Matthew 22:41-42). Sadly, their sluggish response, was tendered with little feeling or emotion. Its dearth of traction was obvious, its inability to generate spontaneity was palpable, its lack of energy to engage enthusiasm was noticeable, its incapacity to spark vitality was evident, and its failure to candidly acknowledge the powerful relationship that can exist between ourselves and God was clear.

Why is it important to strengthen our relationship with the Savior?

The simple questions: "What think ye of Christ?" demands that we dig deeply within ourselves before we bear our witness, because it is all too easy to superficially retreat into colorless and insipid verbiage as the easy way out. If we casually and carelessly steer a course away from Him with offhand, dismissive, and inconsiderate comments, until He is conveniently out of sight and mind, we can realistically expect in return no more than a stupor of thought.

Our baptism
gives us the opportunity
to literally have the best of
both worlds; to live on earth,
but still enjoy a heavenly
peace that surpasses
understanding.

52.

We are baptized that we might enjoy the Sabbath day, as we never have before.

How does baptism help us to obey the Law of the Sabbath?

With baptism, we are introduced to a day of worship and of rest, that we may be far from the tumult of the teeming multitudes of the telestial crowd. He knows that it is easy for us to choke on possessions whose opacity clouds our ability to experience illumination by the Spirit. Focusing on the kingdom, especially on the Sabbath, helps us to maintain our perspective and strengthen our reverence for His work.

For what purpose was the Sabbath day created?

God has prepared the Sabbath Day as a "work release program" to see how we will behave when we are left on our own, after having received unambiguous instruction regarding what we ought to do.

How can baptism help the Sabbath day become more special?

On His day, we "praise (His) great and terrible name, for it is holy." (Psalms 99:3). We no longer put to death those who profane or secularize the Sabbath, and yet we die spiritually when we alienate ourselves from God's influence, because our progression comes to a halt. For "broad is the gate, and wide the way that leadeth to the deaths; and many there are that go in thereat, because they receive me not, neither do they abide in my law." (D&C 132:25).

How can baptism turn our hearts to the Law of the Sabbath?

There is a perpetual battle raging in our hearts. It pits our desire to serve our Master against telestial tendencies that twist our focus inward, toward ourselves and away from our Creator. "Two ways always lie open before us - one leading to an ever lower and lower plane, where are heard the cries of despair and the curses of the poor, where manhood shrivels and possessions wear down the possessor; and the other leading to the highlands of the morning where are heard the glad shouts of humanity, and where honest effort is rewarded with immortality." (John P. Altgeld).

Angels will attend us after we have entered the fold. "For I will go before your face," promised the Lord. "I will be on your right hand, and on your left, and my Spirit shall be in your hearts, and mine angels round about you, to bear you up." (D&C 84:88).

53.

We are baptized that we might reconnect with our spiritual Birth Parents.

How does baptism remind us that we are never really very far from Home?

Truly did Shakespeare write that "the world is all a stage," for life is a Three Act Play. The script was written long before the world was made. The First Act took place in the pre-earth existence, where we, as spirit children of our Heavenly Father, were nurtured by his side. The Second Act takes place on the earth, where we have come for a brief sojourn, to have experiences that only mortality can offer, to develop faith, and to learn to be obedient. The Third Act will take place when physical death overtakes us.

How does our baptism expand our understanding of our divine heritage?

We see the scriptures in a new light, that we are the sons and daughters of "the living God." (Hosea 1:10). "The Spirit itself beareth witness with our spirit, that we are the children of God." (Romans 8:16). We find answers to our yearning to know: "Have we not all one father?" We ask the question: "Hath not one God created us?" (Malachi 2:10).

How does God answer, when we ask: "Father, are you there?"

In a wonderfully whole and complete manner, Heavenly Father is sensitive to our needs and to our prayers, however small or insignificant they may seem to us. He does hear us, because prayer draws upon the virtue present in the Spirit of God. Every time we reach out to God, we are, in effect, touching the Savior's garment. How we do this, no one can describe, for it must be directly experienced. (See Mark 5:27-34).

How is our baptism related to the sealing power of the priesthood?

If we remain true to our covenants, in the eternities, there will be no empty chairs around the table at family gatherings. When we return home from our mortal mission, we will fondly remember the people we met, and those we helped. We will recall how we have grown both physically and spiritually. We will find Mother there, waiting to embrace us, as She stands beside Father, Who will be bursting with pride in our accomplishments. We will brush away tears of happiness on our cheeks. Father will strike hands with us, and then hug us tenderly. Mother will put Her arm around our waist, and escort us to the familiar surroundings of the room that has been prepared for our homecoming

With baptism, we
receive a variety of spiritual
gifts that can be the antidote for
the poisonous telestial tendencies
that suppress the expression
of celestial sureties.

54.

We are baptized that we might enter into God's Rest.

How is God's Rest harmonious with family exaltation?

Our families can be our greatest source of joy in time, as well as in the eternities. In moments of deep reflection, as at the waters of baptism, we envision "stepping on shore, and finding it heaven! We visualize taking hold of a hand, and finding it God's hand. We contemplate breathing a new air, and finding it celestial air. We imagine feeling invigorated, and finding it immortality. We dream of passing from storm and tempest to an unbroken calm, and of waking up, and finding it home." (Anonymous).

How can baptism generate the power to propel us into God's Rest?

Moroni promised: "If it so be that ye believe in Christ, and are baptized, first with water, then with fire and with the Holy Ghost, following the example of our Savior, according to that which he hath commanded us, it shall be well with you in the day of judgment." (Mormon 7:10).

What must we do, in order to be able to enter into God's Rest?

When we gain a perfect knowledge of the divinity of the work, we will no longer suffer from fear, doubt, apprehension of danger, the religious turmoil of the world, or from the vagaries of men. His Rest is born of a settled conviction of the truth in our minds, and is manifest in the peace that follows our obedience to celestial principles.

After our baptism, how can we embark upon our journey to Christ with real enthusiasm?

As we journey through "this vale of tears" (see Wycliffe's Bible, Psalms 84:6), the real journey to Christ has only just begun. Having been born again through baptism, we "lay aside every sin," which beforehand had easily besought us, and had bound us down to destruction. (Alma 7:15).

Simply put, baptism
exposes us to the process
by which we progress. Heavenly
Father designed baptism to test our
mettle. This is why having the courage be
true to our convictions is so intimately tied
to righteousness. Only when we act on the basis
of faith will we receive a confirmation of the
power behind the ordinance of baptism,
as feelings of self-confidence grow
and purposeful action replaces
our tentative overtures.

55.

We are baptized that we might vitalize Heavenly Father's Plan of Happiness in our lives.

How can our baptism help us to internalize the principles that lead to happiness?

Joseph Smith said: "Happiness is the object and design of our existence, and will be the end thereof, if we pursue the path that leads to it, and this path is virtue, uprightness, faithfulness, holiness, and keeping all of the commandments of God." ("Teachings," p. 255).

How does our baptism provide opportunities to re-adjust our priorities?

With baptism, some of us painfully recognize that we have sought "all the days of (our) lives for that which (we) cannot obtain, and ... have sought for happiness in doing iniquity, which thing is contrary to the nature of that righteousness which is in our great and Eternal Head." (Helaman 13:38). Enlightened by the Spirit, the eyes of our understanding are opened. (See D&C 76:12, 110:1, and 138:11).

Why is the Gospel the foundation of real happiness?

Baptism provides insight into the spiritual roots of our relationships that are the products of our interconnectivity and interdependence. These help us to live in the world without being tarnished by it. In the end, "abundance is multiplied unto (the Saints) through the manifestations of the Spirit." (D&C 70:13). Our righteous objectives stay in focus when we pay attention to the guideposts that have been provided by our Heavenly Father. These mile markers help us to stay on track during our journey through mortality.

Why do those who disobey the commandments sometimes seem to be happy?

They may live "after the manner of happiness for a season." They are able to do this because their level of understanding and their behavior harmonize with worldly standards. As long as they can shut out the light of Christ, they may live in the illusion of happiness. But, sooner or later, the discrepancy between their behavior and Gospel ideals will become so great that it cannot be sustained, and their short-lived pleasure in worldly ways will be destroyed. They will ultimately realize that "wickedness never was happiness." (Alma 41:10).

Eight year old
children are so recently removed
from the stability and certainty of the
eternal world, that they are often impatient to
recapture the peaceful security and quiet
serenity of the more relaxed, familiar,
and predictable environment to
which they had become
accustomed.

56.

We are baptized that we might forever thereafter commemorate the birthdate of our immortal souls.

How is our baptism a cause for celebration in heaven?

Bathed in the stunning clarity of light, those who have been baptized often stare in wide-eyed wonder at the beautiful simplicity of the interwoven threads within the pattern of Gospel principles that make up the tapestry of The Plan of Salvation.

How can our baptism commemorate the birthdate of our immortal soul?

With baptism, we choose liberty and eternal life, instead of captivity and spiritual death. We choose to live our lives within the context of the Gospel and its laws. Without it, our unbridled freedom would lead to tyranny. We are free to choose whether or not we wish to be baptized, but we cannot choose to escape the consequences if we choose unwisely. It is Christ's way for us to act for ourselves. (See 2 Nephi 2:27). It is Satan's way for us to be acted upon. Because of the Atonement, the 'perfect law of liberty' allows us to be free according to the flesh. (See James 1:25).

How does our baptism send a message of hope all the way to heaven?

Baptism opens a portal to the principles, ordinances, and covenants that enable us to become sanctified, so that we may be worthy to live once again in a state of holiness in the presence of our Heavenly Father. Because of baptism, all may come unto Christ, and lay hold upon every good gift ... and be perfected in him, (as they) deny (themselves) of all ungodliness." (Moroni 10:30 & 32). Because of baptism, we may all "continue in the supplicating of his grace" to one day stand blameless before Him at His Pleasing Bar. (See Alma 7:3).

Do you think that heavenly beings are given permission to attend baptismal services?

When we stand in holy places, and free ourselves from the cares and concerns of the world, the realities of the eternities illuminate our minds. At our baptism, if we listen very carefully, we can hear the gentle rustling of the wings of angels coming from behind a slightly-parted veil. The company of beings from the unseen world sweeps the cobwebs from our minds that opens up to our view undreamed vistas of otherwise inaccessible experience.

The
world attempts
to make changes
from the outside, and
fails miserably. The Gospel
changes us from the inside, and
succeeds brilliantly. We are thus
created to reach our potential
in both the image and
likeness of God,
our Father.

57.

We are baptized that we might have hope in our Savior, Jesus Christ.

How does our understanding of the principles of The Plan of Salvation expand the scope of our hope in Christ?

Baptism invites us to consider the possibility that we might one day be like the Savior. We believe that His grace consists of the gifts and power by which we may be brought to His perfection and stature, so that we may enjoy not only what He has, but also what He is. We believe in His promise: "If ye by the grace of God are perfect in Christ, and deny not his power, then are ye sanctified in Christ by the grace of God, through the shedding of the blood of Christ, which is in the covenant of the Father unto the remission of your sins, that ye become holy, without spot." (Moroni 10:33).

Is hope in Christ reserved only for members of The Church of Jesus Christ of Latter-day Saints?

Baptism is not prejudicial. It simply levels the playing field for all of Heavenly Father's children. He has enough confidence in The Plan to allows our agency to find expression in myriad ways. The ordinances that are part of The Plan will always stand ready to save our souls, but in the meantime, we may worship Almighty God according to the dictates of our conscience. The "Author of Eternal Salvation" allows us to worship how, where, or what we may. (Hebrews 5:9, see the 11th Article of Faith).

How can baptism make Saints of sinners?

The differences between us matter very little. Saints and sinners are not so very different, after all. Baptism is the great equalizer. (See Acts 10:34).

How does baptism reflect our hope in Christ?

Hope is not wishful thinking, or misguided trust in a promise that cannot be fulfilled, nor is it a high stakes gamble based on a statistical improbability. It is the inevitable reward of well-founded faith, when we have developed the discipline to completely control our desires and emotions within the bounds the Lord has set, and to keep our priorities in harmony with Gospel principles.

The powers of
heaven and earth amplify
each other, and carry us along
on waves of the Spirit. With baptism, all
our trappings and pretenses are shorn away,
outward observance and phylacteries
are stripped from the ritual of
our worship, and only our
true feelings remain.

58.

*We are baptized in a process of generation,
and not just of maturation.
(See Mosiah 27:26).*

How is baptism a mile-post on our journey toward becoming new creatures in Christ? (See Mosiah 27:26).

Mortality has been designed to be a life-long learning laboratory to give each of us the opportunity to mold our nature to more closely resemble that of our Father in Heaven. He initiated baptism to make that metamorphosis possible.

What does it mean to make the journey to Christ?

Baptism is the catalyst that propels us upward toward the discovery of the personal levels of experience with the Savior, for when He speaks of "knowing Him," He must be referring to a special sense of the word. It is not enough that we know about Him by reading the Gospels, or by listening to others speak of Him. We must know Him through the bonds of common experience and common feeling. Thus, our baptism becomes an immersion in the tangible element of Spirit.

How does baptism bind us to Heavenly Father's perfect Plan of Salvation?

Our religion is more involved with recovery than discovery. Our destiny is not union, but reunion with divine realities. Our religious recognition is a re-learning of that which we have already understood. In this context, the word religion may derive from the Latin root "ligare" – "to bind." Thus religion would mean "to bind again." This fits nicely with the perspective linking religion to a reunion with a divine purpose, or a Plan, for Heavenly Father's children.

How does baptism illustrate the genius of our Heavenly Fathers' Plan?

Baptism represents more than the making of resolutions that can be nothing more than promises to ourselves that are generally kept for a few days or weeks at best, before they are abandoned and we return to our previously held lifestyles. The ordinance of baptism has staying power. Baptism has no bias; its basis is belief, nurtured by a rich culture medium that has been infused with faith, repentance and the companionship of the Spirit. (See the 4th Article of Faith).

The unblemished
innocence of little children
who are about to be baptized makes
us optimistic that peace is within our reach.
When we become as little children, "submissive,
meek, humble, patient, (and) full of love,"
the enticings of the Holy Spirit help us
to put off the natural man and
to become saints through the
Atonement of Jesus Christ.
(Mosiah 3:19).

59.

We are baptized that we might enter into
the fold, there to be cared for
by the Good Shepherd.
(See John 10:11).

Why is it dangerous to allow ourselves to become complacent about our baptismal covenant?

"We have paused on some plateaus long enough," declared President Spencer W. Kimball. "Let us resume our journey forward and upward. Let us quietly put an end to our reluctance to reach out to others, whether in our own families, wards, or neighborhoods. We have been diverted at times from fundamentals on which we must now focus, in order to move forward as a person or as a people." (C.R., 4/1979).

How is baptism the gift that keeps on giving?

For many, following their baptism, the feelings they would like to express cannot be formed into words. Suffice to say, that by the grace of their Heavenly Father, their eyes have been opened. The Savior becomes their traveling companion and trusted advisor. He helps them to forget their bad days and to become better; to love their families, and to be more responsible towards others. In a word, to sacrifice themselves through the love of the Lord.

How does baptism re-define itself each time the faithful enter the healing waters?

With our baptism, gone are the days when we would have been content to build upon the sepulchres of the fathers. For too long, the world has been satisfied writing only biographies, histories, and criticisms relating to the mission of the Savior. But we are no longer comfortable with only these third-person accounts. The restored authority to baptize stands as a testament that, once again, it is possible to individually, and not only institutionally, tap directly into the fountain of living water.

How does baptism help us to live in accordance with priesthood principles?

As soon as we learn to govern our lives by the eternally valid principles of The Plan of Salvation, we will find ourselves on the path that leads to God's kingdom. John Taylor correctly taught: "Priesthood is the legitimate rule of God and is the only power that has a right to rule upon the earth, and when His will is done on the earth, as it is done in heaven, no other power will bear rule." (J.D. 5:187).

Reflection can be a good thing, especially when the light of Christ shines on our countenances. As Alma asked the people of Zarahemla, "And now, behold, I ask of you, my brethren of the church, have ye spiritually been born of God? Have ye received His image in your countenances? Have ye experienced this mighty change in your heart?" (Alma 5:14).

60.

We are baptized that we might contribute our own chapter to The Greatest Story Ever Told.

What do you think their reaction will be, when others sit down to read your chapter in The Greatest Story Ever Told?

The Greatest Story Ever Told is meant to be a sign and a wonder to an unbelieving world. It has been designed to give guidance to true believers in the Last Days. It is a story for hard times and for good times. It has the power to dismiss worldly influences that compete with its issues of real substance that should be the focus of our attention.

What tools have we been given to help us to richly illustrate our own chapters in The Greatest Story Ever Told?

David O. McKay taught that the time between our birth and the age of accountability is ideally suited to teaching the principles of the Gospel. In fact, children are like little sponges, soaking up the doctrines of the kingdom.

Have you noticed how your mentors have modified their approach, when teaching you how to write your story?

President McKay further taught that the time between their eighth birthday and their sixteenth year is the ideal period for children to be trained in the application of the principles of the Gospel that have been taught at home and in Church.

How does The Plan of Salvation set us free to reach our potential?

President McKay taught that when we reach the age of sixteen and are emerging into young adulthood, it is time for us to be trusted in the correct application of the principles we have been taught, that have formed the basis of our training, and that have been incorporated, through practice, into our lives.

The
indescribable
peace that follows
obedience to celestial principles
brings a greater reality within our
reach. When we realize that we are not
alone, we have begun a journey that
will carry us to a higher state
of being where we will find
ourselves covered in star
dust, as we mingle
with the
Gods.

61.

We are baptized that our Heavenly
Father might create, in our behalf,
an impenetrable "shield of faith"
in our Lord Jesus Christ.
(Ephesians 6:16).

Why do you think we are baptized individually, and not in large groups?

Each of us has been fitted with a shield of faith that has been tailored to our unique and distinctive needs. Its elements are strengthened by the covenants we make with Heavenly Father. We make these individually, and not collectively, and we renew them repetitively. This protects us from getting caught up in the mechanics of the Church, from killing the articles of its faith, or from permitting form to triumph over spirit. The kingdom is built by something as simple as our ardor and conviction, as we consciously nurture our relationship with God in a process that formally begins with our baptism.

Why is it important to keep our shields of faith bright and shiny?

By its very nature, baptism contributes to "a great division among the people." (2 Nephi 30:10). In the Last Days, our adversaries are jockeying for position to control our minds, just as they did during our pre-mortal existence. Once again, combatants with increasingly polarized ideologies are forming ranks, in preparation for the battle that has already begun. (See Revelation 16:14).

How do our shields of faith encourage accountability?

Baptism banishes ignorance, for all will one day stand accountable for their own decisions. "There is no eye that shall not see, neither ear that shall not hear, neither heart that shall not be penetrated." (DC 1:2). "The voice of warning (shall) be unto all people," and "those who reject the glad message, the rebellious, shall be pierced with much sorrow." (D&C 1:3-4).

Why is baptism integral to our shields of faith?

Baptism compels us to internalize Gospel principles. It teaches us to view our lives from an eternal perspective, which makes it easier to discern the polarized opposites that are so prevalent in our society today. When we see through the clarifying lens of faith, we can more easily distinguish happiness from its worldly counterfeits, such as pleasure, desire, indulgence, decadence, sensuality, gratification, carnality, amusement, and simply "fun." Baptism makes it possible that when we are weighed in the balances after living in the world, we will not to be found wanting. (See Daniel 5:27).

The
world's definition
of peace is remarkably
superficial: often-times peace is
only equated with the lack of bloodshed
or active combatants. The Lord's definition
is quite different. "His peace is not the peace of
the world of ease, of luxury, idleness, absence
of turmoil and strife, but the peace born of
the righteous life, the peace that lifts the
soul, that day by day brings us closer
to the home of Eternal Peace, the
dwelling place of our Father."
(J. Reuben Clark, Jr.).

62.

We are baptized in white clothing, to symbolically express the purity and the proximity of the Spirit.

Why do we wear white clothing at baptismal services?

It comes down to the guidance and instruction we receive in the "General Handbook of Instructions 2 (20.3.6): "A person who performs a baptism and a person who is baptized wear white clothing."

Are young men of the Aaronic Priesthood who administer the ordinance required to wear white clothing when we recommit ourselves to the covenant of baptism during the Sacrament?

No, they are not. However, as Jeffrey R. Holland taught: "For sacred ordinances in the Church, we often use ceremonial clothing, and a white shirt could be seen as a gentle reminder of the white clothing you wore in the baptismal font and in anticipation of the white shirt you will soon wear into the temple and onto your missions." (C.R., 10/1995).

Is there an official Church policy or standard that requires the wearing of white clothing at times other than when performing the baptismal ordinance?

White may be the preferable color of shirt worn by those who administer the sacrament, (but not by those who receive it). However, with the exception of temple clothing, which is generally white, (think of those who witness live sealing ordinances, who simply wear their "Sunday best"), members of the Church may decide for themselves, through the direction of the Spirit, what they believe is appropriate to wear.

How can baptism help us to have clean hands and pure hearts? (See Psalms 24:4).

Though the wearing of white is encouraged while administering the sacrament, it is not required. President David O. McKay expressed the desire that those who do not have a white shirt might come to the Sacrament table "with clean hands, and especially with a pure heart ... anything that will make the young boys feel that they have been called to officiate in the Priesthood in one of the most sacred ordinances in the Church" (C.R., 10/1956).

Our baptism
leaves the world a better place
than when we found it. When we pass
beyond the veil, we will leave with our
loved ones legacies of both tangible and
intangible remembrances. We will leave them
with our testimonies. We will leave them with
gratitude for the privilege and blessing to
have been knit together in a family,
that is the basic building block
of Heavenly Father's great
Plan of Happiness.

63.

We are baptized that the Spirit of the Lord Omnipotent might work "a mighty change in us, or in our hearts, that we have no more disposition to do evil, but to do good continually." (Mosiah 5:2).

How does knowing that we are the children of God help to work a mighty change in our behavior?

Our religious recognition is a re-cognition, a re-knowing, the sum of our existence. Baptism helps us to suppress our natural inclination to suppress that instinctive response. If we thwart the intrinsic Light of Christ, "we are accountable, and to a degree, we condemn ourselves. We knew Christ before this life, we know Him here, and we will know Him hereafter. His sheep do indeed know His voice." (Truman Madsen).

How do we view the world when our nature has been changed through baptism?

Those who demand physical proof of the power of God as a condition for their belief seek to circumvent the process by which both faith and knowledge are developed. They want proof without price. As with the adulterer, they seek the result without accepting the responsibility.

Why does faith always precede the miracle?

Baptism was not conceived to follow the receipt of signs from heaven. Instead, our faith precedes the miracle. Spiritual confirmation always flows along the pathway that has been created by faith. If a witness were given before faith had transformed us, we might have sure knowledge. But it would have come without an expenditure of faith, and so there would be no appreciation of its significance. It is faith that infuses our belief with staying power.

How does our baptism kindle vital faith?

Baptism grounds us to practical belief, but with elements that commit us to "Citius, Altius, and Fortius." However, our subsequent works do not assure us of salvation, nor do they make us good. It is our faith in the grace of God that does so. Wresting the scriptures, and suggesting that we are saved by works, twists holy writ from its true or proper signification, and perverts it from its correct application. Notwithstanding our faith, we are saved by the grace of God, after all we can do. (See 2 Nephi 25:23).

Sometimes,
when we brush against
the veil, we feel inner stirrings
that are the harmonic vibrations of the
music of a heavenly choir, and we hear the
indistinct murmurings of the voices of angelic
messengers. This is one of the reasons that we
are baptized; that while we yet dwell on
the earth, we might nevertheless be
blessed to be "partakers of
the divine nature."
(2 Peter 1:4).

64.

We are baptized "through the infinite goodness of God, (that by) the manifestations of his Spirit (we might) have great views of that which is to come."
(Mosiah 5:3).

How is our spiritual education different from worldly learning?

Rather than simply multiplying mirrors and studying angles without increasing the light, the first principles and ordinances of the Gospel facilitate the illumination of our minds by the Spirit.

What happens when we allow the Spirit to teach us?

We have no proof until we act on the basis of belief. Then comes the ratification of the reality, manifest as a spiritual confirmation, but only after we act in faith. That is the essence of why James taught that "faith, if it hath not works, is dead, being alone." (James 2:17).

How does baptism have the power to change behavior?

Baptism is the outward evidence of our exercise of faith. We gain spiritual maturity until our faith becomes perfect knowledge. Initially, faith is to believe what we do not see, and the reward of faith is to see what we believe. The process by which faith is developed is one of testing. The Lord gives certain principles, and by obedience to them, blessings and power follow.

What happens to those who wait upon the Lord? (See Isaiah 40:31).

The marvel of God's love is that the more we try to serve Him, the more He blesses us. Therefore, we become even more deeply indebted to Him, and remain so forever. That debt is completely beyond our ability to pay. We can do nothing that puts Him in our debt. But God does not ask us to settle our account with Him. He only asks that we keep His commandments, beginning with the commandment to be baptized.

There are no shades of grey after we have received the ordinance of baptism and our minds become "single to God." (D&C 88:68). If we try to have it both ways, our double mindedness will create intellectual instability and spiritual schizophrenia, for we cannot be servants of the Devil while purporting to follow Christ.

65.

> We are baptized that we might evenly distribute
> the weight of our temporal baggage, that
> we might more easily "enter in
> at the strait gate."
> (Matthew 7:13).

How can baptism help us to more comfortably carry our own burdens?

Temporal baggage can create imbalance that leads to confusion. Baptism jars us out of our collective complacency by upsetting the stagnation of the status quo. It invites us to enjoy a settled conviction in our minds by getting our juices flowing, prodding us to constructively expend our energy, and putting our agency to work.

How can temporal baggage get in the way of our spiritual objectives?

Brigham Young taught: "The first principle that ought to occupy our attention and which is the mainspring of all action is the principle of improvement," and this requires us to balance our temporal baggage with our spiritual objectives and not to confuse one for the other. (J.D. 2:91).

How do you think the Lord views our temporal baggage?

The riches of eternity may be something as simple as the blessing to see from the perspective of our Heavenly Father. Our covenants, beginning with baptism, bring these riches within our grasp, by expanding our vision beyond physical laws that pertain only to the temporal world, toward an appreciation of Gospel principles that relate to the eternities. Baptism invites us to touch the garment of the Savior, not with one of the mean five physical senses, but with our incorruptible spiritual sixth sense.

In a world that is overwhelmed by temporal baggage, how can baptism help us to avoid being tainted by it?

We may live in the world as long as our feet are firmly planted on Gospel sod and we recognize sounding brass and tinkling cymbals for what they really are. Baptism catalyzes a mystical and metaphysical transformation wherein we are figuratively born of God, so that, with new eyes, we can more clearly see what is before us. (See Mosiah 5:7).

With baptism,
there comes a familiarity
with principles that stands in sharp
contrast to the values of society that are
continually morphed by the shifting sands of
cultural expediency. The covenants we make at
baptism protect us from these mutating
standards, and provide a stable
moral basis that shapes us as
we develop into the full
stature of our spirits.

66.

We are baptized that the "opposition in all things" to which Lehi alluded, might become a blessing that allows us to more fully engage The Plan of Salvation.
(2 Nephi 2:11).

How can our baptism become the foundation for purposeful action?

At our baptism, we are given an extra measure of resolve to see life through to its successful conclusion. When our challenges are complicated or compromised by opposition, Gospel principles stand ready to offer assistance related to their resolution.

How can baptism help us to view opposition as a blessing in disguise?

A lot depends upon how we handle opposition, and on what we allow it to do to us. It may impede our progress; but on the other hand, we may use it as a stepping-stone to higher achievement. Our baptism can give us the perspective to see adversity as a diamond dust that polishes us to a high luster, rather than as an abrasive that wears us down and grinds us up.

How can we more fully engage the elements of The Plan of Salvation in order to more effectively deal with opposition?

President Heber J. Grant once said: "If we are trying, to the best of our ability, to improve day by day, then we are in the line of our duty. If we are seeking to remedy our own defects, if we are so living that we can ask for light, for knowledge, for intelligence, and above all, for His Spirit that we may overcome weakness, then, I can tell you, we are in the straight and narrow path that leads to life eternal."

How does the Savior help us to manage opposition?

When we face opposition, we are not truly learned, and are not really strong, unless we hearken to the counsel of the Savior. Our covenant of baptism quickens us, that we might use opposition as the key it was intended to be, to open up a portal to the Spirit. We thereby internalize Gospel principles, and in our obedience to priesthood covenants, we may do all things. (See Philippians 4:13).

Baptism helps us to appreciate how all three members of the Godhead work in our behalf to provide the blessing of immortality and eternal life. "For by the water (we) keep the commandment; by the Spirit (we) are justified, and by the blood (we) are sanctified."
(Moses 6:60).

67.

We are baptized that our trials and tribulations might give us experience, and work to our benefit.
(See D&C 122:7).

Since opposition is necessary for free will to be exercised, how does baptism allow us to reach our potential without damaging the stature of our spirits in the process?

"Baptism of repentance for the remission of sins," (Luke 3:3), together with the Sacrament, fuels our actions, charges our spiritual batteries, and energizes our vision with infinite perspective, creating a pulsing stream of inspiration whose flow has no temporal or spatial boundary. We are engulfed by "the grace of the Lord Jesus Christ, and the love of God, and the communion of the Holy Ghost." (2 Corinthians 13:14).

How can our baptism help us to see more clearly from an eternal perspective?

God has endowed our minds with the ability to resonate with recognition when they encounter truth, and to concentrate on matters of importance, so that ultimately "every one that hearkeneth to the voice of the Spirit (will eventually come) unto God, even the Father." (D&C 84:47). We will do so when we "discard the poor lenses of the body, and peer through the telescope of truth into the infinite reaches of immortality" with an eternal perspective. (Helen Keller, "My Religion," p. 76).

How can our baptism help us to increase our spiritually aerobic maximum pulse rate, as well as the capacity of our lungs to fill with celestial air?

In the waters of baptism, we catch a religious fever that elevates our testimony temperature enough to bless us with a sure witness of the truth, and to get our juices flowing with an appreciation of Who the Savior really is. (See Alma 23:6). Only then, will we experience the earth shaking and mind bending theophany that we are His spiritual offspring, that we might recognize the potential of our position.

How can our baptism teach us how to be comfortable in the company of immortal beings?

When we have faith in the atoning power of Christ, and if we furthermore possess the resolve to activate by the ordinance of baptism the spiritual energy that is lying dormant within us, we will achieve an easy familiarity with ministering angels in bodily form.

Baptism and the gift of the Holy Ghost, are the "fruit of the Spirit" that we receive when we have been taught the doctrine of Christ. (Galatians 5:22).

68.

We are baptized that the "redemption exemption," that is a codicil to the Law of Justice, might be activated and the Law of Mercy set in motion, as our lease on life is renegotiated in our favor.

Why do you think Heavenly Father and the Holy Ghost were present at the baptism of Jesus, to witness the validation of His own very special lease on life?

All who enter the waters of baptism have a divine destiny and are the nobility of heaven. They are counted among those of a choice and chosen generation. (See 1 Peter 2:9). The baptism of Jesus was attended by the greatest Witnesses of all, Heavenly Father and the Holy Ghost, and yet, when the ordinance is performed in our day, the names of all three members of the Godhead are similarly invoked.

Following baptism, how can we take advantage of our own brand new lease on life?

We are baptized because none of us would choose to become spiritually depleted, or to perish because of our neglect of the things that matter most. We understand the consequences of spiritual starvation, doctrinal dehydration, and intellectual inhibition. Without baptism, we risk living marginalized lives while only inches away from the bread of life that would have satisfied our hunger, and from the healing fountain of truth that could have slaked our thirst.

How does Heavenly Father encourage us to enhance the terms of our lease on life?

As we think about our baptism, perhaps we will intuitively respond to President Gordon B. Hinckley's invitation to do a little better, to be a little more kind, to be a little more merciful, and a little more forgiving; "to put behind us our weaknesses of the past, and go forth with new energy and increased resolution to improve the world about us, in our homes, in our places of employment," and "in our social activities."

How does baptism strengthen our resolve to be true to our divine destiny?

The covenant is a token of our understanding and acceptance of the principles of The Plan of Salvation, and of our determination to remain faithful through obedience to our Father in Heaven. We think of brave Horatius, the captain of the gate, who said: 'To every man upon this earth, death cometh soon or late. And how can man die better than facing fearful odds, for the ashes of his fathers, and the temples of his gods?" ("Lays of Ancient Rome," by Thomas Babbington McCaulay).

Nephi
explained that
the doctrine of Christ is that
all who have faith in Jesus Christ
and truly repent of their sins, entering
into a baptismal covenant with Him, will
receive the Holy Ghost, Who will then
direct their way, showing them
the things they must do to
merit the grace of God
and inherit salvation.
(See 2 Nephi 31).

69.

We are baptized that
we might make a simple public
statement about a profound
private conviction.

In what ways can our baptism be both unassuming and reflective?

If we love to live, and learn to love, our charity will become infectious.

How do our faith and testimony carry us beyond the physicality of the ordinance to the spirituality of the covenant?

Our baptism focuses our attention on our testimonies, and the covenant encourages us to nurture them. Every day thereafter, we take our testimony temperature, and hope to regularly detect its feverish pitch. As Alma asked: "Have ye spiritually been born of God? Have ye received his image in your countenances? Have ye experienced this mighty change in your hearts?" (Alma 5:14).

How can the simplicity of the ordinance orient us toward the mysteries of the kingdom?

Baptism encourages us to step back, take a moment, inhale deeply, and focus on the things of importance in our busy lives. The covenant gently guides us into the warm embrace of daily spiritual experiences that confirm our faith. (See Mosiah 27:33).

How is it possible that the 25 simple words of the baptismal prayer can have such profound meaning? (See D&C 20:73).

As we respond to the invitation to enter into the fold, the Spirit moves upon us to wash our flesh in water and put on holy garments, that we might be prepared to enter the joy of the Lord. (See Leviticus 16:4, see also Exodus 40:12-13 & Matthew 25:21).

At our baptism, we are blessed with an awakening comprehension, and we begin to understand that our "Father, and the Son, and the Holy Ghost are one," and that they share a palpable divine power and authority. (3 Nephi 11:27).

70.

> We are baptized "that we might speak with the tongue of angels, and shout praises unto the Holy One of Israel."
> (2 Nephi 31:13).

How do you think baptism prepares us to receive spiritual gifts?

We cannot purchase spiritual gifts, such as speaking with the tongue of angels, with the treasures of the earth. Perhaps this is why in their efforts to obtain the sacred records, Lehi's sons were stripped by Laban of all their gold, silver, and precious things. Obtaining the Holy Scriptures was to be accomplished in the Lord's way, by the power of His mighty arm.

How is baptism like the Rosetta Stone of spiritual experience?

Baptism is the first definitive step on our journey to Christ. The path that lies beyond the font leads to the Tree of Life. It is not a freeway, but is a toll road. Until we have paid the price, we cannot hope to comprehend with fluency the language of the Spirit that clearly explains how to make our way to the tree, that we might harvest its delicious fruit.

How can baptism unlock the gift of the interpretation of tongues?

This gift include the ability to hear the words of the prophets, and of the scriptures with a clear and unambiguous understanding. As the Lord told Joseph Smith: "These words are not of men ... but of me; wherefore, you shall testify they are of me ... For it is my voice which speaketh them unto you; for they are given by my Spirit unto you, and by my power you can read them one to another; and save it were by my power you could not have them. Wherefore, you can testify that you have heard my voice, and know my words." (D&C 18:34-36).

How does baptism prepare us to shout praises unto the Holy One of Israel?

The missionaries who serve throughout the world come to mind. Their commission to preach the Gospel and baptize the nations is accompanied by an endowment of priesthood power. We also remember the Nephite children whom Jesus blessed, whose tongues were loosed, and who "did speak unto their fathers great and marvelous things." (3 Nephi 26:14).

Values are beliefs that may change with circumstances because they are culturally or personally determined. Baptism is the tangible expression of a Gospel principle, a truth that is eternally valid. Its correct understanding is essential, because as a foundation ordinance it lies at the very heart of the doctrine of the Gospel of Jesus Christ.

71.

We are baptized that our hearts might be "knit together in unity and in love." (Mosiah 18:21).

How can our baptism help us to make sense of the myriad elements of The Plan of Salvation?

Baptism coherently stitches foundation principles together into an understandable pattern, so that the power of the word and the witness of truth may be conveyed without the need for external warrant.

How can baptism assure us that when our time comes to pass through the veil, we will leave behind legacies that contribute to the establishment of Zion?

God's Plan involves a sequence of steps that prepare those on both sides of the veil to confront eternity. Its principles are the expression of doctrine that identifies activities that must be performed for His strategies to succeed. As we make commitments, He identifies beforehand the cost required to reach our goals. We work within time lines that are flexible enough to allow us to follow through on our plan of action through trial and error, and even to make mistakes along the way, until we have achieved successful outcomes.

Can eight year old children be as spiritually prepared for baptism as eighty year old adults?

The Plan imposes no age restrictions for participation, other than identifying the age of accountability as it relates to the need for baptism. In the Lord's Church, a three year old, a thirty year old, and a ninety year old may all join together to sing "I am a Child of God" with equal fervency.

As baptism knits us together, will there be any missing threads in the pattern He has planned?

The Plan is absolutely non-discriminatory. It was designed for the world's heaviest person, who weighed in at 1,400 pounds, for the world's tallest person, at 8 feet 11 inches, the world's wealthiest person, who boasts $73 billion in assets, the world's smartest person whose I.Q. is 210, as well as for the other 7 billion of us who fall within these extremes.

Baptism
emancipates us from
the self-limiting conditions
that had heretofore blinded us
to a larger view of life. It frees us to
pay closer attention to celestial guideposts
and principles. It invites us to experience more
intense and reflective self-awareness, deeper
and more abiding humility, reinvigorated
confidence, and incomprehensively
more profound and
enduring faith.

72.

We are baptized that we might enjoy the companionship of "the Comforter, which showeth all things, and teacheth the peaceable things of the kingdom."
(D&C 39:6).

How is baptism like a commencement exercise?

At our baptism, we matriculate into a curriculum where we learn to understand with fluency the language of the Spirit. Baptism pays the price, that we might receive the antidote for poisonous telestial tendencies that would otherwise threaten to choke the expression of celestial sureties.

How can baptism help us to conquer our self-defeating behaviors?

After we have received the baptism of fire and the Holy Ghost, we know when the Comforter abides with us, because we sense a holy communion with the Infinite, as we enjoy a consciousness of victory over our telestial tendencies toward carnality, sensuality, and devilishness.

What tools have we been given to nurture our understanding of the peaceable things of the kingdom?

Living water is so crucial to our well-being that the Lord has provided the means to penetrate solid limestone, as it were, so that it may freely flow into our lives. Baptism creates a conduit that is chiseled through our rough exterior and stony nature with the tools of faith, obedience, study, prayer, good works, and other healthy lifestyle choices.

Why is faith without works dead, that it cannot save us? (See J.S.T. James 2:14).

The conduit to living water is created when we not only believe, but also act on our belief, by being honest, true, chaste, benevolent, virtuous, kind, and in doing good to others. Living water has the power to sustain our lives when we are doers, and not only hearers of the word. (See James 1:22).

Baptism open
up windows of opportunity
to better understand the principles
of the Gospel, that are mysteries to those
who have not spiritually prepared themselves for
personal revelation from God. The Lord has
assured us that we "shall know of a
surety that these things are true,
for from heaven will (He)
declare it unto (us)."
(D&C 5:12).

73.

> "We are baptized as a witness and a testimony that we are willing to serve God with all (our) hearts."
> (Mosiah 21:35).

How can the Light of Christ help us to fulfill our baptismal commitment to minister to the needs of others?

It permits us to listen with sensitivity and to be receptive to the cries of the downtrodden and oppressed, to see with a clarity that allows us to be responsive to the needs of our fellow travelers, and to be benevolently blind to their shortcomings.

How is witnessing for Christ like a spiritual aerobic exercise program?

Witnessing for Christ generates the energy to lift us heavenward. Witnessing for the Savior is more than a repetitive exercise to be performed only by the numbers. It helps us to communicate feeling, capture emotion, contour attitude, crystallize thought, compartmentalize action, congeal passion, and convey sentiments that creates spiritual revitalization.

In baptism, how do we follow the example of Aaron?

The Lord Jehovah said: "Thou shalt bring Aaron and his sons unto the door of the tabernacle of the congregation, and wash them with water. And thou shalt put upon Aaron the holy garments, and anoint him, and sanctify him." (Exodus 40:12-13).

What are the ordinances of salvation and exaltation?

We begin with the baptismal covenant, which is an ordinance of sanctification, and then continue to make promises with Heavenly Father, culminating in those made at the altar of the temple, which are ordinances of exaltation, the fulfillment of which will bring us earthly blessings and eternal life. As we focus our attention on our covenant of baptism that leads to the doors of the temple, our thirst will be quenched with the living water provided by the endowment.

In perfect harmony, the
Godhead promote the doctrine of
Christ with one shared goal: To bring
us to the waters of baptism, and
thereafter to the portal of
the Celestial Kingdom.

74.

We are baptized in such a manner that, as we step out of the font, our faces will always be oriented toward the light.

During baptismal services, how does the Spirit help us to reach out and touch the face of God?

At baptismal services in particular, we feel the Spirit through the medium of music. We are reminded that even before the foundations of the earth were laid, music filled the celestial air, when "the morning stars sang together, and all the sons of God shouted for joy." (Job 38:7).

Why is it important to keep our faces oriented toward the light? (See D&C 88:118).

As our circle of knowledge grows, so do the borders of darkness that encroach upon the edge of the light. The more we know, the more we need to learn, in order to deal with the opposition that is a part of all of our undertakings. Baptism is a celestial gyroscope that centers us, and orients us toward the light and away from thick mists of darkness. (See 1 Nephi 8:23).

What can happen to us if we do not steadfastly face the light?

We walk precariously close to personality precipices when we try to negotiate the slippery slope of moral equivocation. Vice can be "a monster of so frightful mien, as to be hated needs but be seen. Yet seen too oft, familiar with her face, we first endure, then pity, then embrace." (Alexander Pope).

If we allow it to be our guide, where will our illuminated path lead us?

Because of our baptismal covenant, one day in the not too distant future, celestial air will be pungent with a heavenly aether that is punctuated by the melodious strains of our native language. Every detail will be just as we had imagined it would be, including the reassuring radiant heat of a consuming fire kindled beforehand by Father. We will know that this is just where we belong, at Home once again, with our heavenly Parents.

Immersion in water
is symbolic of the burial of
Christ. (See 3 Nephi 11:23). Joseph
Smith said the repentant are "baptized
after the manner of his burial, being buried in
the water in his name, and this according to the
commandment which he has given - That
by keeping the commandments they
might be washed and cleansed
from all their sins."
(D&C 76:51-52).

75.

We are baptized that we might pursue the object and design of our existence, which is to be the happiest people upon the face of the earth.

How can we be strengthened, as we continue our journey to Christ after our baptism?

As we feast upon the word of Christ, we will receive health in the navel and marrow in the bones, (see D&C 89:18), strength in the loins and in the sinews (see Job 40:16-17), power in the priesthood (see D&C 107:14), nourishment from the scriptures, and we will be fortified to endure to the end in righteousness, to receive the grace of God, and to enter into His Rest. (See 2 Nephi 31:20).

Do you think our feelings of happiness come from secretions in our brains, or from our Heavenly Father? (Who, after all, created dopamine, in the first place).

With our baptism comes the dawn of recognition that the blessing of happiness is a gift that Heavenly Father weaves into every Gospel principle. When we accept the invitation to "try the virtue of the word of God" and are exposed to the fruit of the Tree of Life, we open our senses to the matchless realm of joy that can be ours only through obedience. (See Alma 31:5).

Why do you think that it is in quiet moments that we most clearly hear the voice of the Spirit?

The Psalmist wrote: "Be still, and know that I am God." (Psalms 46:10). When we tune out the world's cacophony of confusion, and reject the spurious coin of counterfeit currency that is proffered by moneylenders in the temple, we sense that our Heavenly Father is nearby.

What kind of spiritual refreshment is served at baptismal celebrations?

Our baptism unleashes a spiritual cornucopia. We feast upon the nourishing bread of life that has been provided, drink from a well of living water, and with renewed energy, we "lift up (our) heads and receive the pleasing word of God, and feast upon His love." (Jacob 3:2).

"For if we have
been planted together in the
likeness of his death, we shall be
also in the likeness of his resurrection.
Knowing this, that our old man is crucified
with him, that the body of sin might be
destroyed, that henceforth we
should not serve sin."
(Romans 6:5-6).

76.

> We are baptized because, as disciples
> of Christ, it is our lot in life
> to be sent forth as sheep
> in the midst of wolves.
> (See Matthew 10:16).

How can our baptism take us in the direction of our dreams?

One of life's temptations is to confuse dreams with reality, but a defeat of cosmic proportion comes when our dreams are surrendered to the narrow and confining make-believe of the carnal and sensual world, where life becomes nothing more than an overnight stay in a cheap hotel, in a room illuminated only by a bare bulb hanging from a frayed cord.

How can our baptism help us to maintain order in a chaotic world?

The world may have gone mad, but the Church remains an island in the storm, and the Gospel of Jesus Christ provides a refuge from the uncertainties of life. It speaks a language of stability, direction, and purpose to those who are unsure, uncertain, and hesitant. Of the Lord's children, it might be said: "The stars fade away, the sun himself grows dim with age, and nature sinks in years; But thou shalt flourish in immortal youth, unhurt amidst the war of elements, the wreck of matter, and the crash of worlds." (Joseph Addison, "Cato").

How is baptism an expression of self-restraint?

Those who have been baptized stand out against undisciplined souls who have been seduced by the siren song of the sentinels of Satan. Without the stabilizing influence of the Gospel, unprincipled character crumbles when faced with telestial temptations that are tantalizing and yet traumatizing. These treasures of the earth are worthless counterfeits for the blessings that God has reserved for the faithful. It is this substitution of the sacred by the profane that is an abomination in the sight of God.

How can the Light of Christ protect us from the influence of the adversary?

It provides a shield of protection against the spatter of corrosive perspiration cast off by the destroyer, who is insidiously and persistently working overtime to damage our doctrinal defenses, dull our spiritual sensitivities, diminish our charitable capacity, deplete our bountiful reservoirs of sympathy, and destroy our devotions, even as we labor with an equal but opposite intensity to deify our work on the earth.

"Know ye not that, so
many of us as were baptized
into Jesus Christ were baptized into
his death? Therefore, we are buried with
him by baptism into death, that like as Christ
was raised up from the dead by the glory
of the Father, even so we also should
walk in newness of life" through the
symbolism of being born again,
with baptism by immersion.
(Romans 6:3).

77.

We are baptized that we might be blessed with the means to calibrate our lives with the pattern of heaven itself.

How does baptism relate to the Atonement as the pattern of heaven?

Turning our attention to the Atonement after receiving the baptism of fire and of the Holy Ghost gives us a sense of independence, as we learn something new every day. Consecrating our time to the peaceable things of the Kingdom can open our hearts and our minds to a breathtaking expansion of understanding. A learning style that embraces the Spirit establishes the pattern of heaven, that will become our norm.

How does the Light of Christ help us to appreciate the pattern of heaven?

As we confront eternal truth, the Light of Christ tempers our trepidation. The knowledge that we participated in the First Act of the Three Act Play comes as a complete surprise to most of us, because a veil has been drawn across our memory of those events. We take for granted our participation in the Second Act, because it involves the "here and now." Without energizing light, it seems "ordinary." The Third Act fills us with anxiety, because of our inherent fear of the unknown. With the Light of Christ, however, the shadows are always behind us.

How important is it to have a correct understanding of "the age of accountability?"

While those who teach the doctrine of infant baptism believe that children who die without the ordinance will go to hell, the truth is that it is the professors of that doctrine who are themselves "in danger of death, hell, and an endless torment." (Moroni 8:21). The scriptures boldly testify because our eternal welfare depends upon our correct understanding of this doctrine. All else hangs in the balance.

How does our baptism allow us to experience mortality, and at the same time establish an undeniable connection with the eternities?

The entrance requirements for those who would abide the law of heaven are the same for all who have ever walked the earth. We come from the eternal vantage point of the abode of the Gods. This required a resetting of our celestial chronometer. Omniscient, omnipotent, and omnipresent Beings have calibrated it to a temporal scale, whereas the reckoning had been beforehand "the Lord's time, according to the reckoning of Kolob." (Abraham 3:4).

When the law is woven
into the sinews of our souls, that
it becomes the tapestry of our lives and
is the very pattern upon which we trace our
progress along the path of progression, our
"minds become single to God, and the
days will come that (we) shall
see him; for he will unveil
his face" unto us.
(D&C 88:68).

78.

**We are baptized that the Lord might be on our right, and on our left, and in our hearts.
(See D&C 84:88).**

What mentors have accompanied you during your journey to the waters of baptism?

We realize how heavily we borrow from the towering example of those who have been our mystical mentors, our sensible chaperones, our spiritual guides, our surrogate saviors, and our compassionate critics.

As you have made the journey to Christ, how have you felt His presence? (See Alma 37:41).

The Savior becomes our avatar, showing us the way, strengthening our testimonies, and teaching us humility. He is always there to steady our shaking knees and nurture our faltering faith, to bind up our wounds, and to apply the Balm of Gilead to our soul scars. He provides both tangible and immaterial support, emboldens us with words of encouragement, and cheers our spirits with wise counsel.

How does the Savior work through others to guide us?

We are strengthened by a multitude of angels thinly disguised as our family and friends. We remember the words of Sir Isaac Newton, who, when pressed to reveal the great secret behind his accomplishments, simply replied: "I stood on the shoulders of giants."

How does Satan attempt to influence us to abandon the Savior as our traveling companion?

Satan has focused significant energies and has invested immense resources to neutralize the influence of the Holy Ghost. He goes about it by working under the radar. He creates economic burdens to get mothers out of the home and into the workplace. He employs political pressure, under the guise of "equal opportunity." Within the ivory towers of academia, he tutors the rising generation with carefully groomed mentors who are rebels without a cause, and who rail against every proven principle in the name of intellectual curiosity. One does not have to look very far to see Satan at work.

Baptism is of
such power that it drives the
law into our inward parts, so that
it is written upon our hearts. A mighty
change takes place as we experience the
process of sanctification. When we are
born again, the desired result of all
Gospel-oriented teaching has been
achieved, and we have no more
disposition to do evil, but to
do good continually.
(See Mosiah 5:2).

79.

We are baptized that we might more easily memorize our lines in Heavenly Father's Three Act Play that is entitled "The Plan of Salvation."

How can baptism help us to dismiss the distractions that get in the way of the execution of The Plan?

Baptism clears our minds and gives us a sense of purpose. Through the ordinance, we commune with the Infinite and enjoy the consciousness of victory over our self-defeating behaviors.

How does baptism crystalize our understanding of the Fall of Adam and the Atonement of Jesus Christ?

These doctrines liberate us from apostate teachings relating to the baptism of little children. "For awful is the wickedness to suppose that God saveth one child because of baptism, and the other must perish because he hath no baptism. Wo be unto them that shall pervert the ways of the Lord after this manner, for (after they understand the role of accountability as it relates to the fall of Adam, and understand the necessity of the Savior's redemption) they shall perish except they repent." (Moroni 8:15-16).

How does baptism orient us toward the mysteries of eternity that are part of the script of Act Three of The Plan of Salvation?

After our baptism, we are blessed to be able to press forward, not with the crowd who jostles for position in the circus of telestial trivialities, but rather with the Saints who seek "wisdom and ... the mysteries of God" that are those truths that can only be known by revelation from the Holy Ghost. (D&C 11:7).

In the distant past, do you think we shouted for joy upon hearing about The Plan of Salvation?

When we are baptized, we have feelings of deja-vu, that when we exult in our fellowship with the community of the Saints and of the household of God, we have done so before. (See Ephesians 2:19). We vaguely remember that time in the distant past when "the morning stars sang together, and all the sons of God shouted for joy." (Job 38:7).

The
process of
kindling our divine
spark, of igniting the
spirit lying dormant within
each of awakening our divine
potential, and of nurturing
the God in embryo that
is present within each
of us, is to be
born again.

80.

*We are baptized that we might become
as lights that are set on a hill.
(See Matthew 5:14).*

What does it mean to magnify our calling? (See D&C 84:33).

Fulfilling the requirements of our stewardship means to build it up in dignity and importance, to make it honorable and to enlarge and strengthen it, and to simply perform the service that pertains to it. John Taylor taught: "If you do not magnify your calling, God will hold you responsible for those whom you might have saved, had you done your duty." (J.D. 20:23).

How does light manifest itself as inspiration and revelation?

One exciting element of light is the constant stream of inspiration and revelation that cascades down from above. This insures that we may walk along illuminated pathways, and that no individual or institution may legitimately claim or have a monopoly on divine guidance. Its leveling influence is the great equalizer, giving each of us the same privileges to use our faculties of mind, intellect, and spirit to "come unto Christ." (Moroni 10:32).

How does the light that emanates from Christ speak to us?

As in a heavenly language that is rhythmical, melodious, soothing to our ears, and calming to our souls, when we hear the Spirit quietly whisper: "You're a stranger here," we are struck by the realization that we have "wandered from a more exalted sphere." (Eliza R. Snow).

Why is it important to always walk in the light?

Tom Paine wrote that there will be times in our lives that try our souls. Yet we will have this consolation with us: "The harder the conflict, the more glorious the triumph. What we obtain too cheap, we esteem too lightly. 'Tis dearness only that gives everything its value. Heaven knows how to put a proper price upon its goods." ("Common Sense"). It would be strange, indeed, if a celestial article such as baptism should not be highly rated.

When
we have
been spiritually
begotten of Christ, we are
given the invitation to re-write
the record of our lives. We cannot
go back and start a new beginning,
but we can begin now to make
a new ending. Our lives can
become fairytales that
are waiting to
be written.

81.

We are baptized that our vessels might
be filled with the "oil of gladness."
(Hebrews 1:9).

What is the currency of faith that accrues with compound interest to those who have entered the waters of baptism?

As we quietly carry out our work as disciples of Christ, the righteousness of our cause will be revealed to us in marvelous simplicity and plainness. Walls of opposition to our personal progress will crumble and fall away, and the Lord will comfort and succor us with the bread of life.

How can "the Lord ... go before you, and the God of Israel be your rearward?" (Isaiah 52:12).

As we travel through Idumea's harsh and seemingly unforgiving environment, oases will spring up in the deserts of life, and living water will slake our thirst because our roots have been deeply embedded in the rich loam of eternally valid principles.

How do the terms of our lease on life compel us to look with gratitude to the Author of Salvation?

Sir Walter Scott may have been thinking of the eternal blessings related to baptism, as well as to the contrasting element of the stark reality of living month to month, paycheck to paycheck, in the lone and dreary world, when he wrote: "Breathes there the man, with soul so dead, who never to himself hath said, 'This is my own, my native land!' Whose heart hath ne'er within him burned, as home his footsteps he hath turned from wandering on a foreign strand!" In baptism, we find our way home.

How does baptism prevent us from going "down to the vile dust, from whence (we have) sprung, unwept, unhonored, and unsung?"

The poem continues: "If such there breathe, go, mark him well. For him no minstrel raptures swell. High though his titles, proud his name, boundless his wealth as wish can claim; despite those titles, power, and pelf, the wretch, concentered all in self, living, shall forfeit fair renown, and, doubly dying, shall go down to the vile dust, from whence he sprung, unwept, unhonored, and unsung." ("The Lay of The Last Minstrel"). Oh, the urgency of faith, repentance, baptism, and the receipt of the Holy Ghost!

In baptism,
Mercy satisfies Justice,
and the penitent faithful
receive a remission of sins in a
symbolic rite of purification.
(See 2 Nephi 31:17).

82.

We are baptized to sweep away the cobwebs from our minds.

Do little children, or those with diminished mental capacity, need to be baptized?

Little children "are alive in Christ." (Moroni 8:22). They have no need for repentance or for baptism, "for the power of redemption cometh on all them that have no law. Wherefore, he that is not condemned, or he that is under no condemnation, cannot repent, and unto such baptism availeth nothing." (Moroni 8:22).

What discoveries await us, as we "walk in the light of the Lord?" (Isaiah 2:5).

We learn that in the premortal realm, we knew and worshipped our Father and accepted His Plan whereby we could obtain bodies and gain experience to progress toward perfection; ultimately to realize our divine potential as heirs of eternal life. We learn that The Plan of Happiness extends its reach beyond the grave, and that sacred ordinances culminating in the covenants of the temple make it possible for us to return to our Heavenly Father, there to be reunited with our families for eternity.

What is captivating about the behavior changes that follow our baptism?

Baptism addresses the issues of self-denial, meekness, and charity, and asks that we surrender to the greater good our desire for self-actualization, self-renewal, self-determination, self-fulfillment, self-aggrandizement, and self-control. It asks us to concentrate our efforts on behavior that honors God's design, rather than patronizing the twisted temporal theories of emotional or spiritual well-being that lack an upward thrust. It asks us to "let go and let God."

How can we better understand the doctrines of the Gospel of Jesus Christ?

It is within the pages of The Book of Mormon, that we learn that "the first fruits of repentance is baptism; and baptism cometh by faith unto the fulfilling the commandments; and the fulfilling the commandments bringeth remission of sins; and the remission of sins bringeth meekness, and lowliness of heart; and because of meekness and lowliness of heart cometh the visitation of the Holy Ghost, which Comforter filleth with hope and perfect love." (Moroni 8:25-26).

At
our baptism,
we matriculate into
a curriculum where we learn to
understand the language of the Spirit.
With baptism, we pay the price to receive
the antidote for poisonous telestial
tendencies that always threaten
to choke the expression
of celestial sureties.

83.

> We are baptized that the anchors of our
> faith might rest within a foundation
> of rock, and not of sand.
> (See Matthew 7:26).

What are the fruits of faith? (See Alma 32:40).

Testimony is composed of three essential elements. First is recognition of a Gospel principle. Second is an understanding of the Lord's word concerning that principle, and third is direct experience with that principle, which is the fruits of faith.

How does baptism anchor our faith?

Before our baptism, we receive a testimony of Christ through the witness of the Holy Ghost. The experience vitalizes our faith, encourages us to be obedient, convicts us of our sins, and motivates us to repent. Conversion that follows is the fruits of testimony, and may follow our baptism for an indefinite period of time. During this process, spiritual gifts accompany conversion, and are built upon the foundation of testimony.

How can baptism help us to come to "the knowledge of the Son of God?" (Ephesians 4:13).

With our baptism, resources become available that instruct and inspire us to seek out the other ordinances of the Gospel. These allow us to immerse ourselves in the three-fold mission of the Church; to perfect the Saints, preach the Gospel, and cement family relationships in both time and eternity. As we become unified in our faith, we strengthen each other's testimonies of the mission of the Author of Salvation.

How does our baptism provide a foundation of stability in a world that seems to lack moral footings?

What is important is that we live our lives so that every morning when we get out of bed, somewhere in the world Satan exclaims: "Oh no! They are awake again!"

The characteristics of a Zion society are simply the result of a spiritual transformation in the lives of those who have been baptized and confirmed as members of the Church of Jesus Christ.

84.

*We are baptized that we might fan with
faith the fire of our resolve.
(See Jeremiah 20:9).*

What does baptism teach us about self-reliance?

We sink or swim, largely on our own. As we persevere, we hope and pray for the courage to change the things we can, the serenity to accept the things we cannot, and the wisdom to know the difference. But it is always nice to get a little help from our friends, including our Savior, who led the way with His own baptism. (See John 14:6).

In what ways does baptism empower us?

With baptism, we are endowed with the courage to go into the world to spread the Lord's message. He invites "all to come unto him and partake of his goodness; and he denieth none that come unto him, black and white, bond and free, male and female; and he remembereth the heathen; and all are alike unto God, both Jew and Gentile." (2 Nephi 26:33). As we leave the font, we stand independent above all creatures, infused with the knowledge that our sum is now the Church, and that it is far greater than all of its parts.

For how long do you think we can maintain the intensity of the feelings that are generated by baptism?

Alma asked the penetrating question that continues to demand our attention: "And now, behold, I say unto you my brethren, if ye have experienced a change of heart, and if ye have felt to sing the song of redeeming love," that you experienced at your baptism, "I would ask, can ye feel so now?" (Alma 5:26).

How can our baptism help us to move beyond the mediocrity that too often defines the lifestyle of those who are hampered by the values of the every-day world?

Our baptism introduces us to a spotlight coming from above that quickens our minds and opens our hearts to the spiritual realities at the core of our existence. It invites us to move beyond our three-dimensional mortal experience. We look before us, behind us, and to both sides, but we also experience an upward reach that takes us into an other-worldly spiritual dimension. We look up to God, "whose brightness and glory defy all description," and, perhaps for the first time, we really live. (J.S.H. 1:17, see Alma 37:47).

"Heaven
lies about us
in our infancy. Shades
of the prison house begin
to close upon the growing boy.
But he beholds the light and whence
it flows; he sees it in his joy. The youth,
who daily farther from the east must travel,
still is nature's priest. And by the vision splendid,
is on his way attended. At length, the man
perceives it die away, and fade into
the light of common day."
(Wordsworth).

85.

We are baptized that we might leave a light burning for those who are late to arrive at the wedding feast.
(See John Chapter 2).

How can baptism give us a needed boost, when life's burdens weigh us down?

Whether we are professional athletes or practiced panhandlers, living in the fast or the slow lane of life, whether we have rags or riches, are leaders or lepers, are early prodigies or late bloomers, venture capitalists or welfare recipients; no matter our circumstances, we have been entrusted with the responsibility to build bridges over troubled water to those whose tentative steps betray their faltering faith.

What is the fate of those who refuse the invitation to be baptized?

Those who do not believe in the power of God unto salvation, who will not be baptized, will not be able to continue their eternal progression. For others, who might not be aware of the wedding feast in progress, the foundation principles of The Plan of Salvation have been, at least temporarily, suspended. However, the invitations have been sent out across the heavens by our Father, and He is even now waiting for each individual R.S.V.P.. (See D&C 123:12).

As children of light, what can we do to strengthen the testimonies of others?

As the congealed distillate of our life experiences, our thoughts and feelings relating to the Savior stand revealed as our innocent attempts to yoke our emotions to language. We hope that others will find our expressions of faith refreshing, will use them as food for thought, and will be motivated to act upon their expanding awareness and appreciation of the principles of the Plan.

How can you explain the universality of immortal longings that are experienced by so many of Heavenly Father's children?

All of us are entitled to enjoy the influence of the Light of Christ. There are no scholastic prerequisites relating to The Plan of Salvation. Those without formal education are welcome to participate, as are those with advanced degrees from the most prestigious institutions of higher learning. It is the poor in spirit, however, those with broken hearts and contrite spirits, who seem to have an advantage when it comes to acting upon these immortal longings.

"For the gate by which (we) should enter is repentance and baptism by water; and then cometh a remission of (our) sins by fire and by the Holy Ghost." This puts us on the "strait and narrow path that leads to eternal life." (2 Nephi 31:17-18).

86.

*We are baptized that we might learn
how to consecrate to the Lord
our time, talents, means, and
everything else with which
He has blessed us.*

What happens to us when our priorities are out of order?

When we lose sight of our righteous objectives, we lose the power to bring about positive change. Baptism, however, sharpens our perspective, enabling us to comprehend and build upon principles of perfection that are validated by the Spirit and emulated by the example of the Savior.

How does our baptism provide us with opportunities to "give place" or study, pray, and commit ourselves to a purposeful plan of action? (See Alma 32:27).

With our baptism, we feel the word enlarge our souls and enlighten our understanding. As Brigham Young is reported to have said: "Every Gospel principle carries within it a witness that it is true." It is in the economy of the Gospel that "we often catch a spark from the awakened memories of the immortal soul, which lights up our whole being as with the glory of our former home." (Joseph F. Smith).

How does baptism prepare us to more thoughtfully budget our time?

Concentrating on the things that really matter endows us with a greater capacity to manage the gift of time. We learn to take time with discipline, make time with diligence, find time with care, spend time with thoughtfulness, invest time with wisdom, and share time with pleasure.

How can baptism help us to turn our attention to the weightier matters of the law?
(See Matthew 23:23).

Turning our attention to the weightier matters of the law gives us a sense of independence, as we learn something new every day. Learning how to control our time can open our hearts and our minds to a breathtaking expansion of understanding. As we practice a learning style that embraces the Spirit, we discover the pattern of heaven, and it becomes our norm.

After our
baptism, the Holy Ghost
guides us to covenants relating
to the priesthood and the temple.
"I will give unto the children of men
line upon line, precept upon precept, here
a little and there a little; and blessed are
those who hearken unto my precepts, and
lend an ear unto my counsel, for
they shall learn wisdom; for
unto him that receiveth
I will give more."
(2 Nephi 28:30).

87.

**We are baptized that we might accept our Heavenly Father's invitation to join Him in His work and glory, which is to bring about our immortality and eternal life.
(See Moses 1:39).**

How is baptism the key to an understanding of the mission statement of our Father in Heaven? (See Moses 1:39).

Whisperings of the Spirit confirm that there is more to the Gospel than outward observances, obedience, and covenants. The gift of spiritual enlightenment is the key to our discovery of undreamed vistas of otherwise inaccessible experience.

Why can there be only "one Lord, one faith, (and) one baptism?" (Ephesians 4:5).

The ordinance that admits us into the fold of Christ must be carried out according to specific and pointed instruction, without ambiguity, for except we "be born of water and of the Spirit," declared the Savior, we "cannot enter into the kingdom of God." (John 3:5).

Why is the day of our baptism such a happy occasion?

Our baptism rivets our attention on our Heavenly Father's great gift of happiness that accompanies untroubled souls. As members of the Church of Jesus Christ, we have used our free will to choose the Savior and yield our hearts to Him. We ponder the great and terrible consequences of Gethsemane, and travel with Him to Calvary. We enjoy the sweetness of the redeeming power of the Atonement, which is the keystone of The Plan. We determine to keep the laws of God, because we have learned that the Gospel transcends temporal security and worldly comforts. Jacob described these feelings as "that happiness which is prepared for the saints." (2 Nephi 9:43).

How has Heavenly Father provided for us, so that we might have the promise of eternal life following our baptisms?

We very quickly recognize the pathway before us that leads to spiritual transformation and a Christ-centered life. The Sacrament allows us to regularly recommit ourselves to internalize the truths and principles relating to eternal progression, and endows us with the power to endure to the end in righteousness. Some may consider their burdens to be too heavy, but countless witnesses have testified how obedience has become the perfect law of liberty. (See James 1:25).

It was an integral element of The Plan of Salvation, ordained in the Grand Councils in Heaven before the world was, that little children who died before the age of accountability would be saved in the Celestial Kingdom by the power of the Atonement. "If not so, God is a partial God, and also a changeable God, and a respecter of persons; for how many little children have died without baptism!" (Moroni 8:12).

88.

We are baptized that we might rejoice in our characterization as a peculiar people.
(See 1 Peter 2:9).

How can our participation in God's Plan refine us, and thereby become a perfecting process? (See Malachi 3:2).

In the beginning, Heavenly Father knew that Adam would transgress the law, become mortal, and suffer physical and spiritual, death. Therefore, a Savior was provided, Who was the lamb slain from the foundation of the world, that through baptism the posterity of Adam might receive forgiveness for sin and be redeemed by the power of the Atonement, to be crowned with immortality and eternal life.

How does it feel to know that we are on the path of progression?

Christ is the Author of Salvation, (Hebrews 5:9), and the Finisher of our Faith, (Hebrews 12:2), but The Plan was introduced to His spirit children by Heavenly Father. (See 2 Nephi 9:13). By the spirit of revelation, the Holy Ghost testifies of Christ and of the Father's Plan. (D&C 8:2-3). Working in perfect harmony, the three members of the Godhead promote the doctrine of Christ with one shared goal: to bring us in the waters of baptism to the portal of the Celestial Kingdom.

What principles do you think might have been presented at the Council in Heaven before our world was created? (See D&C 138:55).

We who were in attendance at the Council, who so readily and enthusiastically raised our arms to the square to support our Father's proposal, must have felt the import of the moment, that our Elder Brother Jesus Christ made history. (See Job 38:7). In fact, He was creating a binding precedent to re-write history itself. We were eyewitnesses to the vitalization of "The Merciful Plan of The Great Creator." (2 Nephi 9:6).

Why do you think that baptism was one of the hot topics that were discussed at the Council in Heaven? (See D&C 138:56, Abraham 4:26, & 5:2).

We must have palpably sensed the enveloping reach of His love, understood His quintessential example of humility, His supreme act of selflessness, and His superlative expression of altruism. He had just become our personal Redeemer as the power of the Atonement was activated in our behalf, only conditional upon our baptism into His Church.

The
Last Days
mirror those
of Mormon, who
wrote that "there were
sorceries, and witchcrafts,
and magics, and the power of the
evil one was wrought upon all the face
of the land" because of the lack of faith
of the people. (Mormon 1:19). Baptism is
the spiritual equivalent of enjoying a
power bar or energy drink 30
minutes before engaging
in physical activity.

89.

*We are baptized that righteousness might
stay the sword of justice that hangs
over our wicked world.
(See Helaman 13:5).*

Do you think the angels in heaven are taking note of our behavior?

There are no shades of grey after we have received the ordinance of baptism and our minds become "single to God." (D&C 88:68). If we try to have it both ways, our double mindedness will create intellectual instability and spiritual schizophrenia, for we cannot be servants of the Devil while purporting to follow Christ.

Why does amending wicked behavior require a change of hearts, as well?

Evil people can do good, but in the end their works are a blessing neither to themselves nor to those whom they pretend to serve. When a good deed is motivated by selfish desire, it lacks the power to enrich or transform the giver, and it is "not counted unto him for righteousness." (Moroni 7:7).

How can our baptism help us to distinguish good from evil?

We particularly need the gift of discernment when dealing with a media that has done an excellent job of confusing issues of importance. We remember the caution of Mormon, who, in a prescient glimpse of our day, wrote: "Wherefore, take heed, my beloved brethren, that ye do not judge that which is evil to be of God, or that which is good and of God to be of the Devil." (Moroni 7:14).

How can the Light of Christ have the power to lead the children of God to the waters of baptism?

Before our baptism, the Light of Christ may be the sole source of our inspiration. We get by with the tools we have. We take consolation in the fact that Moroni taught that we "should search diligently in the light of Christ, that (we) may know good from evil." (Moroni 7:18-19).

The principles of The Plan carry us from baptism to the covenants of the temple. "For behold, thus saith the Lord God: I will give unto the children of men line upon line, precept upon precept, here a little and there a little; and blessed are those who hearken unto my precepts, and lend an ear unto my counsel, for they shall learn wisdom; for unto him that receiveth I will give more."
(2 Nephi 28:30).

90.

We are baptized that others might be
influenced to follow our Exemplar.
(See John 14:6).

Why is it important to exercise our testimonies as often as possible?

We must venture forth out of the shadows if we want to appreciate the special familiarity that the Lord enjoys with those whom He has characterized as "the children of light." (John 12:36). As we describe to others how we feel about Christ, we learn to recognize the sensations that come naturally to each of us as a result of the stirrings of those deep feelings of intimacy.

How does our baptism unleash the power of God within us, that our shields of faith might be fortified?

When our souls have been illuminated by the burning Spirit of God, we can no longer remain passive. The flickering fire of faith warms our souls and allows us to feel an upward reach within ourselves. It sensitizes us to truth, beauty, and goodness above and beyond our own attainment.

What has our Creator provided for us to make it easier for us to witness in His name?

"All things denote there is a God, yea, even the earth, and all things that are upon the face of it witness that there is a Supreme Creator." (Alma 30:23-60). We exult in the fact that "all things bright and beautiful, all creatures great and small; all things wise and wonderful; the Lord God made them all." (Anglican Hymn, Cecil Alexander).

What are some of the evidences of the spiritual unification of the members of the Church?

By their actions, new converts and well-established Church members alike echo Paul, who declared to the Romans: "We, being many, are one body in Christ." (Romans 12:5). For example, in spite of the many translations of the scriptures used by members worldwide, there is remarkably little disagreement as to their meaning. The Spirit binds us together, "to act in doctrine and principle pertaining to futurity," while allowing us to maintain our agency to act independently across cultural boundaries. (D&C 101:78).

We will always be subject to the effects of adversity and opposition, but without the therapeutic benefits of baptism, we may needlessly suffer from a stiff neck that prevents us from looking up to Heavenly Father for guidance, over to priesthood leaders for counsel, around to seek out those in need, and down in an attitude of humility.

91.

We are baptized that the culture of the
Latter-day Saints might insulate
us from worldly influences.

How powerful is the wind of doctrine?

The wind of doctrine has done a remarkable job substituting "pleasure" for "happiness" in the general lexicon by making sin appear inviting and by emphasizing instant gratification in social media, on TV, in the movies, and in the print media. Without our conscious awareness, the wind of doctrine has shifted the focus of the world's attention, in the span of one generation, from Life, to Look, to People, to Us, and finally to Self.

How can baptism help us to recognize the divisive influence of the wind of doctrine?

The covenant of baptism is unequivocal in the demands it puts upon the disciples of Christ. It alerts them to Satan's misdirection, that would lead them from brilliant, dazzling white, through every shade of grey, to that fathomless black which, by subtraction, is the absence of every uplifting thought, word, deed, or sustaining principle.

Why is it that those who base their math, as well as their faith, on the wind of doctrine always end up with negative sums?

When Satan does the math, the sums always come out negatively even though the equations may be clothed in impressive-looking formulas. His proofs may look good, but his students are always losers in the end. $3 + (-4) = -1$, $4 \times 3 + (-13) = -1$, and $6/3 \times 2 - 5 = -1$. If we allow him the opportunity, when Satan is finished with us, we will be left as lifeless mannequins. Although we may be clothed in costly garments and fine-twined linens, and continue to sport expensive accessories, beneath it all, we will be no more than hollow shells.

How can our baptismal covenant orient us toward the light, so that if there are shadows, they will always be behind us?

In the scriptures, the first recorded words of Heavenly Father were: "Let there be light." (Genesis 1:3). His last recorded words (to date) were: "This is my beloved Son, Hear Him." (J.S.H. 1:17). These two verses are inextricably linked, and are as bookends to our faith. Our own sun rises and sets on our desire to be drawn to His light, to be mesmerized by His magic, and to be baptized by His priesthood servants.

Baptism gives
our spiritual muscles
pliancy and flexibility,
that there might be room for
the companionship of the Holy Ghost,
"which maketh manifest unto the
children of men, according
to their faith."
(Jarom 1:4).

92.

We are baptized that we might not be tempted to "look back," as we flee from Sodom and Gomorrah.
(See Genesis 19:16).

How does the 5th Article of Faith clarify the necessity of authority to baptize?

Professors of religion often "teach for doctrines the commandments of men, having a form of godliness, (while denying) the power thereof." (J.S.H. 1:19). Creeds are an abomination when they God's children away from the truth. Insult is added to injury when hypocrisy further perverts humanized, spiritually impotent dogma, when people do not really believe, but are only "professors" of religion who are quite comfortable maintaining a summer home in Idumea, although their home address is in Zion.

How does Satan use cunning craftiness to penetrate our defenses?

We know that he will make the most of every opportunity afforded him. He will capitalize on excessive behavior when we are overly-dramatic, over-sensitive, over-bearing, over-eating, over-analytical, over-achieving, or over-whelmed. He knows that over-zealous behavior is the fast track to hell. We cannot afford to joy-ride through Babylon, stopping along the way at every road-side cafe to sample its pleasures.

Why don't more people understand that one vote plus God constitutes a majority?

Ultimately, on every issue there are only three significant votes cast. Heavenly Father votes in favor of us, and Satan votes against us. Each of us casts the deciding vote as all eternity holds its collective breath and waits in hushed anticipation to see what the outcome will be. At that moment, there is no yesterday, and there is no tomorrow. There is only this moment in time when we poised to determine to govern our lives by priesthood principles. If we cast our ballot appropriately, we will find ourselves on the path leading to God's kingdom.

How can our sense of temporal security be deceiving?

With deception and a snare, Satan makes us believe that we are gaining when we are really losing. He does this by leading us by the neck "with a flaxen cord, until he (binds us) with his strong cords forever." (2 Nephi 26:22). Thus, he avoids awakening our faculties to a harsh reality. By distorting our perception, he can even twist our blessings into vehicles that amplify our feelings of self-sufficiency. Emancipation from God, however, comes at the cost of a compact with the Devil.

Our
baptism establishes
a covenant relationship
with the Lord that invites Him to
stand with us, to weigh in on our
side of the scale, even as the
counterfeit coin of Satan's
spurious currency clatters
down in a cacophony of
confusion on the other
side of the scale.

93.

**We are baptized that we might become new creatures in Christ.
(See 2 Corinthians 5:17).**

How can the scriptures expand our appreciation of the scope of The Plan of Salvation?

The scriptures are little packets of light that provide just the right amount of illumination in a dark world. At just the right moment, the Holy Ghost directs us to these love letters from God that encourage us to follow the example of the Savior.

How can baptism, and The Plan of Salvation, put us in touch with our spiritual roots?

"To use the preparation and training we receive as a springboard, to be capable of disciplined, controlled procedure and to be receptive to flashes of insight, is what solid Latter-day Saints should have going for them in their lives. The Gospel sets us free to be creative, and sets us creative to become more free. It is the perfect law of liberty." ("My Religion and Me, "Lesson #9). Truly, our baptism amplifies the quiet spiritual stirrings that underlie our mortal experience.

What does it mean to have been created in both the image and the likeness of God?

When God said: "Let us make man in our image, after our likeness," He meant not only that we should have the same physical characteristics as our Parents, but the same spiritual characteristics as well. (Moses 2:26). Like-minded individuals seek each other out, are drawn to each other, have a natural affinity for each other, stand by each other, comfort and encourage each other, and bring out the best in each other.

What provisions doe The Plan make for the acceptance of the Gospel in the Spirit World by those who have died?

There is to be a thousand years of peace on the earth following the Second Coming of the Lord. During the Millennium, "Christ will reign personally upon the earth." (10th Article of Faith). This will allow members of the Church unimpeded access to the temples, where they will perform vicarious work for the dead. Attended by angels, they will perform the ordinances for their ancestors all the way back to Adam and Eve, if necessary.

Our
baptism helps us to
be patient in our afflictions.
Knowing that the Lord is with us
until the end of our days helps us
to endure our trials and tribulations,
even when they are undeserved, or
we cannot understand why we
have been given them.
(See D&C 24:8).

94.

*We are baptized that we might stand tall
for those who may lack the power
to do so themselves.*

Does the Light of Christ influence all of Heavenly Father's children?

Although we must daily travel farther from the East, we are nevertheless oriented toward a radiant glow emanating from that distant horizon. It provides us with the regularly recurring reassurance of a religious recalibration that autocorrects with celestial precision. It envelops us in an intuitive appreciation of where we came from, why we are here, and where we are going.

How might those who do not correctly understand the ordinance of baptism be "in the gall of bitterness?" (Moroni 8:14).

Perhaps they cannot comprehend how a just and loving Father could consign so many of His innocent children to an eternal fate which, on their own merits, they did not deserve. (See Moroni 8:14). They may despair because of their little ones who have died without baptism. (Moroni 8:14). Others may have had their vision clouded by sin, and can see no way out of their miserable situation. (See Moroni 10:22).

What might be the best way to talk to our friends about how we feel about our baptism?

Even if we do not agree on every point of doctrine, we can at least agree to disagree, initiating a dialogue that leads to understanding. We can't get from A to Z without going through some intermediate steps. Perhaps this is what Isaiah meant, when he urged: "Come now, and let us reason together." (Isaiah 1:18).

Why do you think we, as well as the Ephesian Saints, need to hear Paul's instruction relating to unity? (See Ephesians 2:19).

Paul compared members of the Church, whether they be Ephesians, Tongans, or Utahans, to the parts of the body. Just as the head, the ears, the eyes, the nose, the mouth, the neck, the shoulders, the back, the breast, the vitals and bowels, the arms and hands, the loins, and the legs and feet are important in their different functions, so do all of the members of the Church have different skills and talents.

We become the sons and daughters of God, even one in our Savior Jesus Christ, as He is one in the Father, and the Father one in Him, that we may be one. (See D&C 35:2). We retain our distinct individuality, but become unified in every other way.

95.

We are baptized that we might light candles rather than curse the darkness.

Can one baptism make a difference in the world (or can one baptism make a world of difference)?

Every time a child of God is baptized, values are strengthened, the advancing tide of wickedness slows a bit, and the future looks a little brighter. A thousand points of light, when gathered together, cast a very long shadow.

Can one baptism stem the advancing tide of wickedness?

Wickedness cannot be summarily eliminated, but countermeasures can be put in place, to contain the problem. It is easier to hold up an umbrella than it is to turn off the rain, and it is far more effective to light a candle than it is to curse the darkness.

How can baptism prepare us for the coming millennial day?

It may be true that those who compete in the boiler room of commerce don't get what they deserve; rather, they get what they negotiate. But when the earth is cleansed to receive its paradisiacal glory, a higher standard will prevail and each of us will get exactly what we deserve. In the meantime, baptism helps us to conduct our affairs in a conscious anticipation of that millennial day.

How does our baptism place us on a path that follows priesthood direction?

Ultimately, each of us must ask: "Am I going to follow the prophet, or follow the profit?" "Am I going to be a Saturday Saint, a Sabbath day Saint, or a Latter-day Saint?" Priesthood direction defies spiritual Babylons' perverted conception of equality. In its attempts to be inclusive, the world does not understand that if you don't stand for something, you will fall for anything. A permissive society has, by definition, lost its heliocentric orientation on the Son of God as the Master of the universe.

Baptism
helps us to get
off religious roundabouts.
We "come unto Christ, and (are)
perfected in him, and deny (ourselves)
of all ungodliness; and if (we) shall deny
(our)selves of all ungodliness, and love God
with all (our) might, mind and strength,
then is his grace sufficient for (us),
that by his grace (we) may
be perfect in Christ."
(Moroni 10:32).

96.

We are baptized that it might become easier to approach the Lord with our sacrifices.

What is the difference between a donation and a sacrifice?

A chicken and a pig were discussing plans for a potluck dinner. "I'll bring the eggs, and you provide the ham," said the chicken. The pig thought about this for a minute, and then replied, "You know, your contribution is a donation, but mine is surely a sacrifice."

How comprehensive must our sacrifice be, before it is acceptable to the Lord?

Joseph Smith said that a religion that does not require the sacrifice of all things lacks the power to save souls. This is the essence of the Gospel of Jesus Christ. And so, it makes no difference on which principle of the Gospel we may be focusing. The distance to the Celestial Kingdom of God is measured in faith, and not in miles. It is not a question of dollars and cents, but rather of sacrifice.

What is an honest tithe?

A 1970 letter from the First Presidency stated that notwithstanding the fact that members should pay one-tenth of their income as a tithe to the Church, "every member is entitled to make his or her own decision as to what they owe the Lord, and to make payment accordingly." (March 19, 1970). Hence, the exact amount that is paid is far less important than that each member feels that he or she has been honest with the Lord.

How is the payment of tithing a barometer of our spiritual maturity?

In 1881, obedience to the law of tithing became a requirement for temple attendance for those with an income. (J.D. 22:207-208). Payment of a full tithe, it seems, is a good barometer of our spiritual maturity, and provides an easily quantifiable way to measure our core testimony temperature.

As fire in the sky, the air in the theater of life is charged with an electricity that represents the inevitable merger of the universal encouragement of the Light of Christ with the guidance provided by the Holy Ghost. Streaking in tandem across the heavens, their trajectories coalesce to trace a flaming trail that sparkles over a vast cosmic ocean that is alive with energy. Over the ebb and flow of its tide, an effectual bridge of understanding is created, that is buttressed by the cohesive influence of the mighty foundation of faith.

97.

We are baptized that we might be given opportunities to make and to keep the covenants of salvation and exaltation.

What was King Benjamin's simple counsel regarding how we can be obedient to our baptismal covenant?

His ancient but apropos warning was to watch ourselves judiciously, to be the meticulous guardians of our thoughts, the scrupulous custodians of our words, and the prudent caretakers of our deeds, to fastidiously observe the commandments of God, and to continue evenly in the faith. (See Mosiah 4:30).

How does King Benjamin's counsel empower us to fulfill the measure of our creation?

As we hesitantly inch our way through mortality, his admonition invigorates us with renewed energy, and instills in us the desire to make sacred covenants with our Heavenly Father, that we might know the Savior better.

How will our witness for Christ define, delineate, and determine our divine destiny?

Covenants force us to make choices; to be defenders of the faith or ambassadors of the adversary. In the process, all of heaven holds its collective breath, as time stands still and our fate hangs in the air as a dandelion seed caught in the summer doldrums. Covenants define us or destroy us, for they have the power to delineate our dreams, describe our destiny, and determine how, where, and with whom we will spend eternity. Covenants force us to stand and give our sworn deposition before God, angels, and witnesses, thereafter to be counted among the sheep or the goats, on His right hand or His left hand.

How do covenants vitalize the work of the ministry?

Covenants bind us to the work of the ministry, that is in turn linked to Heavenly Father's mission statement, which is to bring to pass our immortality and eternal life. (See Moses 1:39).

Our
baptism carries us, as on
the wings of angels, far from
the madding crowd, to caress the
tender chords of human associations,
of gratitude, loyalty, and appreciation, of
selflessness, helpfulness and forgiveness, of
friendship, love, and compassion. It moves
us with truth discovered and accepted,
of beauty created and enjoyed, of
goodness deepened and made
manifest in life.

98.

We are baptized that we might unite ourselves with the ordained process by which eternal principles are communicated.

How can we participate, after our baptism, in the work of the ministry?

We believe in the power of the Holy Ghost to be a Revelator, and One Who testifies of truth, wherever it may be found. We believe "all that God has revealed, all that He does now reveal, and we believe that He will yet reveal many great and important things pertaining to the Kingdom." (9th Article of Faith).

How can we make sure that our enthusiasm for the ministry does not offend people?

We need to remember that "there are no ordinary people. We have never talked to a mere mortal. It is immortals with whom we joke, work, marry, snub and exploit. Our charity must be a real and costly love. Next to the blessed Sacrament itself, our neighbors," as well as the homeless person with a cardboard sign, "is the holiest object presented to your senses." (C.S. Lewis). His perception was clear and accurate. He could see the autobiographical thread of his neighbors leading all the way to Deity. He understood that even the most hardened soul has within him "the acorn of a potential oak, the unsculpted image of a glorified personality." (Truman Madsen, "Eternal Man," p. 17).

How does the power of Heavenly Father, Jesus Christ, and the Holy Ghost infuse the universe with light?

Particle physics tells us that, at the moment of the Big Bang, an incomprehensible number of photons was created. The number is 1 followed by 89 zeros, which is essentially insignificant when compared to the luminosity of God. At the end of the day, "there is no power but of God." Photons have been "ordained of God" to provide reliable light in a dark and dreary world. (Romans 13:1).

Is there any viable alternative to baptism?

"This is the way," Nephi said, "and there is none other way nor name given under heaven whereby man can be saved in the kingdom of God. And now, behold, this is the doctrine of Christ, and the only and true doctrine of the Father, and of the Son, and of the Holy Ghost, which is one God, without end." (2 Nephi 31:21).

"This thing shall ye teach – repentance and baptism unto those who are accountable and capable of committing sin; yea, teach parents that they must repent and be baptized, and humble themselves as their little children, and they shall all be saved with their little children."
(Moroni 8:10).

99.

We are baptized that, henceforth, we be no more "carried about with every wind of doctrine." (Ephesians 4:14).

What are the winds of doctrine?

Winds of doctrine are those worldly influences that are always playing mind-games with us, as they jockey for position in a competition for market share. Our baptism reminds us that we are heaven-bound in ways that bridge the cultural confusion and doctrinal dilemmas that are thrown up to hedge the way, by a world that staggers to and fro, like a drunkard. (See Job 12:25, and Psalms 107:27).

How does baptism refute the false notion that we can procrastinate the day of our repentance? (See Alma 34).

A favorite tactic of Satan is to trick us into thinking we have all the time in the world, so that we become numb to the reality that "now is the time and the day of (our) salvation; therefore, if (we) will repent and harden not (our) hearts, immediately shall The Great Plan of Redemption be brought about." (Alma 34:31).

How has the wind of doctrine penetrated nearly every aspect of the lives of those around us?

It is evident in the negative peer pressure that can break down our resolve to do good. It is the silent partner of sports figures, and other luminaries whose lifestyles reflect the vulgar tastes of the world. It substitutes the profane for the sacred, allowing words like "almighty dollar" and "movie star" to fall easily from our lips. It manages to substitute "notoriety" for "celebrity," so that the difference can scarcely be understood.

How can our baptism be a shield and a protection against the power of the destroyer, as long as we have a work left to do on the earth?

Obedience throws open the windows of heaven so that the blessings of the Lord may be poured out upon our heads, to the end "that (we) may not be seduced by evil spirits, or doctrines of devils, or the commandments of men." (D&C 46:7).

It is at
our baptisms that we feel
the gentle caress of the hands
of the Master Potter, as He turns our
lives with the hand of time. We give Him
permission, as the Artisan of our destiny, to
mold us and shape us. (See Jeremiah 18:6). We
are the clay, and He is our potter; and we are the
work of His hands. (See Isaiah 64:8). As our
thoughts turn to the Savior, we remain
impressionable and pliable to
the things of the Spirit.

100.

We are baptized that we might not be deceived "by the sleight of men, and cunning craftiness, whereby they lie in wait to deceive." (Ephesians 4:14).

What is "the sleight of men?"

There are evils and designs that exist in the hearts of conspiring men in the last days, that are designed to lead the righteous away from the strait and narrow way. (See D&C 89:4). The sleight of men relies heavily upon illusion, deceit, and outright dishonesty. Those who are misdirected by the sleight of men are as flotsam and jetsam on the sea of life, "driven about as chaff before the wind." (Mormon 5:16).

How is the spirit that is present at a baptismal service the polar opposite of "cunning craftiness?"

Baptismal services are blessed with the scorching holiness of God's presence, because they focus our attention on the dazzling gates of the Celestial Kingdom. For a brief moment in time, participants are refreshingly freed from the worldly reminders of the adversary that are a part of the "opposition in all things" of which Lehi spoke, and that are so much a part of our daily lives. (2 Nephi 2:11).

How can baptism offer protection from those who "lie in wait to deceive?"

With experience, we learn to recognize the tricks of their telestial trade. We guard against placing ourselves in compromising situations, because these make us more susceptible to temptation and enticements to be evil. Our covenant correctly redirects our attention to the seriousness of sin, the necessity of repentance, and the power of forgiveness through the Atonement of Christ.

How can baptism help us to recognize the fingerprints of Satan on the idols with which he tempts us?

Our covenant guards against his groping hands whose toxic touch has compromised and contaminated customs, culture, morals, ethics, the use of leisure time, language, and humor with moral equivocation and cultural expediency. He has distorted the perception of misfortune and opportunity, poverty and prosperity, adversity and privilege, and sickness and health. He has invaded the media, technology, education, health care, and sports. His influence is radioactive, mutating natural tendencies into unrecognizable forms.

"If it so be that ye believe in Christ, and are baptized, first with water, then with fire and with the Holy Ghost, following the example of our Savior, according to that which he hath commanded us, it shall be well with you in the day of judgment." (Mormon 7:10).

101.

We are baptized that we might honor the order of the priesthood.

By what authority is baptism performed?

Its performance requires the authority of God, the sanction of His file leaders, exactness in its execution, and the validation of witnesses. The authority that was restored by John the Baptist will "never be taken again from the earth until…" where "until" suggests a continuing sense; for example, "God be with you until we meet again." (D&C 13:1).

What was Oliver Cowdery's witness, regarding the angelic restoration of the authority to baptize?

He described the events thus: "What joy filled our hearts, and with what surprise we must have bowed … when we received under his hand the Holy Priesthood, as he said, 'Upon you my fellow-servants, in the name of Messiah, I confer this Priesthood and this authority, which shall remain upon earth, that the Sons of Levi may yet offer an offering unto the Lord in righteousness." (Footnote to J.S.H. 1:71).

Who are the sons of Levi that are referred to in Doctrine & Covenants Section 13?

The sons of Levi are "the sons of Moses and also the sons of Aaron (who) shall offer an acceptable offering and sacrifice in the house of the Lord." (D&C 84:31). Joseph taught that "the sons Moses and of Aaron shall be filled with the glory of the Lord, upon Mount Zion in the Lord's house, whose sons are ye." (D&C 84:32).

How does baptism create the opportunity for young men to become the sons of Moses and of Aaron?

When they reach the appropriate age, typically ages 11 - 18, young men who remain faithful will obtain these two priesthoods and "become the sons of Moses and of Aaron, and the seed of Abraham, and the church and kingdom, and the elect of God." (D&C 84:34).

"Follow me."
(John 21:19).

102.

We are baptized that we might be perfected in our Savior, Jesus Christ. (See Moroni 10:32).

How can baptism fortify us with the discipline to go the second mile?

As long as we are learning, our spiritual awakening is acceptable to the Lord. We may take solace in the scriptures, where, although we are admonished 154 times to be perfect, we are also encouraged 129 times to "learn" and 995 times to "begin." Thus, we read in the scriptures how "the people began to repent of their iniquity; and inasmuch as they did, the Lord did have mercy on them." (Ether 11:8).

What happens when we turn to the scriptures to learn about the Father of our spirits?

The message rings loud and clear, and resonates within our hearts: "In him we live, and move, and have our being, as certain also of your own poets have said. For we are also his offspring. (Acts 17:28). He is "the Father of all." Ephesians 4:6). We lived with Him before we were born.

How does it make you feel to realize that, as evidenced in the baptismal prayer, Heavenly Father knows each of us by our first name?

At the end of the day, each of us is a child of God, known to Him by name. Although we worship together as a Church, at our baptism, and during the administration of subsequent ordinances of the priesthood, we are called by name by the officiant, who then invokes the holy names of the Father, the Son, and the Holy Ghost, to seal the covenant promises upon our heads.

Do you think that Moroni might have been speaking to baptismal candidates, as he closed his record?

He exhorted us: "Yea, come unto Christ, and be perfected in him, and deny yourselves of all ungodliness; and if ye shall deny yourselves of all ungodliness, and love God with all your might, mind and strength, then is his grace sufficient for you, that by his grace ye may be perfect in Christ." (Moroni 10:32).

"I will go before your face," promised the Lord. "I will be on your right hand, and on your left, and my Spirit shall be in your hearts, and mine angels round about you, to bear you up."
(D&C 84:88).

103.

We are baptized that, through God's infinite goodness and the manifestations of the Spirit, we might have great views of that which is to come.
(See Mosiah 5:3).

How can baptism help us to achieve spiritual symmetry?

Baptism orients us more to the laws of the eternal world and to the guidance of the Master than to the limitations imposed by the physical world and to the destructive effects of disproportion. Our experience is inexplicable, and yet undeniable. "Whatsoever is born of God (somehow) overcometh the (laws governing the physical) world." (1 John 5:3).

How does our baptism entitle us to the further light and knowledge that the Lord has promised us?

The Church provides a nurturing influence that makes it easier to have lips that have learned to articulate only positive expressions of speech and never speak guile, shoulders that have developed the strength to bear the burdens of our fellow-travelers who have been battered and bruised by the vicissitudes of life and who may yet be faltering under the heavy weight of sorrow and sin, and backs that have become sturdy enough to withstand the fierce winds of adversity and the subtle wiles of the adversary.

What does it mean to have an eternal perspective?

As Aaron taught King Lamoni's father, around a hundred years before the mortal ministry of the Savior: "Since man had fallen he could not merit anything of himself; but the sufferings and death of Christ atone for their sins, through faith and repentance, (and) he breaketh the bands of death, that the grave shall have no victory ... that the sting of death should be swallowed up in the hopes of glory." (Alma 22:14).

How does Heavenly Father link baptism to the precious gift of testimony?

At our baptism, the emanation of familiar and soothing oscillations of energy resonating from within the limitless reserves that are selflessly shared by the Holy Ghost will carry us along on rolling waves of the spirit toward a more sure personal witness of the Savior's divinity.

With our
baptism comes
"the remission of sins
(which) bringeth meekness,
and lowliness of heart; and
because of meekness and lowliness
of heart cometh the visitation of the
Holy Ghost, which Comforter filleth with
hope and perfect love, which love endureth
by diligence unto prayer, until the end
shall come, when all the saints
shall dwell with God."
(Moroni 8:26).

104.

We are baptized that we might understand how and what we worship, that we might come unto our Father in the name of our Savior Jesus Christ.
(See D&C 93:19).

How does baptism grant us access to the mysteries of the kingdom? (See Matthew 13:11).

Our holy scriptures are called "The Standard Works" with good reason, inasmuch as they are the foundation for the administration of the Lord's worldwide priesthood government, and are every member's personal "Handbook of Instructions." They are of no private interpretation. (See 2 Peter 1:20). Instead, their meaning is discerned by the manifestation of the spirit that is universally accessible to those who have been endowed with the Gift of the Holy Ghost.

How does baptism free us to worship God "according to the dictates of (our) own conscience?" (11th Article of Faith).

Our covenants with God place us beyond the reach of the adversary, and obedience gives us the priesthood and spiritual power necessary to overcome evil. In fact, our "salvation consists (in our) being placed beyond the power of (our) enemies, meaning the enemies of (our) progression, such as dishonesty, greediness, lying, immorality, and other vices." (Joseph Smith).

How do you think we felt after The Plan had been fully explained to us in the pre-mortal world?

Imagine the significance of the events that were unfolding before us: The exercise of our free will had just been guaranteed, the principles of The Plan certified, the price of our future offenses successfully negotiated, the guarantee of payment made in advance, and the demands of Justice satisfied and equally balanced against Mercy. Even cherubim and a flaming sword had been prepared to guard the way, in order to guarantee our opportunity to progress. Our Heavenly Father's work and glory had been confirmed, to bring to pass our immortality and eternal life. (See Moses 1:39).

Following our baptism, how can the temple become the pinnacle of our worship?

We receive living water in the House of the Lord, where we are given instruction, are endowed with power and understanding, and are promised peace and joy. We receive living water when, through our faithfulness, we are washed clean from the blood and sins of this generation.

"This is the
Gospel which I have given
unto you - that I came into the
world to do the will of my Father,
because my Father sent me ... And
it shall come to pass, that whoso
repenteth and is baptized in
my name shall be filled."
(3 Nephi 27:13-20).

105.

We are baptized with the realization that when the Lord gives us commandments, He also prepares ways for us to accomplish the tasks that are set before us.
(See 1 Nephi 3:7).

How can sacrifice, in its many forms, have the power to make us feel so happy?

We see what might be best for ourselves and for the Kingdom of God, develop a testimony that it should be, and then work with all our capacity to make it happen, whatever the cost might be. Then, when we are so richly blessed far beyond the measure that we deserve, the price, once paid so painfully, is recalled in gladness. We receive full value. As Brigham Young is reported to have said: "I never count the cost of anything. I just find out what the Lord wants me to do, and I do it."

How can renewing our covenant of baptism help us to lengthen our stride?

Ralph Waldo Emerson declared: "That which we persist in doing becomes easier for us. Not that the nature of the thing has changed, but our power to do is increased." Spencer W. Kimball illustrated this concept when he told the Saints: "What I am asking for is not a flashy, temporary change in performance, but a quiet resolve to lengthen our stride." ((Regional Representative's Seminar, 3 Oct. 1974.)

Why do you think there is a need for repentance before baptism?

"Whosoever repenteth and cometh unto me," said the Lord, "the same is my church. Whosoever declareth more or less than this, the same is not of me, but is against me; therefore he is not of my church." (D&C 10:67-68). Since the day the Church was organized on April 6, 1830, this doctrine has not changed. The Lord's messengers have taught this doctrine without modification since the Restoration of the Gospel on that date.

How can angels from heaven help us to repent before, and after, our baptism?

Angels, who are the servants of Christ, are commissioned to the work. "And the office of their ministry is to call men unto repentance, and to fulfil and to do the work of the covenants of the Father, which he hath made unto the children of men, to prepare the way among the children of men, by declaring the word of Christ unto the chosen vessels of the Lord, that they may bear testimony of him." (Moroni 7:31).

"There is no regularly constituted church on earth, nor any person authorized to administer any church ordinance (such as baptism); nor can there be until new apostles are sent by the Great Head of the Church, for Whose Coming I am seeking." (Roger Williams).

106.

We are baptized to make it easier for us to "pray unto the Lord, (to) call upon his holy name, (and to) make known his wonderful works among the people."
(D&C 65:4).

What is our greatest joy, when we sacrifice for the kingdom?

We are, and will forever be, His junior partners, and never His equals, but we still know what it feels like to be in business with God. When we work tirelessly, and the sweat drips off the ends of our noses, we thank our Father in Heaven for the capacity to work, for the blessing it is to feel physically fatigued, and for whatever talents we have been able to muster, to be put to use for the benefit of the Church and kingdom.

With Heavenly Father taking such good care of us, how can we keep in perspective the blessings He pours out upon our heads?

When we survey the fruits of our labors, we try to envision the purpose for which we have received our blessings. If our talents are multiplied, our greatest enjoyment comes when they are put to use for the benefit of others. Our happiness is like a butterfly. The more we chase it, the more it eludes us. But when we exert ourselves in service to others, happiness comes and rests quietly on our shoulder.

What can we do to better follow the Savior's example?

When we think about maintaining the intensity of feeling we experienced at our own baptisms, we remember the two disciples on the Road to Emmaus, who, after communing with the Resurrected Lord, declared: "Did not our heart burn within us, while he talked with us by the way, and while he opened to us the scriptures?" (Luke 24:32).

Can there be a greater witness than the Holy Ghost?

The Holy Ghost bears the most sacred witness of the validity of every Gospel ordinance. With the baptism of fire and the unimpeachable witness of the Holy Ghost, the Atonement is complete, Mercy satisfies Justice, and the penitent faithful receive a remission of sins in a symbolic rite of purification.

"The harder the conflict, the more glorious the triumph. What we obtain too cheap, we esteem too lightly; 'tis dearness only that gives everything its value. Heaven knows how to put a proper price upon its goods." (Tom Paine, "Common Sense"). It would be strange, indeed, if such a celestial article as baptism should not be highly rated.

107.

> We are baptized so that, although we were an hungered,
> and thirsty, and strangers, we will no longer be
> naked, or sick, or imprisoned within the
> fortress of our own limiting beliefs.
> (See Matthew 25:34-40).

How does baptism help us to break free of our self-imposed limitations?

Baptism helps us to chart the unknown possibilities of existence. We sweep aside the self-limiting belief that "the sky is the limit." In its stead, we substitute the mind and soul expanding certainty that "the wide expanse of heaven is the limit." We are reminded that one of the greatest contributions of Joseph Smith was the "knowledge of what is to come after death. He did much to clarify our understanding of heaven and to make it seem worth working for." ("My Religion & Me" Course Manual).

How can baptism counteract the insidiously destructive nature of limiting beliefs?

Fading light is the consequence of the corrosive nature of sin, or even of the opposition in all things that is a necessary part of our mortal experience. Without baptism, which is the lynchpin of The Plan of Salvation, all must be lost. Fortunately, the Lord reveals truth to all those who are spiritually prepared to understand it, and from the beginning, has provided a pathway to perfection that they might humble themselves as little children.

How was Naaman the Leper an example of one who can be a prisoner of limiting beliefs?

The waters of baptism are a ready invitation to those who are humble, meek, poor in spirit, and pure in heart. When Elisha directed Naaman to wash in the River Jordan seven times in order to be cured of his leprosy, this proud captain of the host of the King of Syria at first refused. But "his servant came near, and spake unto him, and said, My father, if the prophet had bid thee do some great thing, wouldest thou not have done it? How much rather then, when he saith to thee, Wash, and be clean?" Then, with the faith of a little child, "he went down, and dipped himself seven times in Jordan … and his flesh came again like unto the flesh of a little child, and he was clean." (2 Kings 5:13-14).

How can our baptism liberate us from intellectual, philosophical, or spiritual captivity?

The Law of Witnesses enjoys its most profound expression at baptismal services, for "the testimony of two men is true." (John 8:17). Witnesses stand beside the unimpeachable witness of the Holy Ghost to confirm the validity of the ordinance.

"The first fruits of repentance is baptism; and baptism cometh by faith unto the fulfilling the commandments; and the fulfilling the commandments bringeth remission of sins; and the remission of sins bringeth meekness, and lowliness of heart; and because of meekness and lowliness of heart cometh the visitation of the Holy Ghost." (Moroni 8:25-26).

108.

We are baptized that, with uplifted hands unto the Most High, our incomings, our outgoings, and our salutations might be in the name of the Lord.
(See D&C 109:9).

How can witnesses help those who are struggling as they make the journey to Christ?

Witnesses nudge those who are groping about in darkness to move closer to the Light. Jeremiah exercised the power of testimony to exhort the spiritually blind and deaf inhabitants of Jerusalem: "Hear now this, O foolish people, and without understanding; which have eyes, and see not; which have ears, and hear not." (Jeremiah 5:21).

How does the Light of Christ work tirelessly to encourage us to praise God?

It helps us to recognize the hand of God in all things, and to know that there are no coincidences, but instead only an awe-inspiring divine design that beautifully and flawlessly choreographs our lives.

How can the Light of Christ prompt us to lift up our hands and praise God?

The Light of Christ examines what it means to be anxiously engaged, inspires us to plumb the depths of our commitment to the Savior, sensitizes us to the nobility of His work, and makes us more acutely aware of His grace, by bringing the visions of glory into focus.

How is our baptism a re-affirmation of our pre-mortal acceptance of The Plan of Salvation?

In that realm, as spirit sons and daughters, we knew and worshipped God as our Eternal Father, and accepted His Plan by which we could obtain physical bodies and gain earthly experience to progress by faith toward perfection. Thereby, we could ultimately realize our divine destiny as rightful heirs of eternal life. (See Abraham 1:2).

"Wherefore, my beloved brethren, can we follow Jesus, save we shall be willing to keep the commandments of the Father? And the Father said: Repent ye, repent ye, and be baptized in the name of my Beloved Son." (2 Nephi 31:10-11).

109.

> We are baptized that we might find
> greater happiness, peace, and rest; that we
> might obtain the blessings of the fathers,
> including the authority to administer
> the ordinances of the Gospel.
> (See Abraham 1:2).

After the close of the Savior's ministry, how successful was the Church in maintaining strict obedience to the doctrine of Christ?

During the Age of Chivalry, Charlemagne urged his churchmen to faithful Gospel scholarship. "In a letter to abbots and bishops, he complained of illiterate monks: 'What pious devotion had faithfully prompted their hearts, their uneducated tongues could not put into words without stumbling.' Hardly a Bible existed that was not riddled with the gross errors of untutored copyists." (Will Durant, "The Age of Chivalry," p. 61).

How did the Reformation pave the way for the Restoration of the Gospel?

A leader of the Reformation in America, Roger Williams, wrote: "There is no regularly constituted church on earth, nor any person authorized to administer any church ordinance (such as baptism); nor can there be until new apostles are sent by the Great Head of the Church, for Whose Coming I am seeking." ("Picturesque America," p. 502).

What do you think Thomas Jefferson meant when he used the term: "Primitive Christianity"?

He fumed that "the religion builders have so distorted and deformed the doctrines of Jesus, so muffled them in mysticisms, fancies and falsehoods, have caricatured them into forms so inconceivable, as to shock reasonable thinkers. Happy in the prospect of a restoration of Primitive Christianity, I must leave to younger persons to encounter and lop off the false branches which have been engrafted into it by the mythologists of the middle and modern ages." ("Jefferson's Complete Works," 7:210).

How is baptism related to the Restoration of the Gospel?

The Restoration reestablished the authority to act in obedience to the law of heaven. As the Savior taught: "This is the Gospel which I have given unto you - that I came into the world to do the will of my Father, because my Father sent me ... And it shall come to pass, that whoso repenteth and is baptized in my name shall be filled." (3 Nephi 27:13-20).

"The voice of warning (shall) be unto all people, (and) those who reject the glad message, the rebellious, shall be pierced with much sorrow." (D&C 1:3-4).

110.

We are baptized to become more observant followers of righteousness, to possess greater knowledge, to be the progenitors of nations and ambassadors of peace, and to receive instruction, and keep the commandments.
(See Abraham 1:2).

What do the scriptures have to say about the ability of the Church to sustain true doctrine without continual revelation?

Paul had prophesied of the coming apostasy from the faith, when he wrote to the Thessalonian Saints: "Be not soon shaken in mind, or be troubled, neither by spirit, nor by word, nor by letter as from us, as that the day of Christ is at hand. Let no man deceive you by any means. For that day shall not come, except there come a falling away first." (2 Thessalonians 2:2-3).

What did early Church historians have to say about apostasy from the truth?

In the third century A.D., the Church Historian Eusebius provided a glimpse of the falling away that had been spoken of by Paul, and that had already begun. He wrote: "But with our greater freedom a change came over us. We yielded to pride and sloth. We yielded to mutual envy and abuse. We warred upon ourselves as occasion offered, and we used the weapons and the spears of words. Leaders fought with leaders, and laity formed factions against laity. Unspeakable hypocrisy and dissimulation traveled to the farthest limits of evil." ("The Essential Eusebius," p. 177).

Why did the Pharisees of His day remain silent when Jesus was baptized?

"The fact that baptism was practiced in ancient Israel might explain why the Savior was not criticized by the orthodox Jews when He was baptized. The Pharisees were quick to (rebuke) Him whenever He did anything contrary to their law. However, not a single word of criticism concerning the baptism of Jesus Christ is found in the New Testament." ("Commentary on The Book of Mormon" p. 155).

How can the ordinance of baptism help us to be more observant followers of righteousness?

Heavenly Father has ordained a Plan that is all the more beautiful because of its simplicity It is clearly established in the Bible and clarified in companion scriptures. It has been carefully articulated in both The Book of Mormon and the Doctrine and Covenants, in order to silence disputations among the people concerning this vital point of doctrine.

"I will give unto the children of men line upon line, precept upon precept, here a little and there a little; and blessed are those who hearken unto my precepts, and lend an ear unto my counsel, for they shall learn wisdom; for unto him that receiveth I will give more."
(2 Nephi 28:30).

111.

We are baptized that we might become kings and priests, and queens and priestesses; in effect, to become rightful heirs of the blessings that belonged to the fathers.
(See Abraham 1:2).

Why are we baptized individually, and not in large groups?

Heavenly Father purposely designed baptism so that each time the ordinance would be performed, it would be unique, and in its own special way be particularly adapted to the child of God who was then entering the fold. It is at baptismal services that we "hear truth spoken with clarity and freshness, uncolored and untranslated. It speaks from within ourselves in a language original but inarticulate, heard only with the soul." (Hugh B. Brown).

What is the eternal destiny of those who die before they reach the age of accountability?

The breath of fresh air that is manifest in latter-day revelation is unequivocal: "Children who die before they arrive at the years of accountability are saved in the Celestial Kingdom of heaven." (D&C 137:10).

To whom do the blessings of the Abrahamic Covenant apply?

Because of the Atonement, all have equal opportunity before the Lord. All "may have the privilege, living or dead, of accepting the conditions of the great Plan of Redemption provided by the Father, through the Son, before the world was." (John Taylor, "Mediation and Atonement," p. 181).

Where does the pathway lead that begins with baptism?

The pathway to the Celestial Kingdom is illuminated by the principles of true conversion that point us in the direction of a clear recognition of iniquity, and then to a deep godly sorrow for our sins. Next comes inescapable suffering and torment that stimulates an appeal to the Savior, together with our awakening understanding of the power of the Atonement. From Him, comes forgiveness, spiritual enlightenment, and great joy. This motivates us to a lifestyle of righteousness and service. Each time this happens, the endless loop cycles one more time, calibrated to an ever higher plane of existence.

As we respond to the
invitation to enter into the
fold, the Spirit moves upon us to
wash our flesh in water and to put
on holy garments, that we might
be prepared to enter into
the joy of the Lord.
(See Leviticus 16:4).

112.

We are baptized because we have brought forth fruit worthy of repentance.
(See Moroni 6:1).

How does baptism free us from the destructive process of everything that is of a temporal nature to gradually decline into disorder?

When we are "born of God," our orientation is more toward the expansive laws of eternity than to the restrictive confines of the physical world. When we are in harmony with heaven, we are simply in a better state of balance. We overcome the world with a freedom from incarceration to the inexorable immutability of the law of entropy, that governs the temporal world in which we now live. (See 1 John 5:3).

Why do you think baptism has been described as a "narrow gate?" (2 Nephi 33:9).

It can be challenging to muster faith unto repentance that leads us to the strait and narrow gate of baptism. In fact, "few there be that find it." (Matthew 7:14). Those who ultimately pass through this portal will find the way opening up before them because it has been clearly defined by the Atonement of Christ.

Why do faith and repentance precede baptism? (See the 4th Article of Faith).

Baptism is the pinnacle of our experience, when through the Atonement we are liberated by independence from the bondage to sin. This feeling is incalculable, indescribable, and inexplicable, and yet it is undeniable. It is not maturational, but is generational, as we become new creatures in Christ. (see 2 Corinthians 5:17).

After our baptism, when we regularly repent, what happens to the recollection of our former sins?

Regarding sins for which we have repented, we will remember them only insofar as they increase our testimonies and strengthen our resolve to refrain from repeating them, but we will no longer fee the guilt associated with the transgression. The Spirit of the Lord Omnipotent will cause a mighty change to come over us, "that we have no more disposition to do evil, but to do good continually." (Mosiah 5:2).

"This thing shall
ye teach – repentance
and baptism unto those who are
accountable and capable of committing
sin; yea, teach parents that they must
repent and be baptized, and humble
themselves as their little children,
and they shall all be saved
with their little children."
(Moroni 8:10).

113.

We are baptized that we might give away all of our sins, but there are strings attached.
(See Alma 22:18).

What happens when we give away our sins?

With baptism, we realize that "life is a sheet of paper white where each of us may write a line or two, and then comes night. Greatly begin. If thou hast time but for a line, make that sublime. Not failure, but low aim is crime." (James Russell Lowell).

Why do you think the Sacrament has been provided to those who have been baptized?

Without the sustained spiritual nourishment that is repetitively provided by the tokens of the Sacrament, it is inevitable that we would, sooner or later, die spiritually. (See Romans 8:13).

Do you think that we could be happy while living in eternity, if we had not beforehand given away our sins?

Though our sins "be as scarlet, they shall be as white as snow; though they be red like crimson, they shall be as wool." (Isaiah 1:18). The divine Plan of Happiness enables family relationships to be perpetuated beyond the grave. Sacred ordinances, beginning with baptism, culminating in the covenants of the temple, make it possible for God's children to return to His presence in a state of purity and innocence, and for families to be united eternally.

Can you think of anyone who would be willing to take personal responsibility for our sins?

One reason the Atonement is so hard for even the disciples of Christ to grasp is that it was conceived in heaven. It is not of this world, and so if we try to wrap our finite minds around it, we will fail. But it must not be summarily dismissed just because it cannot be rationally explained. "The things which some men esteem to be of great worth ... others set at naught ... Yea, even the very God of Israel do men trample under their feet." (1 Nephi 19:7). The Atonement is one of the mysteries of the kingdom that can only be spiritually discerned. (See 1 Corinthians 2:14).

Baptism allows us
to "press forward" with
complete dedication and with
"steadfastness," or with confidence
and a firm determination in Christ,
"having a perfect brightness of hope," or
perfect faith, and charity, or "a love of God
and of all men." If we do this, "feasting upon
the word of Christ," by receiving strength
and nourishment from the scriptures,
and if we endure to the end, not in
wickedness, but in righteousness,
we "shall have eternal life,"
which is the greatest gift
that God can bestow.
(2 Nephi 31:20).

114.

We are baptized when charity has become the foundation of our faith.

How can we protect ourselves with a "shield of faith?"

The counsel of our Heavenly Father strikes familiar chords within us, even as Satan's fingerprints are more easily identified on the idols with which he tempts us. Little wonder that the Master said that His sheep would recognize His voice, and follow Him." (See John 10:27).

Our shield of faith notwithstanding, why does it sometimes seem as if we are so alone? (See Mark 1:3).

In our day, we need a shield of faith as never before, because Satan has infiltrated government, and has suppressed the will of the silent majority by legitimizing the wild, rabid, and morally indefensible demands of the vocal minority. He has snuffed out freedom of expression within democracy, and with gold and silver he has purchased armies and navies, false priests who oppress, and tyrants with whom he goes about sowing destruction upon the earth. (See Mosiah 7:31).

How can charity strengthen our "shield of faith?"

Baptism inspires us to direct our charity toward others. The covenant fosters empathy, and teaches us to be less concerned with telestial trivia and more focused on celestial sureties. It gently encourages us to be humble and selfless, to be forbearing, and to reflect poise under provocation.

How do those who have been baptized qualify by worthiness to bear a "shield of faith?"

Those who have been baptized think no evil, have no secret agenda, and rejoice not in iniquity, but are instead repulsed by sin. They delight in the truth, believe all things, hope all things, endure many things, and hope to be able to endure all things. They are drawn to light, and are continually open to that which is uplifting. (See Moroni 7:45).

Those who are baptized are "not ashamed of the Gospel of Christ, for it is the power of God unto salvation to every one that believeth." (Romans 1:16).

115.

> We are baptized because we have determined to follow the Savior "with full purpose of heart, acting no hypocrisy and no deception before God."
> (2 Nephi 31:13).

How is our discipleship vitalized as we approach the Savior "with full purpose of heart?"

We follow the Savior when we build up our stewardship responsibilities in dignity and importance, make them honorable and commendable in the eyes of all, enlarge and strengthen them, and simply perform the service that pertains to them. If we do not magnify our callings, God will hold us responsible for those whom we might have saved, had we done our duty. (Discourse delivered in the Tabernacle, Salt Lake City, 7/7/1878).

How can we "give birth" to our witness of Jesus Christ, that it might be borne "with full purpose of heart?"

With our baptism, the night of darkness is followed by the Renaissance, a spiritual rebirth that paves the way for enlightenment. Light banishes darkness and our world blossoms with new ideas and unbridled optimism. Though we "walked in darkness, (we) have seen a great light. They that dwell(ed) in the land of the shadow of death, upon them hath the light shined." (Isaiah 9:2).

Why do you think that people sometimes act with hypocrisy, or "deception before God?"

Perhaps they are embarrassed to be identified as Christians. But those who are baptized are "not ashamed of the Gospel of Christ, for it is the power of God unto salvation to every one that believeth." (Romans 1:16).

What has Heavenly Father provided to make sure that we witness for the Savior with "full purpose of heart?"

When we feel the urge to push His agenda, Heavenly Father has provided us with the Light of Christ to be our labor coach, providing us with just the right amount of encouragement to successfully deliver our witness without being overbearing.

We are the "elect according to the foreknowledge of God the Father, through sanctification of the Spirit, unto obedience and sprinkling of the blood of Jesus Christ."
(1 Peter 1:2).

116.

We are baptized that we might experience liberation from our self-defeating behaviors.

How does baptism prepare us for our magnum opus in the theater of life?

Baptism invites inspiration from heaven. For example, we cannot just determine to be charitable. We need the guidance of the Spirit to lead us to those in need. In doing so, we are doubly blessed.

Why do you think the Gospel is called "the perfect law of liberty?" (See James 1:25).

Obedience to Gospel principles blesses us to "be like the bird who, pausing in her flight awhile on boughs too light, feels them give way beneath her, and yet sings, knowing she hath wings." (Victor Hugo).

How does baptism re-introduce us to the program of the Three Act Play that was imprinted upon our souls before we came to earth?

Baptism invites us to step back, inhale deeply, take time, and focus our energies on the important things, as we scurry about during Act Two of life's Three Act Play that is The Plan of Salvation. The covenant gently introduces us to the warm embrace of daily experiences with the Holy Ghost to bring Act One to our remembrance, and to tantalize us with a taste of the treats that await us when the curtain call comes that signals the commencement of Act Three.

How does baptism bring out the best in us?

Our baptism prepares us to rise to the occasion, and to meet every challenge of mortality. As Mormon said: "I judge better things of you, for I judge that ye have faith in Christ because of your meekness." (Moroni 7:39). He was like wise old Tevya in The Fiddler on The Roof, who told his daughters: "In Anatevka, God knows who you are, and what you may become."

"Wherefore,
my beloved brethren,
can we follow Jesus save
we shall be willing to keep the
commandments of the Father?"
(2 Nephi 31:10).

117.

> We are baptized that we might press forward
> with steadfastness, having a perfect brightness
> of hope and a love of God and of our brothers
> and sisters, feasting upon the scriptures, and
> enduring to the end in righteousness.
> (See Nephi 31:20).

Following baptism, how can the repetition of the Sacrament become a vehicle for our personal growth and development?

At baptism, we are called by our "user name," and then, in a renewal of our covenant during the ordinance of the Sacrament, we are given the password that grants us access to the key of knowledge. This vital information endows us with a perfect brightness of hope and a love of God and of all men, as we feast upon the word of Christ, and endure to the end. (See 2 Nephi 31:20)

How did Joseph Smith feast upon the word of God after reading James 1:2-?

The word of God led him to the Sacred Grove, where he learned that the creeds of Christendom were "an abomination." (J.S.H. 1:19). Organizations or teachings that do not lead us clearly and directly toward salvation and exaltation in the Celestial Kingdom are abominable in the sight of God. It was confusion and the fear of impending condemnation that drove Joseph Smith to his knees and introduced the world to the Dispensation of The Fulness of Times.

How did Joseph Smith receive the gift of the ministering of angels even before his baptism?

His account of the initial appearance of the Angel Moroni is unique. (See J.S.H. 1:29-43). Joseph wrote that late one evening a light started to appear in his bed chamber, and grew brighter and brighter, until it was lighter than at noonday. Suddenly the Angel Moroni appeared before him, standing in the air. Clearly, He did not come through the door when he entered the room. He just "appeared," as if from another world.

How does our baptism become a commencement exercise?

Our baptism can catalyze our resolve, so that our experience can be as it was on the Day of Pentecost, when the words of Peter and the other apostles carried the day by penetrating the hearts of their listeners. Peter was asked: "Men and brethren, what shall we do? Then Peter said unto them, Repent, and be baptized every one of you in the name of Jesus Christ for the remission of sins, and ye shall receive the gift of the Holy Ghost." (Acts 2:37-38).

"For by the water (we) keep the commandment; by the Spirit (we) are justified, and by the blood (we) are sanctified." (Moses 6:60).

118.

> We are baptized that we might hear the voice of the Lord that is unto all, for "there is none to escape; and there is no eye that shall not see, neither ear that shall not hear, neither heart that shall not be penetrated."
> (D&C 1:2).

In what literal and figurative ways does the Savior ask us to follow Him?

The Savior's example demonstrates that entrance into the Church and Kingdom is strait; that is to say, it is narrowly defined. There should be no discussion or variance of opinion regarding the prescribed way. He set the pattern by simply commanding the children of men to follow Him. (See 2 Nephi 31:10).

Can we also follow the Savior by listening to the counsel of His prophet?

Their ecclesiastical responsibility has always been to invite less active members of the Church to return to the fold in full fellowship. This was powerfully demonstrated in Russel M. Nelson's first address, as President of the Church.

Can we really follow the Savior to the waters of baptism if there is confusion regarding the correct administration of the ordinance?

The history of post-apostolic Christianity illustrates the misunderstanding that has taken place concerning the doctrine of Christ. This was presaged by the Savior's instruction to the Nephites: "And there shall be no disputations among you, as there have hitherto been. Neither shall there be disputations among you concerning the points of my doctrine." (3 Nephi 11:28).

How does the baptismal prayer in The Book of Mormon teach us to follow the Savior?

Anciently, Christ gave the Nephite Twelve the specific words that they were to employ in the baptismal prayer, so that there might be no misunderstanding. (See 3 Nephi 11:23-27). Because this prayer authorizes the officiant to invoke the holy names of all three members of the Godhead, its words convey power, and suggest without reservation the sanction and approval of the Father, the Son, and the Holy Ghost.

"If ye will enter in by the way ... it will show unto you all things what ye should do. Behold, this is the doctrine of Christ." (2 Nephi 32:5-6).

119.

We are baptized that we might affirm our support of family values.

Why does it sometimes seem as if the prophets are as lone voices crying in the wilderness? (See Mark 1:3).

Satan has infiltrated government, and has suppressed the will of the silent majority by legitimizing the wild, rabid, and morally indefensible demands of the vocal minority. He has snuffed out freedom of expression with political correctness, and with the treasures of the earth he has purchased false priests who oppress. With armies and navies he goes about sowing horror upon the earth. (See Mosiah 7:31).

How can we fortify ourselves with the words of the prophets?

Truly, the Word is more powerful than the sword. The counsel of the prophets resonates with truth because it strikes familiar chords within us, allowing us to more easily identify the smeared fingerprints of Satan on the idols of wood and stone with which he continually assaults our defenses. How wonderful it is to receive the gifts of the Spirit, recognize the voice of our Master, and build up our strength to resist evil as we obey His teachings. (See John 10:27).

How can baptism empower us to act upon the doctrine of eternal families?

Baptism allows our efforts to be directed toward relationships that are the basic building blocks of eternity. Our baptismal covenant teaches us to be less concerned with telestial trivia, and to be more focused on these celestial sureties, even as Satan loudly and insistently argues his case to destroy the family, before the world court of public opinion.

How can we protect ourselves with the "shield of faith?" (Ephesians 6:16).

Those of us in our sunset years, feel as Victor Hugo, who wrote: "The nearer I approach the end, the clearer I hear around me the immortal symphonies of the world which invite me. For half a century, I have been writing my thoughts, but I feel that I have not said a thousandth part of that which is in me. My work is only a beginning. It is hardly above its foundation. I would gladly see it mounting forever."

The
penitent are
"for all the laws
of God; and their flesh
is cleansed, shining bright
in the waters of purification,
even in the waters of baptism.
They shall be given a new name
in due time to walk perfect
in all the ways of God."
("The Serek Scroll").

120.

We are baptized that we might become saviors
on Mount Zion to our kindred dead.
(See Obadiah 1:2).

How does vicarious work for the dead harmonize with the principles of The Plan of Salvation?

Work for our dead in the House of the Lord harmonizes perfectly with the doctrine that God is no respecter of persons, (see Acts 10:34), that He esteems all flesh as one, (see 1 Nephi 17:35), and that He views all of His children as living. (See Job 33:4). Vicarious work for the dead is an inspired program to knit our eternal families together with the light and knowledge that are received by the power of the Holy Ghost on both sides of the veil.

How can all of Heavenly Father's children have equal opportunity to become heirs of salvation and eternal life?

"Those who did not have the opportunity to hear the message of salvation in this life, but who would have accepted it with all their hearts if such an opportunity had come to them, are the ones who will accept it in the Spirit World. They are the ones for whom we shall perform the ordinances in the temple." (Joseph Fielding Smith, Jr.).

How does baptism for the dead stand beside the Atonement as a vicarious work?

Baptism for the dead is "one of the grand principles of truth revealed through the Prophet Joseph Smith. Obedience allows us to "rejoice in the kingdom of God with our relatives and friends in the grand reunion and assemblage of the saints of the Church of the First Born" (Joseph Fielding Smith, Jr.).

How is baptism for the dead the "most glorious of all subjects belonging to the everlasting gospel." (D&C 128:17).

It is so important that resurrected beings will help the Saints during the Millennium to complete the vicarious work of salvation for the dead. The "will help us correct the mistakes we have made in doing research concerning our dead ancestors. They will also help us find the information we need to complete our records" all the way back to Father Adam and Mother Eve. (Joseph Fielding Smith, Jr.).

"Whoso believeth in me, and is baptized ... shall inherit the kingdom of God." (3 Nephi 11:33).

121.

We are baptized that the Spirit might find expression as a light within each of us.

What do you think will be the outcome of the battle raging in the hearts of men, on Saturday?

Conditions have not yet deteriorated so far that the wicked cannot still be recommended unto God by the priesthood servants of God. (See Mormon 7:21). In fact, Joseph Fielding Smith once declared: "I believe there has never been a moment of time since the creation but what there has been someone holding the priesthood on the earth to hold Satan in check," that the wicked might yet be given time to repent.

How can baptism help us to maintain our individuality?

It can free us to discover the divine design that has been envisioned by our Heavenly Father for each of His children. If Satan can succeed in reducing our distinctive and unique personality signatures to the lowest common denominator, or if we trade our divine birthright for a mess of pottage, he will destroy us. If we surrender the traits that make us unique, we will fade into a shadow and a caricature of what we might have otherwise been.

How does baptism help us to regain and retain our spiritual identities?

When we have paid the price of entry into the waters of baptism, in order to regain our spiritual identity, we will feel liberated. We will enjoy the Light of Christ, and the guidance of the Holy Ghost that expresses itself through our love of God and our fellowmen.

What can happen to us, if we do not enjoy the protection from spiritual identity theft that is afforded by baptism?

If Satan breaches the firewalls of our spiritual security system, he will move quickly to neutralize our defense mechanisms, our intruder-alert warnings will fail, and his infectious virus will be left to spread uncontrollably. The effects of the resulting contamination will be compromise, conflict, and chaos, instead of the stability, order, and direction of those whose lives are Christ-centered.

"The baptismal font was instituted as a similitude of the grave." (D&C 128:13).

122.

We are baptized that Heavenly Father might show us our weaknesses. (See Ether 12:27).

How can our weakness be transformed into a source of strength?

Weakness can be a primer on midwifery, because it can germinate the arduous process of the growth and development of our testimony. Confronting and dealing with weakness by relying upon the power of the Atonement enables us to bear our witness with conviction, when the questions are posed: "What think ye of Christ?" and "Whose son is he?" (Matthew 22:42).

How does the grace of God help us to deal with our imperfections?

The Savior taught: "My grace is sufficient for all men that humble themselves before me; for if they humble themselves before me, and have faith in me, then will I make weak things become strong unto them." (Ether 12:27).

Why would Heavenly Father think to bless us with weaknesses?

Weakness can seed the atmosphere of our inspiration, so that nurturing moisture might fall upon our tender testimonies and facilitate the germination of the seeds of faith that are key to the transformation of our nature. When it is linked to faith, weakness can motivate us to respond to the invitation to do better, and to be kinder, to be more merciful, and to be more forgiving.

How is it possible that a quality like weakness can possibly promote a principle that is as positive and as exhilarating as progression?

Our progression hinges largely upon what do we do with our weaknesses, and what our weaknesses do for us. We may allow weakness to either impede or facilitate our progress. We are fortunate, indeed, if baptism intervenes, and laces our weakness with healthy measures of meekness and humility, in order to amend our narrow perspective, so that we might see supposed stumbling blocks as the very stepping stones that are needed to reinforce our confidence, conquer our fears, and overcome the obstacles to our progression.

We are "baptized after the manner of his burial, being buried in the water in his name, and this according to the commandment which he has given - That by keeping the commandments (we) might be washed and cleansed from all (our) sins."
(D&C 76:51-52).

123.

We are baptized that we might know that we are here, at this place, and in this time, by divine design.
(See 2 Nephi 2:24).

What do you think the Lord meant, when he said: "All these things shall give thee experience, and shall be for thy good?" (D&C 122:7).

The culture medium of our experience is provided by our Heavenly Father as a rich agar to nourish us, as we work out our salvation with fear and trembling. (See Philippians 2:12).

How would you describe the choreography of The Plan of Salvation?

The talents of the best artistic directors of music and dance are recognized with Tony Awards. However, their gifts would need to be infinitely multiplied for us to even begin to understand that Heavenly Father is the Architect of our creation, and that He is Alpha and Omega, and the Beginning and the End of our salvation.

How can The Plan of Salvation be infinite in its scope and yet be so personalized that it meets our individual needs?

There are no coincidences. There are only innumerable examples of the Lord working behind the scenes in our behalf. Everything happens by divine design.

What are divine accoutrements?

We demean ourselves when we only accessorize our lives with Gospel principles, rather than incorporating them into the core of our existence and experience. We must take care that we do not adorn ourselves with fine-twined linen at the cost of the full armor of God. The flaxen cords around our necks that feel so comfortable can far too easily be transformed into heavy chains that are secured to millstones, as we balance our lives on tippy stepping-stones that trace a pattern of uncertainty over swiftly moving currents in deep water. (See 2 Nephi 26:22).

"Know ye not that, so many of us as were baptized into Jesus Christ were baptized into his death? Therefore, we are buried with him by baptism into death, that like as Christ was raised up from the dead by the glory of the Father, even so we also should walk in newness of life" through the symbolism of being born again, with baptism by immersion. (Romans 6:3).

124.

> We are baptized that we might
> honor God and feel His love, as we
> confess His hand in all things, and
> obey His commandments.
> (See D&C 59:21).

Have you ever thought to compare your faith to that of those whom Peter taught on the Day of Pentecost? (See Acts 2:37).

The Restoration ushered in a Pentecostal outpouring of the Spirit, and humble petitioners with a sincere desire to understand the will of God asked anew: "Now that we have heard the message, and have put it to the test of prayerful inquiry, what shall we do?" Their demonstration of faith led to the waters of baptism, where the blessings of continuing commitment, dedicated discipleship, selfless service, and sustained spirituality awaited them.

How is the Angel Moroni a prototype for those who will one day be enveloped in light?

After Moroni appeared to Joseph Smith in his bedchamber, the light began to gather up around him, and he ascended in a conduit right into heaven. One day, light may gather around each of us in a similar manner, as the physical confines of our mortal clay evaporate, and as with pure energy we return to our Maker, amid clouds of glory.

How can baptism provide the mortar that binds together the "Pillars of Creation?"

Jesus Christ is the Architect of the cosmos, including the "Pillars of Creation," elephant trunks of interstellar gas and dust in the Eagle Nebula, 7,000 light years from Earth. In an 1857 sermon entitled "The Condescension of Christ," London pastor Charles Spurgeon used the phrase to describe both the physical world and the force stemming from the divine that binds it all together. "Now wonder, ye angels," Spurgeon wrote of the birth of Christ, "the Infinite has become an infant. He, upon whose shoulders the universe doth hang, nurses at his mother's breast; He who created all things, and bears up the pillars of creation!"

How can the Holy Ghost help us to honor our baptismal covenant?

The creative drive that has guided the children of our Heavenly Father since the dawn of history can be traced back to the Holy Ghost. In the Last Days, as more of the children of God are baptized, we see that the Spirit is being "poured out upon all flesh," and "young men see visions, and old men dream dreams." (Joel 2:28).

"Be humble, and be
submissive and gentle; easy
to be entreated; full of patience
and long-suffering; being temperate
in all things; being diligent in keeping the
commandments of God at all times; asking for
whatsoever things ye stand in need, both spiritual
and temporal, always returning thanks unto
God for whatsoever things ye do receive.
And see that ye have faith, hope, and
charity, and then will ye always
abound in good works."
(Alma 7:23-24).

125.

We are baptized to remind ourselves that the poor, the unlearned, the common person, and the native born, may equally come unto Christ. (See Acts 10:24).

How can baptism temper our experiences?

Paul assured the Saints that if they remained steadfast, in no matter what circumstances they might find themselves, no matter what cards they might have been dealt in life, in no matter what twist of fate they might think themselves trapped, ultimately, all things would be theirs, for they were "Christ's, and Christ is God's." (1 Corinthians 3:21-23).

How does the Gospel exert an equalizing influence upon all of God's children?

The Gospel is designed to generate enthusiasm. Its teachings create confidence, and rather than assigning blame, they show how to fix mistakes. Its doctrines and principles define authority, but still delegate responsibility. Its Author, the Carpenter of Nazareth, knew how, but more often showed how. He never reduced work to drudgery, but rather elevated it to excitement. Instead of concentrating power, he generated co-operation. He never drove His disciples forward, but was always out in front, leading them to green pastures and oases of still waters.

Have you ever heard the couplet, penned by Lorenzo Snow, that reads: "As man is, God once was. As God is, man may be?"

Alma spoke of a "restoration (that) shall come to all, both old and young, both bond and free, both male and female, both the wicked and the righteous; and even there shall not so much as a hair of their heads be lost; but every thing shall be restored to its perfect frame." (Alma 11:44). Although "it doth not yet appear what we shall be, (nevertheless) we know that, when he shall appear, we shall be like him, for we shall see him as he is." (1 John 3:2). Our hope of a glorious resurrection hinges upon this truth.

How is the Gospel of Jesus Christ like our own personal play-book in the game of life?

The beauty of the Gospel is that one size fits all. It is designed to meet the needs of all of Heavenly Father's children. It is universally applicable, allowing each of us to break free from our personalized limiting beliefs, those stories we tell ourselves that cause us to sabotage our own best efforts. In every case, its doctrines can unleash the power of our potential. It is full of magical principles patiently waiting for our wits to grow sharper, so that we can be inspired by them.

The worth of principles
is validated through personal
witness, or testimony. Our desire to be
baptized becomes the outward expression
of our personal dedication to obedience. It
is the public manifestation of the desire to
have a private covenant relationship with
God. It is the voluntary surrender
of agency to a higher power,
the subjugation of our
will, to His will.

126.

We are baptized because this life is the time for us to prepare to meet our Heavenly Father.
(See Alma 32:34).

How can we withstand those who deceitfully try to keep us from knowing God?

Those who are deceitful falsely represent themselves. They write checks they cannot cash because they are spiritually and morally bankrupt. Their gas tank is running on empty and there is no reserve. "Who shall ascend into the hill of the Lord," asked the Psalmist, "or who shall stand in his holy place? He that hath clean hands, and a pure heart, who hath not lifted up his soul unto vanity, nor sworn deceitfully." (Psalms 24:3-4).

How can we safeguard our free will, as we prepare for our heavenly homecoming?

We must acknowledge the constant and unrelenting assaults of Satan upon our spiritual identities. We must come to believe that it is only the power of God that can restore us to complete spiritual health. We must turn our lives over to His care and keeping, while constantly re-evaluating the stability and integrity of our moral shields. We must acknowledge the power of the priesthood as a key ally in our fight against Satan's onslaughts. Rather than relying upon our own puny efforts, we must be ready to allow the power of God to defeat Satan. We must ask Jesus Christ to come to our rescue, and in particular to allow the Atonement to heal the damage done in consequence of the weaknesses in our own armor.

How can baptism help us to exercise agency to act independently?

We must be true to our friends, family, and acquaintances; be true to our word, and honor our commitments, in order to draw upon the power of God through ordinances and covenants. We must be absolutely honest in our dealings with our fellow warriors, and right whatever wrongs for which we are responsible. We must constantly monitor our defensive network of systems designed to resist Satan, recognize when they fail, accept responsibility for the outcomes that are a consequence of our weakness, and take steps to restore our integrity by drawing upon the power of the Atonement.

How can the Atonement prepare us to meet God?

We must maintain open lines of communication with the powers of heaven. We must not only believe in Christ, but also believe Him when He says that He can heal us through His Atonement, which is His secret weapon in the defense of our spiritual identity.

Following our baptism, we discover that obedience is no longer inconvenient, but has become our quest. In that moment, said Ezra Taft Benson, God endows us with power. When we are diligent in our obedience, our agency enjoys its greatest expression. This is one of the hardest things for the unconverted to understand.

127.

We are baptized to guard ourselves against spiritual identity theft.

How bold is Satan in his efforts to steal our spiritual identity?

He is so brash that he even tried to steal the Savior's identity on the Mount of Temptations. He brazenly demanded that Jesus renounce His citizenship in the Kingdom of Heaven in exchange for pride, the honors of men, and the admiration of the world. "If thou be the Son of God," he cried, "command that these stones be made bread." (Matthew 4:3). "If thou be the Son of God," he urged, "cast thyself down." (Matthew 4:6). "All these things will I give thee," he promised, "if thou wilt fall down and worship me." (Matthew 4:10).

Where do the scriptures testify that Heavenly Father know each of us?

On one occasion, He spoke to Joseph Smith and said: "Thou art Joseph." (D&C 3:9). He likewise told a great Book of Mormon prophet: "Thou art Nephi." (Helaman 10:6), and He told Moses: "Thou art my son." (Moses 1:4). On another occasion, He explained: "Thou art one in me, a son of God; and thus may all become my sons." (Moses 6:68). Thus, was Moses inspired to exclaim: "Thou hast said, I know thee by name." (Exodus 33:12).

How can we be protected against spiritual identity theft?

Baptism helps us to discern good from evil, because Satan wears many hats and is the great deceiver. (See D&C 52:14). He is an honorary member of the Screen Actor's Guild, and a sought-after image consultant. He cruises the Internet, and is a permanent resident of chat-rooms. He is the great deceiver who bombards us with spam emails. He is a prize-winning author, and a talented lyricist, composer, and scriptwriter. He is the creative influence behind media too numerous to mention. He is a fashion designer, travel agent, vintner and beer distributor, an actor, newscaster, politician, scientist and power broker. He may even be a teacher, or wear clerical robes.

How does baptism reinforce the concept that we are children of God?

Of the truth that we have a Father in Heaven, there is no question, for "the Spirit itself beareth witness with our spirit, that we are the children of God." (Romans 8:16). We know this intuitively. How sweet it is to hear Primary age children as young as three sing the songs of Zion that declare we are the children of God.

"All those who humble themselves before God, and desire to be baptized (who) have truly repented of all their sins ... shall be received by baptism into his church."
(D&C 20:37).

128.

We are baptized as a testament that "the works, and the designs, and the purposes of God cannot be frustrated, neither can they come to naught." (D&C 3:1).

What is The Merciful Plan of The Great Creator? (See 2 Nephi 9:6).

"Mercy claimeth the penitent, and Mercy cometh because of the Atonement; and the Atonement bringeth to pass the resurrection of the dead; and the resurrection of the dead bringeth back men into the presence of God. For behold, Justice exerciseth all his demands, and also Mercy claimeth all which is her own; and thus, none but the truly penitent are saved." (Alma 42:23-24, underlining mine). Our desire to be baptized is ignited by the celestial spark of God that is designed to save our souls.

What is The Plan of Our God? (2 Nephi 9:13).

The covenant of baptism was "prepared from the foundation of the world." (Alma 42:26). John Taylor taught: "To the Son is given the power of the resurrection, the power of the redemption, the power of salvation, the power to enact laws for the carrying out and accomplishment of the design. Hence, life and immortality are brought to light, the Gospel is introduced, and He becomes the Author of eternal life and exaltation." ("Mediation and Atonement," p. 171-172).

What is The Great and Eternal Plan of Deliverance From Death? (2 Nephi 11:5).

A key provision of The Plan is that we came into this world to die. "And now behold, I say unto you that if it had been possible for Adam to have partaken of the fruit of the tree of life at that time, there would have been no death, and the word would have been void." (Alma 12:23). It was clearly understood before we came to earth that our experience here would be a critical part of The Great and Eternal Plan of Deliverance From Death. When Adam and Eve were placed in the Garden, it was understood that they would transgress God's law and become mortal. (See Moses 6:64). It was no coincidence that shortly thereafter, they were baptized.

What is The Plan of Salvation? (Alma 24:14).

The Plan of Salvation is The Plan of Redemption, The Plan of Mercy, and The Plan of Happiness, because it makes possible the resurrection of otherwise imperfect beings to eternal lives of glory. If it had not been for The Plan of Salvation, "which was laid from the foundation of the world, there could have been no resurrection of the dead." (Alma 12:25).

"Ye must repent, and be baptized in my name, and become as a little child, or ye can in nowise inherit the kingdom of God." (3 Nephi 11:38).

129.

We are baptized as a testament that we are willing to participate in "God's eternal plan."
(Official Declaration 2).

What is The Plan of Redemption? (Alma 29:2).

"According to Justice, The Plan of Redemption could not be brought about and "Mercy could not take effect except it should destroy the work of Justice." (Alma 42:13). The beauty of the perfect Plan of Redemption, then, is that it meets the demands of Justice through the infinite mercy of a loving Heavenly Father. With masterful reconciliation, The Plan allows God to be both just and merciful at the same time. Cherubim and a flaming sword guarded the way to the Tree of Life, but The Plan provided Adam and Eve with a way, through the Atonement, to fulfil the measure of their creation.

What is The Great Plan of The Eternal God? (Alma 34:9).

If we take The Great Plan of The Eternal God for granted, or if we abandon its core principles, its power to bless our lives may slip away and be lost forever. Because The Plan guarantees free will, it gives us wide latitude to use our agency; even to do so inappropriately to make poor choices. The Plan provides us with currency sufficient for our needs, but also allows us to substitute for legal tender wads of counterfeit cash good only for late payments with interest tacked on for bad behavior.

What is The Great and Eternal Plan of Redemption? (Alma 34:16).

The principles governing the Fall of Adam and the Atonement of Jesus Christ, were "great and eternal purposes (that) were prepared from the foundation of the world." (Alma 42:26).

What is The Great Plan of Redemption? (Alma 34:31).

The Plan of Redemption required that "an Atonement should be made. Therefore God Himself atoneth for the sins of the world, to bring about The Plan of Mercy, to appease the demands of Justice, that God might be a perfect, just God, and a merciful God also." (Alma 42:15). The Atonement allowed God to become the Master of the situation by placating Justice while still mercifully reclaiming us from physical and spiritual death. Through sacrifice, the debt would be paid, redemption made, the covenant fulfilled, Justice satisfied, the will of God done, and all power given to the Son.

We must baptized
for the remission of sins. The
foundation principle upon which
the ordinance is anchored is based
upon an injunction found throughout
the canon of scripture: "Repent, and
ne baptized every one of you in
the name of Jesus Christ for
the remission of sins."
(Acts 2:38).

130.

> We are baptized we might lend support
> to the declaration of the Gods
> "that their plan was good."
> (Abraham 4:21).

What is The Plan of Restoration? (Alma 41:2).

Adam fell that we might come to earth in order to prepare for a resurrection. (See Alma 12:24). Through the Atonement, we will be raised in the resurrection clothed in the kinds of bodies needed to dwell in the various degrees of glory to which we have qualified.

What is The Great Plan of Salvation? (Alma 42:5).

Without baptism, we are doomed to suffer in the shadows where we experience only illusions of reality. Without obedience, the discrepancy between our marginalized behavior and the ideals of The Plan become so great that our short-lived pleasure in worldly ways must evaporate as the morning dew in the light of day. Sooner or later, when this disparity becomes so great that it reaches "critical mass," a requisite readjustment tears down the façade of corruption and hypocrisy to allow the cultivation of a more nurturing lifestyle only made possible by the Atonement of Jesus Christ, and related obedience to the principles of The Plan.

What is The Great Plan of Happiness? (Alma 42:8).

Without repentance we must ultimately be in a wretched state, living forever in our sins. (See Alma 12:26). Without baptism, if we were to partake of the fruit of the tree of life, which is eternal life or the highest expression of the love of God, it would not be possible to sustain a celestial existence, inasmuch as in our present condition we would be incapable of obedience to celestial principles. Thus, The Great Plan of Happiness would be frustrated. Mercy and Justice were placed before Adam and Eve, to bar the way to the Tree of Life until they had the opportunity to participate in the saving ordinances of the Gospel. (See Alma 12:21, 42:2, and Moses 4:31).

What is The Plan of Mercy? (Alma 42:15).

Because of The Plan of Mercy, the principle of agency could be honored, allowing us to encounter opposition in a mortal setting and to gain experience, in spite of the fact that Justice must be served should we violate eternal law in the process. When Jesus Christ stepped forward as the Lamb Slain From the Foundation of the World, The Plan swung into action, allowing us to die without jeopardizing our eternal destiny.

"Follow me,
and do the things which
ye have seen me do ... with full
purpose of heart, acting no hypocrisy
and no deception before God, but
with real intent, repenting of your
sins, witnessing unto the Father
that ye are willing to take
upon you the name of
Christ by baptism."
(2 Nephi 3:12-13).

131.

> We are baptized with the assurance of "eternal life, which God, that cannot lie, promised before the world began."
> (Titus 1:2).

What is The Plan of Happiness? (Alma 42:16).

Cherubim insured that The Plan would not be frustrated, by guarding the way to eternal life. For "if Adam had put forth his hand immediately, and partaken of the Tree of Life, he would have lived forever (in his sins), according to the word of God, having no space (to allow the Atonement to kick into gear, thereby allowing time) for repentance." (Alma 42:5). The Atonement allowed Adam and Eve, and their posterity, to follow after their own will, to know the good from the evil, to follow The Plan to its successful conclusion, and to have joy therein.

What is The Great Plan of Mercy? (Alma 42:31).

If we fail to live up to all of the laws of the Gospel, The Great Plan of Mercy will intervene in our behalf, through Repentance. If we Recognize our mistakes, experience Remorse for having made them, attempt to make Restitution if our behavior has wronged others, learn from the error and Reform our ways, and Resolve to Refrain from Repeating it, we will be free to continue the path of progress, with a complete Resolution because of the Atonement of our Redeemer, of what would have otherwise been incapacitating short-comings.

What do the scriptures teach about our pre-mortal life?

The Lord told Jeremiah: "Before I formed thee in the belly I knew thee, and before thou camest forth out of the womb, I sanctified thee, and I ordained thee a prophet unto the nations." (Jeremiah 1:5). Job likewise described a time before we were born, "when the sons of God came to present themselves before the Lord." (Job 1:6).

Do you think that you came to your family here on earth by divine design?

We were chosen "before the foundation of the world, that we should be holy and without blame before him in love." (Ephesians 1:4). He also taught: "We have had fathers of our flesh which corrected us, and we gave them reverence. Shall we not much rather be in subjection unto the Father of spirits, and live?" (Hebrews 12:9). "The Preacher wrote: "Then shall the dust return to the earth as it was: and the spirit shall return unto God who gave it." (Ecclesiastes 12:7).

"Adam cried unto the Lord, and he was caught away by the Spirit of the Lord, and was carried down into the water, and was laid under the water, and was brought forth out of the water. And thus he was baptized, and the Spirit of God descended upon him, and thus he was born of the Spirit, and became quickened in the inner man." (Moses 6:65-66).

132.

We are baptized that, with the gentle instruction of the Spirit, we might become better at building relationships.

Why is it important that we "press forward with a steadfastness in Christ, having a perfect brightness of hope, and a love of God and of all men?" (2 Nephi 31:20).

President David O. McKay once said: "Let me assure you that some day you will have a personal Priesthood interview with the Savior, Himself. If you are interested, I will tell you the order in which He will ask you to account for your earthly responsibilities.

What do you think President McKay said would be the Savior's very first question?

"First, He will request an accountability report about your relationship with your wife."

Since families are the basic building block of eternity, can you imagine what was second on the list of questions?

"Second, He will ... request information about your relationship to each and every child."

Since we have all come from God, Who is our Home. what do you think was next on the list?

"Third, he will want to know what you have personally done with the talents you were given in your pre-mortal existence."

Baptism speaks
to our spirits, for every
Gospel principle carries within
itself a witness that it is true. Its
language is universal, and when the
Holy Ghost illuminates our minds, we
enjoy fluency, familiarity, and ease
with the doctrines, and comfort
with the revealed word of
God that opens up vistas
of eternal proportion
before our eyes.

133.

We are baptized that we might bow our knees "unto the Father of our Lord Jesus Christ, of whom the whole family in heaven and earth is named."
(Ephesians 3:14-15).

After family, why do you think that active participation in the programs of the Church is important to the Savior?

President McKay said that in our personal interview with the Savior, "He will want a summary of your activity in your Church assignments."

Since we are all one community, do you think the Savior will be interested in how we have treated our neighbors?

The next thing the Savior will ask, according to President McKay is: "Were you honest in all your dealings?"

How can the earth be "full of the knowledge of the Lord, as the waters cover the sea?" (Isaiah 11:9).

Finally, President McKay said the Savior "will ask for an accountability report on what you have done to contribute in a positive manner to your community, state, country and the world."

How does baptism prepare us for our heavenly reunion with our Father?

"Now are we the sons of God, and it doth not yet appear what we shall be: but we know that, when he shall appear, we shall be like him, for we shall see him as he is." (1 John 3:2).

Baptism
at the age of eight
captures the heart of a little
child before it has been exposed to
the cankering influence and corrosive
elements of the world, before their hearts
are set upon temporal things, and their
spirituality has been so weakened that
the things of God are no longer part
of their daily experience. Better than
the rest of us, little children have a
capacity to "lay aside the things
of this world, and seek for
the things of a better."
(D&C 25:10).

134.

We are baptized that those who have died without having had the opportunity to hear about The Plan of Salvation might also partake of eternal life.

What does a "patron" do, in the House of The Lord?

The Atonement is the Gold Standard of vicarious work. In our day, the Savior has delegated authority to the members of His Church to follow His example, to act in behalf of the dead, of those who are unable to perform saving ordinances for themselves, since they have passed beyond the veil and are living in the Spirit World while they await the resurrection.

What is vicarious work? (See D&C 138:33).

The ordinances performed by patrons in the temple, beginning with baptism on behalf of those who have passed beyond the veil, are vicarious works that establish a covenant relationship with our Father that are equal in power and authority to our own demonstrations of obedience. Vicarious work is a key element of The Plan of Salvation, for the Atonement of Jesus Christ itself is such a work.

How does Section 2 of the Doctrine & Covenants relate to baptism for the dead?

The prophecy concerning the coming of Elijah was the first revelation Joseph Smith received and is one of the most carefully documented prophecies of all time, appearing in all four of the Standard Works. (Malachi 4:5-6, 3 Nephi 24 & 25, J.S.H. 1:36-39, & D&C 2 & 110). In fact, "It is the keystone of the wonderful Gospel arch, and if that center stone should weaken and fall out, the whole Gospel structure would topple down in unorganized doctrinal blocks." (John Widtsoe).

Why do you think the wording of Malachi's prophecy is not identical in all four of the Standard Works?

The wording in Malachi in the Bible is identical to 3 Nephi 25:5-6 in The Book of Mormon, but differs from that in the Doctrine and Covenants and the Pearl of Great Price, which are also identical. When Moroni quoted the prophecy to Joseph Smith, his alterations from the Bible and Book of Mormon texts were probably for emphasis and clarification, rather than for correction. The wording helps Latter-day Saints to better understand this prophecy concerning the sealing power of the priesthood.

He Who was
our Exemplar descended
beneath us all, both physically
and symbolically, when He was
baptized in Jordan, the lowest
body of fresh water upon
the face of the earth.

135.

We are baptized as a witness that "the Lord God will do nothing, but he revealeth his secret unto his servants the prophets."
(Amos 3:7).

How does Section Two in The Doctrine & Covenants read?

"Behold, I will reveal unto you the Priesthood, by the hand of Elijah the prophet, before the coming of the great and dreadful day of the Lord. And he shall plant in the hearts of the children the promises" or covenants "made to the fathers," that is to say, Abraham, Isaac, and Jacob, "and the hearts of the children shall turn" or bind or seal "to their fathers. If it were not so," if the sealing power of the priesthood were not restored, "the whole earth would be utterly wasted at his coming" because The Plan of Salvation would be thwarted. (This is the curse mentioned in Malachi 4:6; see below).

How does the prophecy read in The Old Testament?

Malachi wrote: "Behold, I will send you Elijah the prophet before the coming of the great and dreadful day of the Lord: And he shall turn the heart of the fathers to the children, and the heart of the children to the fathers, lest I come and smite the earth with a curse." (Malachi 4:5-6).

How does the prophecy read in The Pearl of Great Price?

"Behold, I will reveal unto you the Priesthood by the hand of Elijah the prophet, before the coming of the great and dreadful day of the Lord … And he shall plant in the hearts of the children the promises" or covenants "made to the fathers," that is to say, Abraham, Isaac, and Jacob, "and the hearts of the children shall turn" or bind or seal "to their fathers. If it were not so," if the sealing power of the priesthood were not restored, "the whole earth would be utterly wasted at his coming." (J.S.H. 1:38-39).

How does the prophecy read in The Book of Mormon?

The Lord quoted Malachi during His ministry among the Nephites: "Behold, I will send you Elijah the prophet before the coming of the great and dreadful day of the Lord. And he shall turn the heart of the fathers to the children, and the heart of the children to their fathers, lest I come and smite the earth with a curse." (3 Nephi 25:6).

"The Lamb of God ... fulfil(ed) all righteousness in being baptized by water." (2 Nephi 31:6).

136.

> We are baptized that we might be "easy to be entreated (and) firm to keep the commandments." (Helaman 7:7).

What literary devices have the ancient prophets used in their entreaties?

They have employed aphorisms, that are proverbial statements or theological profundities. These are linked to hokmahs, which are peculiar Hebrew figures of speech. Together, these comprise many of the foundation scriptures in the liturgy of the Church. The fact that authentic hokmahs are sprinkled throughout The Book of Mormon testifies to the accuracy of Joseph Smith's translation of this ancient Hebrew text.

How can baptism help us to be "firm to keep the commandments?"

To initiate the conflagration of sin, all that needed is combustible fuel, an ignition temperature, and oxygen. We must live in the world, but we don't have to be of the world. (See John 15:19). We can't allow the heat of the moment get the better of us. Baptism has been deigned to introduce us to the strait and narrow way, that we might be safely guided past the ammunition dumps of the Devil.

What can you do to better remember your own baptismal covenant?

The intoxicating alcohol of the adversary has been distilled to dull our senses, if we are so careless as to indulge in the sin of excess. If we are not careful, "the hobnailed boots of indiscretion's marathon dancer will tap a rowdy two-step across the terracotta of our consciousness. If excess is our master, reason must surely be cast into the rumble seat of our libidinous juggernaut. Then, the piper must be paid!" (Pogo, The Cartoon Philosopher).

What are the mists of darkness that threaten to detour us from the strait and narrow way?

We are always at risk of being detoured by doctrinal dilemmas, conceptual cul-de-sacs, and religious roundabout, that lead to faltering faith, crises of confidence, and character crippling compromises.

When we walk
in the footsteps
of Jesus Christ with real
intent, by repenting of our
sins, we witness unto the Father
that we are willing to take upon
ourselves the name of Christ, by
baptism – yea, by following
our Lord and our Savior
down into the water.
(See 2 Nephi 31:13).

137.

> We are baptized that we might be "slow to be led to do iniquity; and quick to hearken unto the words of the Lord."
> (Helaman 7:7).

How does our baptism help us to be "slow to be led to do iniquity?"

There must needs be opposition in all things, but even the righteous can be seduced by corrosive cocktails of convenience, adroitly offered by a bartender named Beelzebub. The Devil's designer drinks are poisonous potions whose naturally bitter taste is attenuated by all of his counterfeits concoctions, such as pleasure, decadence, indulgence, hedonism, intemperance, and self-gratification.

What blessings do we receive when we are quick to hearken to the words of the Lord?

The Gospel Firearms Safety Course cautions us to never play with loaded weapons, for Satan stands like a sentinel, ready at any time to discharge his assault rifle in the direction of doctrine. Beelzebub's high velocity bullets of unbelief may harmlessly ricochet off the bedrock of well-grounded faith. However, they can be dangerous, and can even mortally wound the eternal identity of those who have not put on the whole armor of God. His explosive devices may be improvised, but they are insidious and insincere, incorrect, immoral, and impulsively disingenuous.

Can those who play poker with the Devil hope to win every hand?

Those who equivocate walk the slippery slope above a personality precipice, while proper prior priesthood preparation prevents poor performance. In any event, those who are distracted by the cacophony of confusion and cornucopia of comfort created by their carnal creations must ultimate crash and burn in the perfect storm of a train wreck in slow motion that was orchestrated by poor choices.

How can aphorisms help us to remember our baptismal covenant?

The scriptures are full of aphorisms, many of which have made their way into the lexicon of the people: Ask and you shall receive. Take up your cross, and follow me. Wickedness never was happiness. There must needs be opposition in all things. Come unto Christ and be perfected in him. Be ye therefore perfect. Keep the commandments. Charity never faileth. Mercy satisfieth Justice. Endure to the end. My yoke is easy, and my burden is light. Come follow me. Faith without works is dead, being alone. And, of course, Repent, and be baptized.

"My people have gone astray from my precepts, and have not kept mine ordinances, which I gave unto their fathers. And they have not observed mine anointing, and the burial, or baptism wherewith I commanded them."
(J.S.T. Genesis 17:5).

At the end of the day,
as Ignatius Loyola observed, we are baptized...

That we might toil, and not seek for rest...

That we might give and not count the cost...

That we might fight, and not heed the wounds...

That we might labor, and not ask for any reward save that of knowing that we do God's will.

The Psalmist wrote: "Be still, and know that I am God." (Psalms 46:10). When we tune out the world's cacophony of confusion, and reject the spurious coin of counterfeit currency that is proffered by moneylenders in the temple, we sense that our Heavenly Father is nearby.

Appendices 1 - 9

Those who have been baptized
stand out against undisciplined souls who have been
seduced by the siren song of the sentinels of Satan. Without the
stabilizing influence of the Gospel, unprincipled character
crumbles when faced with telestial temptations that
are tantalizing and yet traumatizing. These
treasures of the earth are worthless
counterfeits for the blessings
that God has reserved
for the faithful.

One Hundred and One Reasons Why We Are Baptized

1. We are baptized in submission to the law of heaven.

2. We are baptized as a witness that we are willing to follow in the footsteps of the Savior.

3. We are baptized to demonstrate our obedience to the will of the Savior.

4. We are baptized in similitude of the supreme act of humility by the Savior.

5. We are baptized to "fulfill all righteousness." (Matthew 3:15).

6. We are baptized to receive a remission of our sins, if we have reached the age of accountability.

7. We are baptized to gain admission to the Lord's church, which is "the only true and living church upon the face of the whole earth" with which He is pleased. (D&C 1:31).

8. We are baptized that we might experience sanctification through fire and the Holy Ghost. (See Mosiah 5:7).

9. We are baptized that we might be spiritually begotten of Christ. (See Mosiah 5:7).

10. We are baptized that our hearts might be changed through faith on the name of Jesus Christ. (See Mosiah 5:7).

11. We are baptized that we might be born of Jesus Christ. (See Mosiah 5:7).

12. We are baptized in a symbolic re-birth, as we pass through a tangible portal in the similitude of the grave.

13. We are baptized in order to qualify for the blessings that are found in the other ordinances of the Gospel.

14. We are baptized that we might be better prepared to travel the established path that leads to the Celestial Kingdom of God.

15. We are baptized in the temporal expression of a spiritual reality.

16. We are baptized that we might overcome spiritual death, and come into the presence of the Father, the Son, and the Holy Ghost.

17. We are baptized in a palpable expression of the Doctrine of Christ.

18. We are baptized to facilitate the temporal implementation of The Plan of Salvation. (See D&C 3:1).

19. We are baptized that we might have opportunities to bear each other's burdens. (See Mosiah 18:8).

20. We are baptized that we might be given the privilege to "mourn with those that mourn." (Mosiah 18:9).

21. We are baptized that we might "comfort those that stand in need of comfort." (Mosiah 18:9).

22. We are baptized that we might have the courage to "stand as witnesses of God at all times and in all things, and in all places that (we) may be in." (Mosiah 18:9).

23. We are baptized that we might "be redeemed of God, and be numbered with those of the first resurrection, that (we might) have eternal life." (Mosiah 18:9).

24. We are baptized as a witness that we have made a covenant to serve God "and keep his commandments, that he (might) pour out his Spirit more abundantly" upon us. (Mosiah 18:10).

25. We are baptized that we might be given the tools we need to lengthen our stride.

26. We are baptized that we might no more be "strangers and foreigners," but instead, "fellow citizens with the saints, and of the household of God." (Ephesians 2:19).

27. We are baptized that we might join the ranks of member missionaries.

28. We are baptized that we might continue "steadfastly in the apostles' doctrine and fellowship, and in breaking of bread, and in prayers." (Acts 2:41-42).

29. We are baptized that we might be clothed with spiritual chain-mail, as protection against the fiery darts of the adversary. (See 1 Nephi 15:24).

30. We are baptized that we might be released from bondage to sin. (See D&C 84:49).

31. We are baptized that we might participate in the foundation ordinance of The Plan of Salvation.

32. We are baptized by immersion in water, that we might feel not only the spiritual significance, but also the physical intensity, of the covenant we make with our Heavenly Father.

33. We are baptized as Jesus Christ invites us, by name, to become His disciples.

34. We are baptized in a dramatic validation of the influence of the Light of Christ, and of the power of the Holy Ghost.

35. We are baptized to affirm the innocence of little children.

36. We are baptized that we might experience spiritual delight, without the rush of sensory over stimulation that is prevalent in our technological world.

37. We are baptized "for the perfecting of the saints, for the work of the ministry, (and) for the edifying of the body of Christ." (Ephesians 4:12).

38. We are baptized that we might "all come in the unity of the faith, and of knowledge of the Son of God...unto the measure of the stature of the fulness of Christ." (Ephesians 4:13).

39. We are baptized "that we henceforth be no more children, tossed to and fro." (Ephesians 4:14).

40. We are baptized that we might speak "the truth in love, (and) grow up into him in all things, which is the head, even Christ." (Ephesians 4:15).

41. We are baptized "unto the confounding of false doctrines and laying down of contentions." (2 Nephi 3:12).

42. We are baptized that the light of our lives might grow "brighter and brighter until the perfect day." (D&C 50:24).

43. We are baptized that the earth might "be full of the knowledge of the Lord, as the waters cover the sea." (Isaiah 11:9).

44. We are baptized to capture the promise of the "peace of God, which passeth all understanding." (Philippians 4:7).

45. We are baptized that we might pause, and reflect upon the things that are really important in our lives.

46. We are baptized that we might affirm our faith in the immortality of our souls, because we feel, within ourselves, immortal longings.

47. We are baptized that we might learn to abide by the laws of the Celestial Kingdom, even as we dwell upon the earth, that our hearts might burn within us, as the Spirit speaks to us and opens the scriptures to our understanding. (See Luke 24:32).

48. We are baptized that we might think less about self-sufficiency, and more about our Christ dependency.

49. We are baptized that we might be given the tools to burst free of our self-imposed limitations.

50. We are baptized "in consequence of the evils and designs which do and will exist in the hearts of conspiring men (and women) in the last days." (D&C 89:4).

51. We are baptized that we might publish peace and tidings of great joy, endure to the end, and be lifted up at the last day, to inherit eternal life. (See 1 Nephi 13:37).

52. We are baptized that we might enjoy the Sabbath day, as we never have before.

53. We are baptized that we might re-connect with our spiritual Birth Parents.

54. We are baptized that we might enter into God's Rest.

55. We are baptized that we might vitalize Heavenly Father's Plan of Happiness in our lives.

56. We are baptized that we might forever thereafter commemorate the birthdate of our immortal souls.

57. We are baptized that we might have hope in our Savior, Jesus Christ.

58. We are baptized in a process of generation, and not just of maturation. (See Mosiah 27:26).

59. We are baptized that we might enter into the fold, there to be cared for by the Good Shepherd. (See John 10:11).

60. We are baptized that we might contribute our own chapter to The Greatest Story Ever Told.

61. We are baptized that our Heavenly Father might create, in our behalf, an impenetrable "shield of faith" in our Lord Jesus Christ. (Ephesians 6:16).

62. We are baptized in white clothing, to symbolically express the purity of the ordinance and the proximity of the Spirit.

63. We are baptized that the Spirit of the Lord Omnipotent might work "a mighty change in us, or in our hearts, that we have no more disposition to do evil, but to do good continually." (Mosiah 5:2).

64. We are baptized "through the infinite goodness of God, (that by) the manifestations of his Spirit (we might) have great views of that which is to come." (Mosiah 5:3).

65. We are baptized that we might evenly distribute the weight of our temporal baggage, that we might more easily "enter in at the strait gate." (Matthew 7:13).

66. We are baptized that the "opposition in all things" to which Lehi alluded, might become a blessing that allows us to more fully engage The Plan of Salvation. (2 Nephi 2:11).

67. We are baptized that our trials and tribulations might give us experience, and work to our benefit. (See D&C 122:7).

68. We are baptized that the "redemption exemption" that is a codicil to the Law of Justice might be activated and the Law of Mercy set in motion, as our lease on life is renegotiated in our favor.

69. We are baptized that we might make a simple public statement about a profound private conviction.

70. We are baptized "that we might speak with the tongue of angels, and shout praises unto the Holy One of Israel." (2 Nephi 31:13).

71. We are baptized that our hearts might be "knit together in unity and in love." (Mosiah 18:21).

72. We are baptized that we might enjoy the companionship of "the Comforter, which showeth all things, and teacheth the peaceable things of the kingdom." (D&C 39:6).

73. We are "baptized as a witness and a testimony that (we are) willing to serve God with all (our) hearts." (Mosiah 21:35).

74. We are baptized in such a manner that, as we step out of the font, our faces will always be oriented toward the light.

75. We are baptized that we might pursue the object and design of our existence, which is to be the happiest people upon the face of the earth.

76. We are baptized because, as disciples of Christ, it is our lot in life to be sent forth as sheep in the midst of wolves. (See Matthew 10:16).

77. We are baptized that we might receive the means to calibrate our lives with the pattern of heaven itself.

78. We are baptized that the Lord might be on our right, and on our left, and in our hearts. (See D&C 84:88).

79. We are baptized that we might more easily memorize our lines in Heavenly Father's Three Act Play that is entitled "The Plan of Salvation."

80. We are baptized that we might become as lights that are set on a hill. (See Matthew 5:14).

81. We are baptized that our vessels might be filled with the "oil of gladness". (See Hebrews 1:9 & Matthew 25:1).

82. We are baptized to wash away the cobwebs from our minds.

83. We are baptized that the anchors of our faith might rest within a foundation of rock, and not of sand. (See Matthew 7:26).

84. We are baptized that we might fan with faith the fire of our resolve. (See Jeremiah 20:9).

85. We are baptized that we might leave a light burning for those who are late to arrive at the wedding feast. (See John Chapter 2).

86. We are baptized that we might learn how to consecrate to the Lord our time, talents, means, and everything else with which He has blessed us.

87. We are baptized that we might accept our Heavenly Father's invitation to join Him in His work and glory, which is to bring about our immortality and eternal life. (See Moses 1:39).

88. We are baptized that we might rejoice in our characteriztion as a peculiar people. (See 1 Peter 2:9).

89. We are baptized that righteousness might stay the sword of justice that hangs over a wicked world. (See Helaman 13:5).

90. We are baptized that others might be influenced to follow our Exemplar. (See John 14:6).

91. We are baptized that our Latter-day Saint culture might help to insulate us from worldly influences.

92. We are baptized that we might not be tempted to "look back," as we flee from Sodom and Gomorrah. (See Genesis 19:16).

93. We are baptized that we might become new creatures in Christ. (See 2 Corinthians 5:17).

94. We are baptized that we might stand tall for those who may lack the power to do so themselves.

95. We are baptized that we might light candles rather than curse the darkness.

96. We are baptized that it might become easier to approach the Lord with our sacrifices.

97. We are baptized that we might be given opportunities to make and keep the covenants of salvation and exaltation.

98. We are baptized that we might unite ourselves with the ordained process by which eternal principles are communicated.

99. We are baptized that, henceforth, we be no more "carried about with every wind of doctrine." (Ephesians 4:14).

100. We are baptized that we might not be deceived "by the sleight of men, and cunning craftiness, whereby they lie in wait to deceive." (Ephesians 4:14).

101. We are baptized that we might honor the order of the priesthood.

Baptism provides a
shield against the spatter
of corrosive perspiration cast
off by the destroyer, who is insidiously
working overtime to damage our doctrinal
defenses, dull our spiritual sensitivities, diminish
our charitable capacity, deplete our bountiful
reservoirs of sympathy, and destroy our
devotions, even as we labor with an
equal but opposite intensity
to deify our work
on the earth.

Three dozen additional reasons why we are baptized.

102. We are baptized that we might be perfected in our Savior, Jesus Christ. (See Moroni 10:32).

103. We are baptized that, through God's infinite goodness and the manifestations of the Spirit, we might have great views of that which is to come. (See Mosiah 5:3).

104. We are baptized that we might understand how and what we worship, that we might come unto our Father in the name of our Savior Jesus Christ. (See D&C 93:19).

105. We are baptized with the realization that when the Lord gives us commandments, He also prepares ways for us to accomplish the tasks that are set before us. (See 1 Nephi 3:7).

106. We are baptized to make it easier for us to "pray unto the Lord, (to) call upon his holy name, (and to) make known his wonderful works among the people." (D&C 65:4).

107. We are baptized so that, although we were an hungered, and thirsty, and strangers, we will no longer be naked, or sick, or imprisoned within the fortress of our own limiting beliefs. (See Matthew 25:34-40).

108. We are baptized that, with uplifted hands unto the Most High, our incomings, our outgoings, and our salutations might be in the name of the Lord. (See D&C 109:9).

109. We are baptized that we might find greater happiness, peace, and rest; that we might seek for the blessings of the fathers, including the authority to administer the ordinances of the Gospel. (See Abraham 1:2).

110. We are baptized to become more observant followers of righteousness, to possess greater knowledge, to be the progenitors of nations and ambassadors of peace, and to receive instruction, and keep the commandments. (See Abraham 1:2).

111. We are baptized that we might become kings and priests, and queens and priestesses; in effect, to become rightful heirs of the blessings that belonged to the fathers. (See Abraham 1:2).

112. We are baptized because we have brought forth fruit worthy of repentance. (See Moroni 6:1).

113. We are baptized that we might give away all of our sins, but there are strings attached. (See Alma 22:18).

114. We are baptized when charity has become the foundation of our faith.

115. We are baptized beause we have determined to follow the Savior "with full purpose of heart, acting no hypocrisy and no deception before God." (2 Nephi 31:13).

116. We are baptized that we might experience liberation from our self-defeating behaviors.

117. We are baptized that we might press forward with steadfastness, having a perfect brightness of hope and a love of God and of our brothers and sisters, feasting upon the scriptures, and enduring to the end in righteousness. (See Nephi 31:20).

118. We are baptized that we might hear the voice of the Lord that is unto all, for "there is none to escape; and there is no eye that shall not see, neither ear that shall not hear, neither heart that shall not be penetrated." (D&C 1:2).

119. We are baptized that we might affirm our support of family values.

120. We are baptized that we might become saviors on Mount Zion to our kindred dead. (See Obadiah 1:2).

121. We are baptized that the Spirit might find expression as a light within each of us.

122. We are baptized that Heavenly Father might show us our weaknesses. (See Ether 12:27).

123. We are baptized that we might know that we are here, at this place, and in this time, by divine design. (See 2 Nephi 2:24).

124. We are baptized that we might honor God, and feel His love, as we confess His hand in all things, and obey His commandments. (See D&C 59:21).

125. We are baptized to remind ourselves that the poor, the unlearned, the common person, and the native born, may equally come unto Christ. (See Acts 10:24).

126. We are baptized because this life is the time for us to prepare to meet our Heavenly Father. (See Alma 32:34).

127. We are baptized to guard ourselves against spiritual identity theft.

128. We are baptized as a testament that "the works, and the designs, and the purposes of God cannot be frustrated, neither can they come to naught." (D&C 3:1).

129. We are baptized as a testament that we are willing to participate in "God's eternal plan." (Official Declaration 2).

130. We are baptized that we might lend support to the declaration of the Gods "that their plan was good." (Abraham 4:21).

131. We are baptized with the assurance of "eternal life, which God, that cannot lie, promised before the world began." (Titus 1:2).

132. We are baptized that, with the gentle instruction of the Spirit, we might become better at building relationships.

133. We are baptized that we might "bow our knees unto the Father of our Lord Jesus Christ, of whom the whole family in heaven and earth is named." (Ephesians 3:14-15).

134. We are baptized that those who died without having had the opportunity to hear about The Plan of Salvation might also partake of eternal life.

135. We are baptized as a witness that "the Lord God will do nothing, but he revealeth his secret unto his servants the prophets." (Amos 3:7).

136. We are baptized that we might be "easy to be entreated, (and) firm to keep the commandments." (Helaman 7:7).

137. We are baptized that we might be "slow to be led to do iniquity, and quick to hearken unto the words of the Lord." (Helaman 7:7).

138. Finally, as Ignatius Loyola declared, we are baptized that we might give and not count the cost, that we might fight and not heed the wounds, that we might toil and not seek for rest, and that we might labor and not ask for any reward save that of knowing that we do God's will.

How many more reasons to be baptized do you think you can find in the scriptures?

"Our minds being now enlightened, we began to have the scriptures laid open to our understandings, and the true meaning and intention of their more mysterious passages revealed unto us in a manner which we never could attain to previously, nor ever before had thought of."
(J.S.H. 1:74).

Over 500 Discussion Questions

With baptism,
the Savior becomes
our shepherd, showing us the way,
strengthening our testimonies, and teaching
us humility. He is always there to steady our shaking
knees and nurture our faltering faith, to bind up
our wounds, and to apply the Balm of Gilead
to our soul scars. He provides both tangible
and immaterial support, emboldens us
with words of encouragement,
and cheers our spirits
with wise counsel.

1. We are baptized in submission to the law of heaven.

Do you think baptism has always been performed in the Lord's own way?

How do some people "wrest the scriptures" that relate to baptism? (D&C 10:63).

Do you think the Savior's Apostles administered baptism correctly?

What happened when the priesthood authority of the Apostles died with them?

2. We are baptized as a witness that we are willing to follow in the footsteps of the Savior.

What does it mean to follow the Savior with full purpose of heart? (See Mosiah 7:33).

Why doesn't The Book of Mormon make any special mention of the manner of baptism among the Nephites?

When was the ordinance of baptism first administered?

In the scriptures, where do we learn about Adam's baptism?

We are baptized to demonstrate our obedience to the will of the Savior.

How did the voice of the Lord teach Nephi about the ordinance of baptism?

How difficult is it to follow the commandment to be baptized?

What happens when we surrender our will to the guidance of our Heavenly Father?

How can baptism influence our attitude about obedience?

We are baptized in similitude of the supreme act of humility by the Savior.

Why do you think the Savior chose to be baptized in the Jordan River?

How can our baptism help us to feel good about ourselves?

How is baptism related to the Atonement of Jesus Christ?

Why do you think the age of eight is described as the age of accountability? (See D&C 29:47).

We are baptized to fulfill all righteousness.
(See Matthew 3:15).

How can envisioning our own baptism make us feel so good inside?

Why do you think the Savior, Who was without sin, submitted to baptism?

How can parents help their children to "fulfill all righteousness" by encouraging them to be baptized? (2 Nephi 31:5).

What else can parents do to prepare their children for baptism?

We are baptized to receive a remission of our sins, if we have reached the age of accountability.

What has the Atonement of Jesus Christ got to do with baptism?

Why do you think God has given us the commandment to be baptized?

Who are the only perfect examples of those who are free from the stain of sin?

What can happen to the innocence of children if they are not baptized at the age of eight?

We are baptized to gain admission to the Lord's church, which is "the only true and living church upon the face of the whole earth" with which He is pleased. (D&C 1:30).

How is baptism Heavenly Father's formal invitation to come into the Savior's fold and to be called His people? (See Mosiah 18:8).

What other qualities must we have, before we are baptized?

How does baptism help to create a Zion society?

To whom is admission to the Lord's Church reserved?

We are baptized that we might experience sanctification through fire and the Holy Ghost. (See Mosiah 5:7).

What is one of the special responsibilities of the Holy Ghost?

How does it make you feel to know that Heavenly Father is a party to every Gospel covenant, including baptism?

Why must we be baptized before we can receive the gift of the Holy Ghost?

What kinds of worldly influences are constantly at work to drive away the Spirit?

9. We are baptized that we might be spiritually begotten of Christ. (See Mosiah 5:7).

What was the experience of Joseph Smith following his own baptism?

What did Jesus teach Nicodemus about being "born again," (John 3:3) and about being "spiritually begotten?" (Mosiah 5:7).

How does The Plan of Salvation make it easier for us to be more sensitive to the whisperings of the Spirit?

How can baptism help us to edit the story of our lives?

10. We are baptized that our hearts might be changed through faith on the name of Jesus Christ. (See Mosiah 5:7).

How is our desire to be baptized linked to faith?

What blessings do we receive as our hearts are changed through faith?

How would you describe your faith in Christ?

How did you develop your faith?

11. We are baptized that we might be born of Jesus Christ. (See Mosiah 5:7).

Why would the prophets teach that it is necessary to be born again? (See Mosiah 5:7).
How can baptism help us to internalize eternal principles? (See Jeremiah 31:33).
For what purpose is the law driven into our inward parts? (See Jeremiah 31:33).
How can baptism heal our spiritual blindness? (See John 9:39-41).

12. We are baptized in a symbolic re-birth, as we pass through a tangible portal in the similitude of the grave.

What is the "similitude of the grave?" (D&C 128:13).
To what end are we re-born?
What did the Savior teach the Nephites about the symbolism of baptism?
What was the instruction given by the Apostle Paul, that related to baptism?

13. We are baptized in order to qualify for the blessings that are found in the other ordinances of the Gospel.

What has the Savior promised to give us when we are baptized?
What blessings may we receive when we are baptized?
How does our baptism qualify us to call ourselves Christians? (See Acts 26:28).
Are the guidelines for baptism subject to private interpretation? (See 2 Peter 1:20).

14. We are baptized that we might be better prepared to travel the established path that leads to the Celestial Kingdom of God.

How does baptism make it easier for us to return to our Heavenly Home?
After our baptism, how does the path that leads back Home open up before us?
How does the Plan hold "the key to the mysteries of the kingdom?" (D&C 84:19).
In what ways is baptism our R.S.V.P. to the invitation that has been sent out across the heavens from our Heavenly Father?

15. We are baptized in the temporal expression of a spiritual reality.

How is baptism a "type?"

How are Gospel principles different from the shifting values of the world?

Why do you think Heavenly Father chose water as the medium to convey spiritual truth?

How is baptism related to our adoption into the House of Israel?

16. We are baptized that we might overcome spiritual death, and come into the presence of the Father, the Son, and the Holy Ghost.

Why do you think the baptismal prayer addresses Heavenly Father, as well as Jesus Christ, and the Holy Ghost?

Why do you think Heavenly Father bore His testimony at the baptism of His Son?

How does the Light of Christ influence us to come to the waters of baptism?

Have you ever wondered how the Holy Ghost completes the "Holy Trinity?"

17 We are baptized in a palpable expression of the Doctrine of Christ.

Where in the scriptures has the Doctrine of Christ been most clearly articulated?
Whose doctrine is it that finds expression in the Gospel?
How does the Holy Ghost help us to recognize the Doctrine of Christ?
How does baptism help us to maintain our focus on the Doctrine of Christ?

18 We are baptized to facilitate the temporal implementation of the Plan of Salvation. (See D&C 3:1).

Have you ever thought about how brilliantly The Plan of Salvation has been scripted, to prepare us to be reunited with our Heavenly Father?
For what purpose was The Plan of Salvation conceived?
How does The Plan of Salvation help us to bridge the gap between mortality and eternity?
How do the 7 "Rs" prepare us to meet our Heavenly Father?

19. We are baptized that we might have opportunities to bear each other's burdens. (See Mosiah 18:8).

How can we help to bear each other's burdens?

How can we give more freely of ourselves?

How can we provide help to those in need of temporal, emotional, or spiritual assistance without enabling them?

What should we do if we feel someone is not deserving of our help?

20. We are baptized that we might be given the privilege to "mourn with those that mourn." (Mosiah 18:9).

How can our covenant of baptism help us to put smiles on the faces of those who mourn?

How can baptism help those who mourn to look at life with new eyes?

How difficult would it be to face life's hardships without the support of the Gospel?

How does knowing that we are the children of God help us to face the adversity that is a part of life?

21

We are baptized that we might comfort those that stand in need of comfort." (Mosiah 18:9).

Why is "Comforter" an appropriate name for the Holy Ghost?
Why do you think we are asked to provide comfort to the downtrodden?
How does baptism help us to choose the harder right, instead of the easier wrong?
How does baptism empower us to choose wisely?

22

We are baptized that we might have the courage "to stand as witnesses of God at all times and in all things, and in all places that (we) may be in." (Mosiah 18:9).

What is our responsibility to bear witness of the truth?
How seriously must we take our witness of Christ?
How is our witness of Christ quickened, after our baptism?
Is it possible for all of Heavenly Father's children to be witnesses of Christ?

23

We are baptized that we might "be redeemed of God, and be numbered with those of the first resurrection, that (we might) have eternal life." (Mosiah 18:9).

Why do you think that so many people ignorantly worship an "unknown" God?

How does our desire to be baptized stand in contrast to those who have adopted a lifestyle that falls short of obedience to true principles?

After baptism, what takes places within our hearts as we consecrate our lives to the Savior?

Why is the desire for the world's goods so traumatizing?

24

We are baptized as a witness before our Heavenly Father that we have made a covenant to "serve him and keep his commandments, that he may pour out his Spirit more abundantly" upon us. (Mosiah 18:10).

How does baptism encourage us to listen to the spiritual promptings that nudge us in the direction of our dreams?

As we make covenants with God, how are we transformed?

How do the whisperings of the Spirit encourage us to follow the Savior?

What does it mean to be "elect according to the foreknowledge of God?" (1 Peter 1:2).

We are baptized that we might be given the tools we need to lengthen our stride.

After baptism, why does lengthening our stride sometimes cause discomfort?

Why would the Savior urge us to go the second mile? (See Matthew 5:41).

How are we fortified as we lengthen our stride?

How does lengthening our stride push us out of our comfort zones?

We are baptized that we be no more "strangers and foreigners," but instead, "fellow citizens with the saints, and of the household of God." (Ephesians 2:19).

How can we enjoy the companionship of the Saints?

What concern did Brigham Young express, relating to the temporal welfare of the Saints?

Why is it important to maintain associations with the Saints?

How does fellowship with the Saints positively influence our ability to live in obedience to the principles of the Gospel?

We are baptized that we might join the ranks of member missionaries.

Why did Paul say that we need not be embarrassed by the Gospel of Jesus Christ?

Who are the "elect according to the foreknowledge of God?" (1 Peter 1:2).

Who, among all of Heavenly Father's children, are candidates for baptism?

After we are baptized, how can we be good missionaries? (See D&C 13:1).

We are baptized that we might continue "steadfastly in the apostles' doctrine and fellowship, and in breaking of bread, and in prayers." (Acts 2:41-42).

What does it mean to be "firm and steadfast in the faith?" (Helaman 15:8).

After our baptism, what qualities must we develop if we are to provide Gospel instruction to others?

Who are "ministering angels?"

After baptism, how are we prompted by the Spirit?

29

We are baptized that we might be clothed with spiritual chain-mail as protection against the fiery darts of the adversary. (See 1 Nephi 15:14).

How can Heavenly Father help us to resist Satan's temptations?
How does immersion in the waters of baptism extinguish the fiery darts of the adversary?
How can keeping our eyes focused on the Savior help us to look past the temptations of the world?
How are free will, opposition, and baptism related?

30

We are baptized that we might be released from bondage to sin. (See D&C 84:49).

What are the key points of King Benjamin's counsel, that explained how to free ourselves from the stain of sin? (See Alma 5:21).
How do you feel about having prophets to whom we can turn for counsel and guidance?
When we are baptized, Whose name do we take upon ourselves?
Without the guidance of our Heavenly Father, how can we hope to effectively deal with opposition in our lives?

31

We are baptized that we might participate in the foundation ordinance of The Plan of Salvation.

What are "days of probation?"

Why has baptism been likened to being reborn? (See John 3:3).

Why is baptism an essential element in the learning laboratory of life?

How can focusing our thoughts on the Savior make our baptismal covenant more meaningful to us?

32

We are baptized by immersion in water, that we might feel not only the spiritual significance, but also the physical intensity, of the covenant we make with our Heavenly Father.

After our baptism, what can we do to reach out and touch the face of God?

How can baptism help us to discover the personal levels of experience with the Savior?

What might we record in our journals about how we felt at our baptisms?

How can we tingle with the consciousness of our kinship with the infinite?

33 We are baptized as Jesus Christ invites us, by name, to become His discipes.

Is it possible that Heavenly Father knows each of us by our name?
How is the covenant of baptism a two-way promise?
What does our Heavenly Father promise, in return?
What does it mean to have His Spirit to be with us?

34 We are baptized in a dramatic validation of the influence of the Light of Christ, and of the power of the Holy Ghost.

What does it feel like, when Heavenly Father inspires us by the "unspeakable gift of the Holy Ghost?" (D&C 121:26).
For how long will the Holy Ghost strive with us?
How does the Light of Christ lead us to the Holy Ghost?
How can the Light of Christ protect us from the influence of the adversary?

35. We are baptized to affirm the innocence of little children.

How can it be, that from the foundation of the world, little children have been saved? (See D&C 137:10).

Why is the practice of infant baptism heretical?

What did Moroni have to say about baptism and accountability?

How did Moroni link accountability to the baptism of little children?

36. We are baptized that we might experience spiritual delight, without the rush of sensory overstimulation that is prevalent in our technological world.

In what ways is baptism an ordinance dating back to an earlier time, when the pace of life was less hectic?

How does baptism invite us to stay in touch with our five physical senses, while enhancing contact with our spiritual sixth sense?

How is baptism the physical confirmation of a spiritual reality?

How do the Light of Christ and the Gift of the Holy Ghost work together to provide unmatched sensory stimulation?

We are baptized "for the perfecting
of the saints, for the work of the
ministry, (and) for the edifying
of the body of Christ."
(Ephesians 4:12).

What is the three-fold mission of the Church?

What did Paul mean by the term: "the body of Christ?"

What does it mean to edify the body of Christ?

How can those who have been baptized help to edify the body of Christ?

We are baptized that we might "all come in the unity
of the faith, and of the knowledge of the Son
of God...unto the measure of the stature
of the fulness of Christ."
(Ephesians 4:13).

Why is it important for members of the Church to be unified in their faith?

Why is unity in the faith critical to our survival?

How can baptism help us to become perfect in Christ? (See Moroni 10:32).

What happens to us as we mature in the Gospel?

39

We are baptized "that we henceforth be no more children, tossed to and fro." (Ephesians 4:14).

How does our baptism help us to face the adversity in even our well-balanced mortal experiences?

How does our baptism help us to strengthen our relationship with Jesus Christ?

How should we interact with those who are as children because they do not understand the principles of the Gospel?

How can we nurture understanding when our friends express confusion about the doctrine of baptism?

40

We are baptized that we might speak "the truth in love, (and) grow up into him in all things, which is the head, even Christ." (Ephesians 4:15).

How is it easier to "speak the truth in love" after our baptism?

How can baptism help us to "grow up into him in all things?"

Can the Savior be our head, if we are unwilling to submit to baptism?

How does speaking the truth in love cleanse our inner vessel? (See Alma 60:23).

441

We are baptized "unto the confounding of false doctrines and laying down of contentions." (2 Nephi 3:12).

How does baptism prepare us to confound false doctrines?

In what ways are members of the Church prepared to deal with the laying down of contentions?

How can baptism help us to be more patient as we face our adversaries?

Why is baptism as important a principle today as it has ever been in the past?

442

We are baptized that the light of our lives might grow "brighter and brighter until the perfect day." (D&C 50:24).

What is the light of our lives? (See Mosiah 27:29).

When we came to earth from our heavenly home, do you think we were full of light?

How can we protect our light from encroachment by the darkness that is all around us?

How can our baptism help us to be drawn to the light?

We are baptized that the earth might "be full
of the knowledge of the Lord, as
the waters cover the sea."
(Isaiah 11:9).

Why is our participation in The Plan of Happiness important?

How can the baptism of just one person make a positive difference in the world?

How does baptism help us to trace our royal lineage, and teach us who we really are?

How can the knowledge of the Lord increase in the earth, when we are true to our baptismal covenant?

We are baptized to capture the promise of
"the peace of God, which passeth all
understanding." (Philippians 4:7).

How can baptism define the pathway to peace?

How can we find peace in the world today?

How does the world's concept of peace differ from that to which baptism invites us?

Without baptism, can we ever truly be at peace?

45

We are baptized that we might pause and reflect upon those things that are really important in our lives.

Whose reflection do we see when we look down into the still waters of baptism?

What kind of change comes over us at our baptism?

How does the world seek change?

Why is the worship of idols of any kind so destructive?

46

We are baptized that we might affirm our faith in the immortality of the soul, because we feel, within ourselves, immortal longings.

How does it change our outlook on life, to know that we are spiritual beings having mortal experiences?

What does it feel like when the veil seems to be very thin?

What is magical about putting our lives in harmony with the principles of The Plan of Salvation?

Why was the commandment to be baptized given, in the first place?

47

We are baptized that we might learn to abide by the laws of the Celestial Kingdom, even as we dwell upon this telestial world. (See D&C 88:22).

What can happen to us if we wait another day to take advantage of repentance?

What happens if we neglect to honor our baptismal covenant to rely upon the Atonement of Christ by continually repenting of our sins?

When the wicked have no intention of repenting, what do you think will happen when "critical mass" is reached?

Do you think angels take notice of our efforts to be obedient to the laws of heaven?

48

We are baptized that we might think less about self-sufficiency, and more in terms of our Christ dependency.

What do you think it means to "come unto Christ?" (Moroni 10:32).

What are some of the divine attributes that we can all work on after our baptisms?

How does baptism prepare us deal with the challenges of life?

How is our baptism an expression of our conviction that the Savior is the sole source of our protection?

49

We are baptized that we might be given the tools to burst free of our self-imposed limitations.

What happens to us when we keep the Savior in our thoughts?

What happens to us when we lose the guidance of the Holy Ghost?

What happens to us when we are attuned to the whisperings of the Spirit?

Why do we use the expression: "The healing waters of baptism?"

50

We are baptized in consequence of the "evils and designs which do and will exist in the hearts of conspiring men (and women) in the last days." (D&C 89:4).

How does baptism invite the protection of heaven?

How can our baptism help us to maintain adequate reserves in our spiritual bank accounts?

How can something as simple as baptism protect us against the comprehensive and organized forces of evil?

What is our best defense against evil?

We are baptized that we might publish peace and tidings of great joy, endure to the end, and be lifted up at the last day, to inherit eternal life.
(See 1 Nephi 13:37).

How does the Gospel bring the world news of great joy and peace?
What happens to us as we publish peace and glad tidings?
Without baptism, can we generate the spiritual horsepower to worship the Savior with fervency?
How can we strengthen our relationship with the Savior, that He might lift us up at the last day unto eternal life?

We are baptized that we might enjoy the Sabbath day, as we never have before.

How does baptism help us to obey the Law of The Sabbath?
For what purpose was the Sabbath day created?
How can baptism help the Sabbath day become more special?
How can baptism turn our hearts to the Law of the Sabbath?

53 We are baptized that we might re-connect with our spiritual Birth Parents.

How does our baptism allow us to experience mortality while maintaining our connection with the eternities?

How does our baptism expand our understanding of our divine heritage?

How does God answer, when we ask: "Father, are you there?"

How is our baptism related to the sealing power of the priesthood?

54 We are baptized that we might enter into God's Rest.

How is God's Rest harmonious with family exaltation?

How can baptism generate the power to propel us into God's Rest?

What must we do, in order to be able to enter into God's Rest?

After our baptism, how can we reach out and touch the face of God?

We are baptized that we might vitalize Heavenly Father's Plan of Happiness in our lives.

How can our baptism help us to internalize the principles that lead to happiness?
How does our baptism provide opportunities to re-adjust our priorities?
Why is the Gospel the foundation of real happiness?
Why do those who disobey the commandments sometimes seem to be happy?

We are baptized that we might forever thereafter commemorate the birthdate of our immortal souls.

Why is our baptism a cause for celebration in heaven?
How does the day of our baptism commemorate the birthdate of our immortal soul?
How does our baptism send a message to heaven that all is well on our mission in mortality, and that one day we will be headed back Home?
Do you think that heavenly beings are given permission to attend baptismal services?

We are baptized that we might have hope in our Savior, Jesus Christ.

How does our knowledge of The Plan of Salvation expand the scope of our hope in Christ?
Is hope in Christ reserved only for members of The Church of Jesus Christ of Latter-day Saints?
How can baptism make Saints of sinners?
How does baptism reflect our hope in Christ?

We are baptized in a process of generation, and not just of maturation. (See Mosiah 27:26).

How is baptism a mile post on our journey toward becoming new creatures in Christ? (See Mosiah 27:26).
What does it mean to make the journey to Christ?
How does baptism bind us to Heavenly Father's perfect Plan of Salvation?
How does baptism illustrate the genius of our Heavenly Fathers' Plan?

59
We are baptized that we might enter into the fold, there to be cared for by the Good Shepherd.

Why is it dangerous to allow ourselves to become complacent about our baptismal covenant?

How is baptism the gift that keeps on giving?

How does baptism re-define itself each time the penitent faithful enter the healing waters?

How does baptism help us to live in accordance with priesthood principles?

60
We are baptized that we might contribute our own chapter to The Greatest Story Ever Told.

What do you think their reaction will be, when others sit down to read your chapter in The Greatest Story Ever Told?

What tools have you been given to help you to richly illustrate your own chapter in The Greatest Story Ever Told?

Have you noticed how your mentors have modified their approach, when teaching you how to write your story?

How does The Plan of Salvation set us free to reach our potential?

61

We are baptized that our Heavenly Father might create, in our behalf, an impenetrable "shield of faith" in the Lord Jesus Christ. (Ephesians 6:16).

Why do you think we are baptized individually, and not in large groups?
Why is it important to keep our shields of faith bright and shiny?
How do our shields of faith encourage accountability?
Why is baptism integral to our shields of faith?

62

We are baptized in white clothing, that we might symbolically express the purity of the ordinance and our proximity to the Spirit.

Why do we wear white clothing at baptismal services?
Are those who administer the ordinance required to wear white clothing during the Sacrament?
Is there an official Church policy or standard that requires the wearing of white clothing at times other than when performing the baptismal ordinance?
How can baptism help us to have clean hands and pure hearts? (See Psalms 24:4).

We are baptized that the Spirit of the Lord Omnipotent might work "a mighty change in us, or in our hearts, that we have no more disposition to do evil, but to do good continually." (Mosiah 5:2).

How does knowing that we are the children of God help to work a mighty change in our behavior?

How do we view the world when our nature has been changed through baptism?

Why does faith always precede the miracle?

How does our baptism kindle vital faith?

We are baptized "through the infinite goodness of God, (that by) the manifestations of his Spirit (we might) have great views of that which is to come." (Mosiah 5:3).

How is our spiritual education different from worldly learning?

What happens when we allow the Spirit to teach us?

How does baptism have the power to change behavior?

What happens to those who wait upon the Lord? (See Isaiah 40:31).

We are baptized that we might evenly distribute the weight of our temporal baggage, that we might more easily "enter in at the strait gate." (Matthew 7:13).

How can baptism help us to more comfortably carry our own burdens?
How can temporal baggage get in the way of our spiritual objectives?
How do you think the Lord views our temporal baggage?
In a world that is overwhelmed by temporal baggage, how can baptism help us to avoid being tainted by it?

We are baptized that the "opposition in all things" to which Lehi alluded, might become a blessing that allows us to more fully engage The Plan of Salvation.
(2 Nephi 2:11).

How can our baptism become the foundation for purposeful action?
How can baptism help us to view opposition as a blessing in disguise?
How can we more fully engage the elements of The Plan of Salvation, in order to more effectively deal with opposition?
How does the Savior help us to manage opposition?

> **67**
> We are baptized
> that our trials and tribulations
> might give us experience, and
> work to our benefit.
> (See D&C 122:7).

Since opposition is necessary for free will to be exercised, how does baptism allow us to reach our potential without suffering damage to the stature of our spirits?

How can our baptism help us to see more clearly from an eternal perspective?

How can our baptism help us to increase our spiritually aerobic maximum pulse rate, as well as the capacity of our lungs to be filled with celestial air?

How can our baptism teach us how to be comfortable in the company of immortal beings?

> **68**
> We are baptized that the "redemption exemption," that is
> a codicil to the Law of Justice, might be activated
> and the Law of Mercy set in motion, as our
> lease on life is renegotiated in our favor.

Why do you think Heavenly Father and the Holy Ghost were present at the baptism of Jesus, to witness the validation of His very special lease on life?

Following baptism, how can we take advantage of our own brand new lease on life?

How does Heavenly Father encourage us to enhance, to our benefit, the terms of our lease on life?

How does baptism strengthen our resolve to be true to our divine destiny?

69. We are baptized that we might make a simple public statement about a profound private conviction.

In what ways can our baptism be unassuming and reflective?

How do our faith and testimony carry us beyond the physical ordinance to the spiritual covenant?

How can the simplicity of the ordinance orient us toward the mysteries of the kingdom?

How is it possible that the 25 simple words of the baptismal ordinance can have such profound meaning?

70. We are baptized "that we might speak with the tongue of angels, and shout praises unto the Holy One of Israel." (2 Nephi 31:13).

How do you think baptism prepares us to receive spiritual gifts?

How is baptism like the Rosetta Stone of spiritual experience?

How can baptism unlock the gift of the interpretation of tongues?

How does baptism prepare us to shout praises unto the Holy One of Israel?

71

We are baptized that our hearts might be "knit togther in unity and in love." (Mosiah 18:21).

How can our baptism help us to make sense of the myriad elements of The Plan of Salvation?

How can baptism assure us that when our time comes to pass through the veil, we will leave behind legacies that contribute to the establishment of Zion?

Can eight year old children be as spiritually prepared for baptism as eighty year old adults?

As baptism knits us together, will there be any missing threads in the pattern He has planned?

72

We are baptized that we might enjoy the companionship of "the Comforter, which showeth all things, and teacheth the peaceablethings of the kingdom." (D&C 39:6).

How is baptism like a commencement exercise?

How can baptism help us to conquer our self-defeating behaviors?

What tools have we been given to nurture our understanding of the peaceable things of the kingdom?

Why is faith without works dead, that it cannot save us? (See J.S.T. James 2:14).

73

We are baptized as a
witness and a testimony
that we are "willing to serve
God with all (our) hearts."
(Mosiah 21:35).

How can the Light of Christ help us to fulfill our baptismal commitment to minister to the needs of others?

How is witnessing for Christ like a spiritually aerobic exercise program?

How can we follow the example of Aaron?

What are the ordinances of salvation and exaltation?

74

We are baptized in such a manner that, as
we step out of the font, our faces will
always be oriented toward the light.

During baptismal services, how can we invite the Spirit, that we might reach out and touch the face of God?

Why is it important to keep our faces oriented toward the light? (See D&C 88:118).

What can happen to us if we do not steadfastly face the light?

If we allow it to do so, where will our illuminated path lead us?

75

We are baptized that we might pursue the object and design of our existence, which is to be the happiest people upon the face of the earth.

How can we be strengthened, as we continue our journey to Christ after our baptism?

Do you think our feelings of happiness come from secretions in our brains, or from our Heavenly Father, Who, ironically, created dopamine in the first place?

Why do you think that it is in quiet moments that we most clearly hear the voice of the Spirit?

What kind of spiritual nourishment is served at baptismal celebrations?

76

We are baptized because, as disciples of Christ, it is our lot in life to be sent forth as sheep in the midst of wolves. (See Matthew 10:16).

How can our baptism take us in the direction of our dreams?

How can our baptism help us to maintain order in a chaotic world?

How is baptism an expression of the self-restraint that is required by those who would call themselves disciples of Christ?

How can the Light of Christ protect us from the influence of the adversary?

> We are baptized that we might receive the
> means to calibrate our lives with the
> pattern of heaven itself.

How is baptism related to the Infinite Atonement?

How does the Light of Christ work behind the scenes, to help us fill the measure of our creation?

How important is it to have a correct understanding of "the age of accountability" as it relates to baptism?

How does our baptism allow us to experience mortality, and at the same time establish an undeniable connection with the eternities?

> We are baptized that the Lord might be on our
> right, and on our left, and in our hearts.
> (See D&C 84:88).

What mentors have accompanied you during your journey to the waters of baptism?

As you have made the journey to Christ, how have you felt His presence? (See Alma 37:41).

How does the Savior work through others to guide us?

How does Satan attempt to influence us to abandon the Savior as our traveling companion?

We are baptized that we might more easily memorize
our lines in Heavenly Father's Three Act Play
that is entitled "The Plan of Salvation."

What kinds of distractions does Satan employ to disrupt the execution of The Plan?
How does baptism crystalize our understanding of the Fall of Adam and the Atonement of Jesus Christ?
How does baptism orient us toward the mysteries of eternity that are part of the script of Act Three of The Plan of Salvation?
In the distant past, do you think we shouted for joy upon hearing about The Plan of Salvation?

We are bapized that we might become
as lights that are set on a hill.
(See Matthew 5:14).

What does it mean to magnify our callings? (See D&C 84:33).
How does light manifest itself as inspiration and revelation?
How does the light that emanates from Christ speak to us?
Why is it important to always, always, walk in the light?

81

We are baptized that our vessels might be filled with the "oil of gladness." (See Hebrews 1:9 & Matthew 25:1).

What is the currency of faith that accrues with compound interest to those who have entered the waters of baptism?

How can "the Lord…go before you; and the God of Israel be your rearward?" (Isaiah 52:12).

How do the terms of our lease on life compel us to look with gratitude to the Author of Salvation?

How does baptism prevent us from going "down to the vile dust, from whence (we have) sprung, unwept, unhonored, and unsung?"

82

We are bapized to wash away the cobwebs from our minds.

How does The Book of Mormon clear up confusion in the world regarding the need for those with diminished mental capacity to repent and be baptized?

What discoveries await us, as we "walk in the light of the Lord" following our baptism? (Isaiah 2:5).

What is captivating about the positive behavior changes that follow baptism?

How can The Book of Mormon help us to better understand the basic principles and doctrines of the Gospel of Jesus Christ?

83

We are baptized that the anchors of our faith might be secured within a foundation of rock, and not of sand. (See Matthew 7:26).

What are the fruits of faith? (See Alma 32:40).

What did the Savior teach the Nephites about baptism?

How can baptism help us to come to "the knowledge of the Son of God?" (Ephesians 4:13).

How does our baptism provide a foundation of stability in a world that seems to lack moral footings?

84

We are baptized that we might fan with faith the fire of our resolve. (See Jeremiah 20:9).

What does baptism teach us about self-reliance?

In what ways does baptism empower us?

For how long do you think we can maintain the intensity of the feelings that are generated by baptism?

How can our baptism help us to move beyond the mediocrity that too often defines the lifestyle of those who are mired in the values of the every-day world? (See Isaiah 55:9).

We are baptized that we might leave a light burning for those who are late to arrive at the wedding feast. (See John Chapter 2).

Who among us needs a boost, when life's burdens weigh them down and slow their progress along the path that leads to the waters of baptism?

What is the fate of those who refuse the invitation to be baptized?

As children of light, what can we do to strengthen the testimonies of others?

How can you explain the universality of immortal longings that are experienced by so many of Heavenly Father's children?

We are baptized that we might learn how to consecrate to the Lord our time, talents, means, and everything else with which He has blessed us.

What happens to us when our priorities are out of order?

How does our baptism provide us with opportunities to "give place" or study, pray, and commit ourselves to a purposeful plan of action? (See Alma 32:27).

How does baptism prepare us to more thoughtfully budget our time?

How can baptism help us to turn our attention to the weightier matters of the law? (See Matthew 23:23).

We are baptized that we might accept our Heavenly
Father's invitation to join Him in His work
and glory, which is to bring about our
immortality and eternal life.
(See Moses 1:39).

How is baptism the key to an understanding of the mission statement of our Father in Heaven? (See Moses 1:39).

What do you think Paul meant, when he taught that there is "one Lord, one faith, (and only) one baptism?" (Ephesians 4:5).

Why is the day of our baptism such a happy occasion?

How has Heavenly Father provided for us, so that we might be assured of eternal life following our baptisms?

We are baptized that we might rejoice in our
characterization as a peculiar people.
(See 1 Peter 2:9).

How can our participation in God's Plan refine us, and thereby become a perfecting process? (See Malachi 3:2).

How does it feel to know that we are on the path of progression?

What principles do you think might have been introduced at the Council in Heaven before our world was created? (See D&C 138:55).

Do you think that baptism might have been one of the hot topics that were discussed at the Council in Heaven? (See D&C 138:56, Abraham 4:26, & 5:2).

89

We are baptized that righteousness might stay the sword of justice that hangs over a wicked world. (See Helaman 13:5).

Do you think the angels in heaven are, even now, taking note of our behavior?

Why does amending behavior require a change of heart, as well?

How can our baptism help us to distinguish good from evil?

How can the Light of Christ have the power to lead the children of God to the waters of baptism?

90

We are baptized that others might be influenced to follow our Exemplar. (See John 14:6).

Why is it important to exercise our testimonies as often as possible?

How does our baptism unleash the power of God within us, that our shields of faith might be fortified?

What has our Creator provided for us to make it easier for us to witness in His name?

What are some of the evidences of the spiritual unification of the members of the Church?

91. We are baptized that our Latter-day Saint culture might help to insulate us from worldly influences.

How powerful is the wind of doctrine?

How can baptism help us to recognize the divisive influence of the wind of doctrine?

Why is it that those who base their math on the wind of doctrine always wind up with negative sums?

How can our baptismal covenant help us to face the light, so the shadows will always be behind us?

92. We are baptized that we might not be tempted to "look back," as we flee from Sodom and Gomorrah. (See Genesis 19:16).

Is it necessary to have authority to baptize?

How does Satan use cunning craftiness to penetrate our defenses?

Why don't more people understand that one vote plus God constitutes a majority?

How can our sense of temporal security be deceiving?

93
We are baptized that we might become new creatures in Christ. (See 2 Corinthians 5:17).

How can the scriptures expand our appreciation of the scope of The Plan of Salvation?
How can baptism, and The Plan of Salvation, put us in touch with our spiritual roots?
What does it mean to have been created in both the image and the likeness of God?
How is it to be accomplished, that the dead might accept the Gospel in the Spirit World?

94
We are baptized that we might stand tall for others who may lack the power to do so themselves.

Does the Light of Christ influence all of Heavenly Father's children?
How might those who do not correctly understand the ordinance of baptism be "in the gall of bitterness?" (Moroni 8:14).
What might be the best way to talk to our friends about how we feel about our baptism?
Why do you think we, as well as the Ephesian Saints, need to hear Paul's instruction relating to unity? (See Ephesians 2:19).

We are baptized that we might light candles rather than curse the darkness.

Can one baptism make a difference in the world, or can one baptism make a world of difference?

Can one baptism stem the advancing tide of wickedness?

How can baptism prepare us for the coming millennial day?

How does our baptism place us on a path that follows priesthood direction?

We are baptized that it might become easier to approach the Lord with our sacrifices.

What is the difference between a donation and a sacrifice?

How comprehensive must our sacrifice be, before it is acceptable to the Lord?

What is an honest tithe?

How is the payment of tithing a barometer of our spiritual maturity?

97

We are baptized that we might be given opportunities to make and to keep the covenants of salvation and exaltation.

What was King Benjamin's simple counsel regarding how we can be obedient to our baptismal covenant?

How does King Benjamin's counsel empower us to fill the measure of our creation?

How will our witness for Christ define, delineate, and determine our divine destiny?

How do covenants vitalize the work of the ministry?

98

We are baptized that we might unite ourselves with the ordained process by which eternal principles are communicated.

How can others help us to "give birth" to our participation in the work of the ministry?

How can we make sure that our ministry does not offend people?

How can Heavenly Father, Jesus Christ, and the Holy Ghost infuse the universe with light?

Is there any viable alternative to baptism?

99

We are baptized that, henceforth, we be no more "carried about with every wind of doctrine." (Ephesians 4:14).

What are the winds of doctrine?

How does baptism refute the false notion that we can avoid the consequences of sin by procrastinating the day of our repentance? (See Alma 34).

How has the wind of doctrine penetrated nearly every aspect of the lives of those around us?

How can our baptism be a shield and a protection against the power of the destroyer, as long as we have a work left to do on the earth?

100

We are baptized that we might not be deceived "by the sleight of men, and cunning craftiness, whereby they lie in wait to deceive." (Ephesians 4:14).

What is "the sleight of men?"

How is the spirit that is present at a baptismal service the polar opposite of "cunning craftiness?"

How can baptism offer protection from those who "lie in wait to deceive?"

How can baptism help us to recognize the fingerprints of Satan on the idols with which he tempts us?

101 We are baptized that we might honor the order of the priesthood.

By what authority is baptism performed?
What was Oliver Cowdery's witness, regarding the angelic restoration of the authority to baptize?
Who are the sons of Levi that are referred to in Doctrine & Covenants Section 13?
How does baptism create the opportunity for young men to become the sons of Moses and of Aaron?

102 We are baptized that we might be perfected in our Savior, Jesus Christ. (See Moroni 10:32).

How can baptism fortify us with the discipline to go the second mile?
What happens when we turn to the scriptures to learn about the Father of our spirits?
How does it make you feel to know that Heavenly Father knows each of us by our first name?
How can our baptismal covenant help us to become perfect in our repentance? (See Matthew 5:48).

103

We are baptized that, "through the infinite goodness of God, and the manifestations of the Spirit," we might "have great views of that which is to come." (Mosiah 5:3).

How can baptism help us to achieve spiritual symmetry?

How does our baptism entitle us to the further light and knowledge that the Lord has promised us?

What does it mean to have an eternal perspective?

How does Heavenly Father link baptism to the precious gift of testimony?

104

We are baptized that we might understand how and what we worship, that we might come unto our Father in the name of our Savior Jesus Christ. (See D&C 93:19).

How does our baptism grant us access to the mysteries of the kingdom of heaven? (See Matthew 13:11).

How does baptism free us to worship God "according to the dictates of (our) own conscience?" (11th Article of Faith).

How do you think we felt about coming to earth, after The Plan had been fully explained to us in the pre-mortal world?

Following our baptism, how can the ordinances of the temple become the pinnacle of our worship?

105

We are baptized with the realization that when the Lord gives us commandments, He also prepares ways for us to accomplish the tasks that are set before us. (See 1 Nephi 3:7).

How can sacrifice have the power to make us feel so happy?
How can renewing our covenant of baptism help us to lengthen our stride?
Why do you think there is a need for regular repetitive repentance?
How can angels from heaven help us to repent?

106

We are baptized to make it easier for us to "pray unto the Lord, (and to) call upon his holy name, (and to) make known his wonderful works among the people." (D&C 65:4).

What is our greatest joy, when we sacrifice for the kingdom?
With Heavenly Father taking such good care of us, how can we keep our blessings in perspective?
What is one of the best ways to follow the Savior's example of missionary work?
Can there be a greater witness than the Holy Ghost?

107

We are baptized because, although we were an hungered, and thirsty, and strangers, we are no longer naked, or sick, or imprisoned within the fortress of our own limiting beliefs. (See Matthew 25:34-40).

How does baptism help us to break free of our self-imposed limitations?
How can baptism counteract the fading light of limiting beliefs?
How was Naaman the Leper a prisoner of limiting beliefs?
How can our baptism liberate us from intellectual, philosophical, or spiritual captivity?

108

We are baptized that our incomings, our outgoings, and all our salutations may be in the name of the Lord, with uplifted hands unto the Most High. (See D&C 109:9).

How can witnesses help those who are struggling as they make the journey to Christ?
How does the Light of Christ work tirelessly to encourage us to praise God?
How can the Light of Christ prompt us to lift up our hands and praise God?
How is our baptism a re-affirmation of our pre-mortal acceptance of The Plan of Salvation?

We are baptized that we might find greater happiness, peace, and rest; that we might obtain the blessings of the fathers, including the authority to administer the ordinances of the Gospel.
(See Abraham 1:2).

109

After the close of the Savior's ministry, how successful was the Church in maintaining strict obedience to the Doctrine of Christ?

How did the Reformation pave the way for the Restoration of the Gospel?

What do you think Thomas Jefferson meant, when he used the term: "Primitive Christianity"?

How is baptism related to the Restoration of the Gospel?

We are baptized to become more observant followers of righteousness, to possess greater knowledge, to be the progenitors of nations, ambassadors of peace, and to receive instruction, and keep the commandments.
(See Abraham 1:2).

110

What do the scriptures have to say about the ability of the Church to sustain true doctrine without continual revelation?

What did early Church historians have to say about apostasy from the truth?

Why did the Pharisees of His day remain silent when Jesus was baptized?

How can the ordinance of baptism help us to be more observant followers of righteousness?

111

We are baptized that we might become kings and
priests, and queens and priestesses; in effect,
to become rightful heirs of the blessings
that belonged to the fathers.
(See Abraham 1:2).

Why are we baptized individually, and not in large groups?
What is the eternal destiny of those who die without baptism before they reach the age of accountability?
To whom do the blessings of the Abrahamic Covenant apply?
Where does the pathway lead that begins with baptism?

112

We are baptized because we have brought
forth fruit worthy of repentance.
(See Moroni 6:1).

How does baptism free us from the natural process of entropy, wherein everything that is of a temporal nature gradually declines into disorder?
Why do you think baptism has been described as a "narrow gate?" (2 Nephi 33:9).
Why do faith and repentance precede baptism? (See the 4th Article of Faith).
After our baptism, when we regularly repent, what happens to the recollection of our former sins?

113
We are baptized that we might give away all of our sins, but there are strings attached. (See Alma 22:18).

What happens when we give away our sins?

Why do you think the Sacrament has been provided to those who have been baptized?

Do you think that we could be happy while living in eternity, if we had not beforehand given away our sins?

Can you think of anyone who would be willing to take personal responsibility for our sins?

114
We are baptized when charity has become the foundation of our faith.

How can we protect ourselves with a "shield of faith?"

Our shield of faith notwithstanding, why does it sometimes seem as if we are so alone? (See Mark 1:3).

How can charity strengthen our "shield of faith?"

How do those who have been baptized qualify by worthiness to bear a "shield of faith?"

We are baptized because we have determined to follow the Savior "with full purpose of heart, acting no hypocrisy and no deception before God." (2 Nephi 31:13).

How is our discipleship vitalized as we approach the Savior with full purpose of heart?

How can we give birth to our witness of Jesus Christ, that it might be borne "with full purpose of heart?"

Why do you think that people sometimes act with hypocrisy, or "deception before God?"

What has Heavenly Father provided to make sure that we witness for the Savior with full purpose of heart?

We are baptized that we might experience liberation from our self-defeating behaviors.

How does baptism prepare us for our magnum opus in the theater of life?

Why do you think the principles of the Gospel are called "the perfect law of liberty?" (See James 1:25).

How does baptism re-introduce us to the program of the Three Act Play that was imprinted upon our souls before we came to earth?

How does baptism brings out the best in us?

We are baptized that we might press forward with steadfastness, having a perfect brightness of hope and a love of God and of our brothers and sisters, feasting upon the scriptures, and enduring to the end in righteousness. (See Nephi 31:20).

Following baptism, how can we personalize the ordinance of the Sacrament, so that in its repetition, it might become a powerful vehicle for our growth?

How did Joseph Smith feast upon the word of God after reading James 1:2-3 in the New Testament?

Why do you think Joseph Smith received the gift of the ministering of angels even before his baptism?

How does our baptism become a commencement exercise?

We are baptized that we might hear the voice of the Lord that is unto all, for "there is none to escape; and there is no eye that shall not see, neither ear that shall not hear, neither heart that shall not be penetrated." (D&C 1:2).

In what literal and figurative ways does the Savior ask us to follow Him?

How can we follow the Savior by listening to the counsel of His prophet?

How can we follow the Savior if there is confusion regarding the correct administration of the ordinance of baptism?

How does the baptismal prayer in The Book of Mormon help us to follow the Savior?

119
We are baptized that we might affirm our support of family values.

Why does it sometimes seem as if the prophets are as lone voices crying in the wilderness? (See Mark 1:3).

How can the words of the prophets fortify us?

How can baptism empower us to act upon the principles contained in The Proclamation on The Family?

How can baptism protect our family memories from tarnishing?

120
We are baptized that we might become saviors on Mount Zion to our kindred dead.
(See Obadiah 1:21).

How does vicarious work for the dead harmonize with the principles of The Plan of Salvation?

How can all of Heavenly Father's children have equal opportunity to become heirs of salvation and eternal life?

How does baptism for the dead stand beside the Atonement as a vicarious work?

How is baptism for the dead the "most glorious of all subjects belonging to the everlasting gospel?" (D&C 128:17).

121 We are baptized that the Spirit might find expression as a light within each of us.

What do you think will be the outcome of the battle raging in the hearts of men, on Saturday?

Why is it important for us to maintain our unique personality signatures?

How does baptism help us to regain and retain our spiritual identities?

What can happen to us, if we do not enjoy the protection from spiritual identity theft, that is afforded by baptism?

122 We are baptized that Heavenly Father might show us our weaknesses. (See Ether 12:27).

How can our weakness be transformed into a source of strength?

How does the grace of God help us to deal with our weaknesses and imperfections?

Why would Heavenly Father think to bless us with weaknesses?

How can a quality like weakness possibly promote a principle that is as positive as progression?

123
We are baptized that we might know that we are here,
at this place, and in this time, by divine design.

What do you think the Lord meant, when He said: "All these things shall give thee experience, and shall be for thy good?" (D&C 122:7).

How would you describe the choreography of The Plan of Salvation?

How can The Plan of Salvation be infinite in its scope and yet be so personalized that it meets our individual needs?

What are divine accoutrements?

124
We are baptized that we might honor God and feel His love,
as we confess His hand in all things, and obey His
commandments. (See D&C 59:21).

Have you ever thought to compare your faith to that of those whom Peter taught on the Day of Pentecost? (See Acts 2:37).

How is the Angel Moroni a prototype for those who will one day be enveloped in light?

How can baptism provide the mortar that binds together the foundation principles of the Pillars of Creation?

How can the Holy Ghost help us to honor our baptismal covenant?

125
We are baptized to remind ourselves that the poor, the unlearned, the common person, and the native born, may equally come unto Christ.

Why do our mortal experiences sometimes build us up, while at other times they seem to tear us down?

How does the Gospel exert an equalizing influence?

Have you ever heard the couplet, penned by Lorenzo Snow, that reads: "As man is, God once was. As God is, man may be?"

As we participate in the game of life, in what ways is the Gospel of Jesus Christ like our own personal play-book?

126
We are baptized because this life is the time for us to prepare to meet our Heavenly Father.
(See Alma 32:34).

How can baptism heal our wounds?

How can we safeguard our free will, as we prepare to meet God?

How can baptism help us to exercise agency to act independently?

How can the Atonement prepare us for our heavenly homecoming?

127. We are baptized to guard ourselves against spiritual identity theft.

How bold is Satan in his efforts to steal our spiritual identity?

Do the scriptures reassure us that we are the treasures of heaven?

How can we be protected against spiritual identity theft?

How does baptism reinforce the concept that we are children of God?

128. We are baptized as a testament that "the works, and the designs, and the purposes of God cannot be frustrated, neither can they come to naught." (D&C 3:1).

What is The Merciful Plan of The Great Creator? (2 Nephi 9:6).

What is The Plan of Our God? (2 Nephi 9:13).

What is The Great and Eternal Plan of Deliverance From Death? (2 Nephi 11:5).

What is The Plan of Salvation? (Alma 24:14).

129

We are baptized as a testament that we are willing to participate in "God's eternal plan." (Official Declaration 2).

What is The Plan of Redemption? (Alma 29:2).
What is The Great Plan of The Eternal God? (Alma 34:9).
What is The Great and Eternal Plan of Redemption? (Alma 34:16).
What is The Great Plan of Redemption? (Alma 34:31).

130

We are baptized we might lend support to the declaration of the Gods "that their plan was good." (Abraham 4:21).

What is The Plan of Restoration? (Alma 41:2).
What is The Great Plan of Salvation? (Alma 42:5).
What is The Great Plan of Happiness? (Alma 42:8).
What is The Plan of Mercy? (Alma 42:15).

131
We are baptized with the assurance of "eternal life, which God, that cannot lie, promised before the world began." (Titus 1:2).

What is The Plan of Happiness? (Alma 42:16).
What is The Great Plan of Mercy? (Alma 42:31).
What do the scriptures teach about our pre-mortal life?
Do you think that you came to your family here on earth by divine design?

132
We are baptized that, with the gentle instruction of the Spirit, we might become better at building relationships.

Why is it important that we "press forward with a steadfastness in Christ, having a perfect brightness of hope, and a love of God and of all men?" (2 Nephi 31:20).
What do you think President McKay said would be the Savior's very first question?
Since families are the basic building block of eternity, can you imagine what was second on the list of questions?
Since we have all come from God, Who is our Home, what do you think was next on the list?

133

We are baptized that we might bow our knees "unto the Father of our Lord Jesus Christ, of whom the whole family in heaven and earth is named." (Ephesians 3:14-15).

After family, why do you think that active participation in the programs of the Church is important to the Savior?

Since we are all one community, do you think the Savior will be interested in how we have treated our neighbors?

How can the earth be "full of the knowledge of the Lord, as the waters cover the sea?" (Isaiah 11:9).

How does baptism prepare us for our heavenly reunion with our Father?

134

We are baptized that those who have died without having had the opportunity to hear about the Plan of Salvation might also partake of eternal life.

What does a "patron" do, in the House of The Lord?

What is vicarious work? (See D&C 138:33).

How does Section 2 of the Doctrine & Covenants relate to baptism for the dead?

Why do you think the wording of Malachi's prophecy is not identical in all four of the Standard Works?

135

We are baptized as a witness that "the Lord God will do nothing, but he revealeth his secret unto his servants the prophets." (Amos 3:7).

How does Section Two in The Doctrine & Covenants read?
How does the prophecy read in The Old Testament?
How does the prophecy read in The Pearl of Great Price?
How does the prophecy read in The Book of Mormon?

136

We are baptized that we might be "easy to be entreated, (and) firm to keep the commandments." (Helaman 7:7).

How can scriptural aphorisms help us to be "easily entreated?"
How can aphorisms help us to be "firm to keep the commandments?"
Would your own aphorisms help you to remember your baptismal covenant?
Can your own aphorisms help you to walk the strait and narrow way?

We are baptized that we might be "slow to be led to do iniquity; and quick to hearken unto the words of the Lord." (Helaman 7:7).

How does our baptism help us to be "slow to be led to do iniquity?"
What blessings do we receive when we are "quick to hearken unto the words of the Lord?"
Can those who play poker with the devil hope to win every hand?
How can hokmahs help us to remember our baptismal covenant?

Finally, as Ignatius Loyola declared, we are baptized that we might give and not count the cost, that we might fight and not heed the wounds, that we might toil and not seek for rest, and that we might labor and not ask for any reward save that of knowing that we do God's will.

Baptism clears our minds and gives us a sense of purpose. Through the ordinance, we commune with the Infinite and enjoy the consciousness of victory over our self-defeating behaviors.

Baptismal Prayers in The Scriptures

Doctrine & Covenants

"The person who is called of God and has authority from Jesus Christ to baptize, shall go down into the water with the person who has presented himself or herself for baptism, and shall say, calling him or her by name: Having been commissioned of Jesus Christ, I baptize you in the name of the Father, and of the Son, and of the Holy Ghost. Amen." (D&C 20:73).

Pearl of Great Price

"And he gave unto me a commandment that I should baptize in the name of the Father, and of the Son, which is full of grace and truth, and of the Holy Ghost, which beareth record of the Father and the Son." (Moses 7:11).

Book of Mormon

"Behold, ye shall go down and stand in the water, and in my name shall ye baptize them. And now behold, these are the words which ye shall say, calling them by name, saying: Having authority given me of Jesus Christ, I baptize you in the name of the Father, and of the Son, and of the Holy Ghost. Amen. And then shall ye immerse them in the water, and come forth again out of the water. And after this manner shall ye baptize in my name." (3 Nephi 11:23-27).

Holy Bible

"And Jesus came and spake unto them, saying, All power is given unto me in heaven and in earth. Go ye therefore, and teach all nations, baptizing them in the name of the Father, and of the Son, and of the Holy Ghost." (Matthew 28:18-19).

When we are baptized,
we have feelings of deja-vu,
that when we exult in our fellowship
with the community of the Saints and of the
household of God, we have done so before. (See
Ephesians 2:19). We vaguely remember the
time in the distant past when "the
morning stars sang together,
and all the sons of God
shouted for joy."
(Job 38:7).

The Fourth Article of Faith

We believe that the first principles and ordinances of the Gospel are:
first, Faith in the Lord Jesus Christ; second, Repentance; third,
Baptism by immersion for the remission of sins; fourth,
Laying on of hands for the gift of the Holy Ghost.

As we travel through Idumea's harsh
and seemingly unforgiving environment,
oases will spring up in the deserts of life,
and living water will slake our thirst
because our roots have been deeply
embedded in the rich loam
of eternally valid
principles.

Bible Dictionary - Baptism

From a Greek word meaning to "dip" or "immerse." Baptism in water is the introductory ordinance of the Gospel and must be followed by baptism of the Spirit in order to be complete.

It is associated with faith in the Lord Jesus Christ, repentance, and the laying on of hands for the gift of the Holy Ghost. Baptism has always been practiced whenever the Gospel of Jesus Christ has been on the earth and has been taught by men holding the holy priesthood who could administer the ordinances.

Although there is some obscurity in the Bible as to the antiquity of baptism before the time of Jesus, from latter-day revelation it is clear that Adam was baptized (see Moses 6:64-68) and that the patriarchs and prophets since his time have taught the Gospel and administered the ordinances that pertain to the Gospel. This includes both water baptism and the laying on of hands for the Holy Ghost. (See Moses 8:23-24). The Book of Mormon also shows that baptism was taught and practiced long before the coming of Jesus Christ. (See 2 Nephi 31 and Mosiah 18:8-17).

In the New Testament, Paul speaks of the children of Israel being baptized by Moses "in the cloud and in the sea." (1 Corinthians 10:1-4). Noah and Abraham are spoken of as "preachers of righteousness," which means they taught the Gospel and administered its ordinances. (See Galatians 3:8, Hebrews 4:1-2, 2 Peter 2:5, and Moses 8:23-24).

Baptism symbolizes death, burial, and resurrection and can only be done by immersion. It is clear that John the Baptist and Philip baptized in that manner. (See Matthew 3:16, Acts 8:37-39, Romans 6:1-6, Colossians 2:12, D&C 20:72-74 & 128:12-13). Any other method is not baptism.

We learn from latter-day revelation, which confirms the teaching in the Bible, that the Aaronic Priesthood has authority to baptize with water, whereas the Melchizedek Priesthood has power to baptize not only with water but also to confer the Holy Ghost. (See D&C 13 & J.S.H. 1:68-72). We note also that John the Baptist, who had the Aaronic Priesthood, recognized this distinction and used it to illustrate one of the differences between his mission and the mission of Jesus, who had the priesthood.

Baptism is not optional if one wishes the fulness of salvation. Jesus said a person must be born of water and of the Spirit. (See John 3:3-5). When He sent forth the Twelve Apostles to teach the Gospel, He told them that whosoever believed and was baptized would be saved, and whosoever did not believe would be damned. (See Mark 16:16). Jesus Himself was baptized "to fulfil all righteousness." (See Matthew 3:15 & 2 Nephi 31:4-11). But the Pharisees, being unwilling to accept the Gospel, "rejected the counsel of God against themselves, being not baptized." (Luke 7:30).

Baptism in water has several purposes. It is for the remission of sins, for membership in the Church, and for entrance into the celestial kingdom; it is also the doorway to personal sanctification when followed by the reception of the Holy Ghost.

The age at which baptism should be administered is not specified in the Bible, although it is evident that candidates were to be old enough to be capable of belief and have some understanding. In latter-day revelation, we learn that the Lord has set the age at eight years as the time when a person begins to become accountable and can be baptized. (See D&C 20:71 & 68:25-28). This was also the age given in Old Testament times. (See J.S.T. Genesis 17:11).

Baptism is a most sacred ordinance, which a person, having received it, can remember throughout life as a reminder of the personal commitment to Jesus Christ. Its symbolism is beautiful, and its consequences ever so desirable. John the Baptist had the signal honor among all men to take the Son of God into the water and baptize Him, after which he saw the Holy Ghost descend upon Jesus. By being baptized, Jesus obeyed the law Himself and set the example for all mankind.

Before our baptism, we receive a testimony of Christ through the witness of the Holy Ghost. The experience vitalizes our faith, encourages us to be obedient, convicts us of our sins, and motivates us to repent. Conversion that follows is the fruits of testimony, and may follow our baptism for an indefinite period of time. During this process, spiritual gifts accompany conversion, and are built upon the foundation of testimony.

Topical Guide

Over 100 References to Baptism in the Scriptures

Baptism (36)

1. Jesus, when he was baptized - Matthew 3:16
2. Baptizing them in the name of the Father - Matthew 28:19
3. John did...preach the baptism of repentance for the remission of sins - Mark 1:4
4. Baptized of John in Jordan - Mark 1:9
5. Believeth and is baptized shall be saved - Mark 16:16
6. Except a man be born of water - John 3:5
7. John also was baptizing - John 3:23
8. Repent, and be baptized - Acts 2:38
9. Into the water...and he baptized - Acts 8:38
10. Be baptized, and wash away thy sins - Acts 22:16
11. Buried with him by baptism - Romans 6:4
12. Baptized unto Moses in the cloud - 1 Corinthians 10:2
13. Baptized into Christ have put on Christ - Galatians 3:27
14. Buried with him in baptism - Colossians 2:12
15. Of the doctrine of baptisms - Hebrews 6:2
16. Even baptism doth also now save us - 1 Peter 3:21
17. Waters of Judah, or...of baptism - 1 Nephi 20:1
18. Lamb of God...baptized by water - 2 Nephi 31:5
19. Gate...is repentance and baptism by water - 2 Nephi 31:17
20. Baptized in the name of the Lord - Mosiah 18:10
21. Baptized as a witness...willing to serve God - Mosiah 21:35
22. Many were baptized in...Sidon - Alma 4:4
23. Come and be baptized unto repentance - Alma 7:14
24. After this manner shall ye baptize - 3 Nephi 11:27
25. Believeth not in me, and is not baptized, shall be damned - 3 Nephi 11:34
26. Believe...and be baptized - 3 Nephi 12:2
27. First fruits of repentance is baptism - Moroni 8:25
28. I confer...keys...of baptism - D&C 13
29. Remission of sins by baptism - D&C 19:31
30. Go ye into all the world...baptizing - D&C 68:8
31. Gospel of repentance and of baptism - D&C 874:27

32. Vicarious baptism for the remission of sins - D&C 138:33
33. Be born again...of water - Moses 6:59
34. I confer...keys...of the gospel...of baptism - J.S.H. 1:69
35. After...baptized, we experienced great and glorious blessings - J.S.H. 1:73
36. First principles...Baptism by immersion - 4th Article of Faith
37. Suffer it to be so now...to fulfil all righteousness - Matthew 3:15.

Baptism is Essential (23)

38. Teach all nations, baptizing them - Matthew 28:19
39. Jesus came...and was baptized of John - Mark 1:9
40. He that believeth and is baptized shall be saved - Mark 16:6
41. Jesus also being baptized - Luke 3:21
42. Rejected the counsel of God...being not baptized - Luke 7:30
43. Except a man be born of water...he cannot enter into the Kingdom of God - John 3:5
44. Repent, and be baptized every one of you - Acts 2:38
45. Commanded them to be baptized - Acts 10:48
46. Be baptized, and wash away thy sins - Acts 22:16
47. One Lord, one faith, one baptism - Ephesians 4:5
48. Saved us, by the washing of regeneration - Titus 3:5
49. Baptism doth also now save us - 1 Peter 3:21
50. Commandeth all men that they must...be baptized - 2 Nephi 9:23
51. Need have we, being unholy, to be baptized - 2 Nephi 31:5
52. Whoso believeth in me, and is baptized...shall be saved - 3 Nephi 11:33
53. The commandment: Repent...and be baptized - 3 Nephi 27:20
54. As many as repent and are baptized...and endure...shall be saved - D&C 18:22

Baptism by Immersion (17)

55. After...baptized...a remission of your sins - D&C 55:1
56. They are they who...were baptized...according to the commandment - D&C 76:51
57. Not baptized...shall be damned - D&C 84:74
58. Turn unto me...repent...and be baptized - Moses 6:52

59. Ye must be born again...of water - Moses 6:59
60. When he was baptized, went up straightway out of the water - Matthew 3:16
61. Baptized of him in the river - Mark 1:5
62. Coming up out of the water - Mark 1:10
63. Baptizing...because there was much water there - John 3:23
64. Went down both into the water - Acts 8:38
65. Buried with him by baptism - Romans 6:4
66. One Lord, one faith, one baptism - Ephesians 4:5
67. Buried with him in baptism - Colossians 2:12
68. Were buried in the water - Mosiah 18:14
69. Immerse them in the water - 3 Nephi 11:26
70. Went down into the water and was baptized - 3 Nephi 19:11
71. Had come up out of the water - 3 Nephi 19:13
72. Immerse him or her in the water - D&C 20:74
73. Baptized ... being buried in the water - D&C 76:51
74. Baptism by water, to be immersed D&C 128:12
75. Laid under the water - Moses 6:64
76. Baptism by immersion - 4th Article of Faith
77. Baptized...in the river...confessing - Mark 1:5
78. He that believeth and is baptized - Mark 16:16
79. Repent, and be baptized - Acts 2:38

Qualifications for Baptism (25)

80. They that gladly received his word were baptized - Acts 2:41
81. If thou believest with all thine heart - Acts 8:37
82. Believe on the Lord Jesus Christ - Acts 16:31
83. The baptism of repentance - Acts 19:4
84. Be baptized...having perfect faith - 2 Nephi 9:23
85. Witnesseth...he would be obedient - 2 Nephi 31:7
86. Witness...ye have entered into a covenant - Mosiah 18:10
87. Baptized as a witness... willing to serve God - Mosiah 21:35
88. Whosoever is baptized...shall believe in my name - Mosiah 26:22
89. Who repented of their sins - Alma 6:2
90. Must repent, and be born again - Alma 7:14
91. As many as did believe were baptized - Alma 19:35
92. Whoso repenteth...and desireth to be baptized - 3 Nephi 11:23
93. Become as a little child - 3 Nephi 11:38
94. See that ye are not baptized unworthily - Mormon 9:29
95. Came forth with a broken heart and a contrite spirit - Moroni 6:2
96. Took upon them the name of Christ, having a determination to serve - Moroni 6:3
97. Who humble themselves ... and desire to be baptized - D&C 20:37
98. Arrived unto the years of accountability - D&C 20:71
99. Children shall be baptized...when eight years old - D&C 68:27

100. Received the testimony of Jesus, and believed on his name - D&C 76:51
101. All men...must repent - Moses 6:57
102. What shall they do which are baptized for the dead - 1 Corinthians 15:29

Baptism for The Dead (5)

103. Baptized for those who are dead - D&C 124:29
104. In relation to the baptism for your dead - D&C 127:5
105. Baptism for the dead - D&C 128:1
106. Vicarious baptism for the remission - D&C 138:33

Brigham Young's Testimony Relating to His Baptism

"If all the talent, tact, wisdom, and refinement of the world had been sent to me with the Book of Mormon, and had declared, in the most exalted of earthly eloquence, the truth of it, undertaking to prove it by learning and worldly wisdom, they would have been to me like the smoke which arises only to vanish away. But when I saw a man without eloquence, or talents for public speaking, who could only say, 'I know, by the power of the Holy Ghost, that the Book of Mormon is true, that Joseph Smith is a Prophet of the Lord,' the Holy Ghost proceeding from that individual illuminated my understanding, and light, glory, and immortality were before me.

I was encircled by them, filled with them, and I knew for myself that the testimony of the man was true.... My own judgment, natural endowments, and education bowed to this simple, but mighty testimony. There sits the man who baptized me, brother Eleazer Miller. It filled my system with light, and my soul with joy.

The world, with all its wisdom and power, and with all the glory and gilded show of its kings or potentates, sinks into perfect insignificance, compared with the simple, unadorned testimony of the servant of God." ("Journal of Discourses," 1:91).

Before our baptism, we receive a testimony of Christ through the witness of the Holy Ghost. The experience vitalizes our faith, encourages us to be obedient, convicts us of our sins, and motivates us to repent. Conversion that follows is the fruits of testimony, and may follow our baptism for an indefinite period of time. During this process, spiritual gifts accompany conversion, and are built upon the foundation of testimony.

Lorenzo Snow's Testimony Relating to His Baptism

Lorenzo Snow was baptized and confirmed in June 1836. Recalling his developing testimony, he later said: "I believed the Latter-day Saints had the true religion, and I joined the Church. So far my conversion was merely a matter of reason." He remembered: "I was perfectly satisfied that I had done what was wisdom for me to do under the circumstances." Although he was content for a time with this understanding, he soon yearned for a special manifestation of the Holy Ghost. He said, "I had no manifestation, but I expected one."

"This manifestation did not immediately follow my baptism, as I expected," he recalled. "But, although the time was deferred, when I did receive it, its realization was more perfect, tangible and miraculous than even my strongest hopes had led me to anticipate. One day, while engaged in my studies, some two or three weeks after I was baptized, I began to reflect upon the fact that I had not obtained knowledge of the truth of the work — that I had not realized the fulfillment of the promise: 'He that doeth my will shall know of the doctrine;' and I began to feel very uneasy."

"I laid aside my books, left the house, and wandered around through the fields under the oppressive influence of a gloomy, disconsolate spirit, while an indescribable cloud of darkness seemed to envelop me. I had been accustomed, at the close of the day, to retire for secret prayer to a grove, a short distance from my lodgings, but at this time I felt no inclination to do so. The spirit of prayer had departed, and the heavens seemed like brass over my head. At length, realizing that the usual time had come for secret prayer, I concluded I would not forego my evening service, and, as a matter of formality, knelt as I was in the habit of doing, and in my accustomed retired place, but not feeling as I was wont to feel."

"I had no sooner opened my lips in an effort to pray, than I heard a sound, just above my head, like the rustling of silken robes, and immediately the Spirit of God descended upon me, completely enveloping my whole person, filling me from the crown of my head to the soles of my feet, and O, the joy and happiness I felt! No language can describe the instantaneous transition from a dense cloud of mental and spiritual darkness into a refulgence of light and knowledge, as it was at that time imparted to my understanding. I then received a perfect knowledge that God lives, that Jesus Christ is the Son of God, and of the restoration of the Holy Priesthood, and the fulness of the Gospel."

"It was a complete baptism — a tangible immersion in the heavenly principle or element, the Holy Ghost; and even more real and physical in its effects upon every part of my system than the immersion by water; dispelling forever, so long as reason and memory last, all possibility of doubt or fear in relation to the fact handed down to us historically, that the 'Babe of Bethlehem' is truly the Son of God; also the fact that He is now being revealed to the children of men, and communicating knowledge, the same as in the apostolic times. I was perfectly satisfied, as well I might be, for my expectations were more than realized, I think I may safely say, in an infinite degree."

"I cannot tell how long I remained in the full flow of this blissful enjoyment and divine enlightenment, but it was several minutes before the celestial element, which filled and surrounded me, gradually began to withdraw. On arising from my kneeling posture, with my heart swelling with gratitude to God beyond the power of expression, I felt — I knew that he had conferred on me what only an Omnipotent Being can confer — that which is of greater value than all the wealth and honors worlds can bestow." (Juvenile Instructor, January 15, 1887).

Lorenzo Snow

Phil Hudson's Testimony

I know that the Book of Mormon is the word of God through His servants the prophets to His children in the Last Days. The Spirit has repeatedly borne witness of this to me as I have feasted upon the words of this book. I testify that this companion to the Holy Bible is a second witness of Jesus Christ, and that we will draw near to God by obedience to the principles contained in this inspired work.

I know that Joseph Smith was an instrument in Heavenly Father's hands to usher in the Restoration of the Gospel of Jesus Christ and to prepare the world for the Second Coming of the Savior. It is my testimony that he was a holy apostle who held the fulness of the keys of the priesthood of God, and that by the authority given him by angelic messengers, he established The Church of Jesus Christ of Latter-day Saints.

I know that, in the words of Daniel, the Gospel will roll forth as a stone cut out of a mountain, until it fills the whole earth. I testify that missionaries have been called and set apart to preach the Gospel, that they do so with power and authority beyond their mortal capacity, and that they are saviors on Mount Zion to those who will hearken to their words.

I testify that the ordinances of the Gospel, beginning with baptism, are available to all of Heavenly Father's children.

I testify that the heavens are open, and that today God not only communicates with us through His prophets, but also that He speaks to each of us individually by the power of the Holy Ghost. I know by my own experience that the Light of Christ illuminates the way before us. I know that The Plan of Salvation is The Plan of Redemption. I know that Heavenly Father's spirit children are so important to Him that He conceived a Plan whereby they might return to His presence in the full stature of their spirits.

I know that I may one day stand before Him in spotless white garments, free of the stain of sin, because of the sacrifice of our Savior Jesus Christ. While I may not fully comprehend His Atonement, I know that it is real, because I feel my Heavenly Father's forgiveness and unconditional love when I have repented of my sins. I have felt that love ever since I was received into the Church through the portal of baptism.

It is my testimony that through my membership in The Church of Jesus Christ of Latter-day Saints, I may participate in all of the saving ordinances of the Gospel, and that, in particular, the ordinances of the temple will bind my family together forever.

I know that family exaltation in the Celestial Kingdom of God is the crown jewel of immortality and eternal life, and that God's Plan is designed to bring my family happiness in this life, and a fulness of joy in the life to come.

I know that God's Rest is within my grasp if I listen to the voice of the Spirit, am prompted to act, and endure to the end in righteousness.

Philip M. Hudson

Alma asked the question that continues to demand our attention: "And now, behold, I say unto you my brethren, if ye have experienced a change of heart, and if ye have felt to sing the song of redeeming love," that you experienced at your baptism, "I would ask, can ye feel so now?" (Alma 5:26).

About The Author

Phil Hudson and his wife Jan have 7 children and over 20 grandchildren. They enjoy spending time with their family at their cabin nestled in the Selkirk Mountains, on the shore of Priest Lake, the crown jewel of North Idaho. Phil had a successful family dental practice in Spokane, Washington for 43 years, before retiring in 2015. He has an eclectic mix of hobbies, and enjoys riding motorcycles and ATVs. In his free time, he can be found hiking, boating, cycling, snow biking, and traveling with Jan. He always finds time, however, to record his thoughts on his laptop. He understands Isaac Asimov's response when he was asked: "If you knew that you only had 10 minutes left to live, what would you do with your time?" He answered: "I'd type faster."

When this volume was published, Phil and Jan were serving as missionaries for The Church of Jesus Christ of Latter-day Saints, in the Kingdom of Tonga. While there, they celebrated their 50th wedding anniversary.

There are
no shades of grey
after we have received
the ordinance of baptism and
our minds become "single to God."
(D&C 88:68). If we try to have it both
ways, our double mindedness will create
intellectual instability and spiritual
schizophrenia, for we cannot
be servants of the Devil
while purporting to
follow Christ.

By The Author

Essays

- Volume One: Spray From The Ocean Of Thought
- Volume Two: Ripples On A Pond
- Volume Three: Serendipitous Meanderings
- Volume Four: Presents Of Mind
- Volume Five: Mental Floss
- Volume Six: Fitness Training For The Mind And Spirit

First Principles and Ordinances Series

- Faith - Our Hearts Are Changed
- Repentance - A Broken Heart and a Contrite Spirit
- Baptism - One Hundred And One Reasons Why We Are Baptized
- The Holy Ghost - That We Might Have His Spirit To Be With Us
- The Sacrament - This Do In Remembrance Of Me

Book of Mormon Commentary

- Volume One: Born In The Wilderness
- Volume Two: Voices From The Dust
- Volume Three: Journey To Cumorah

Doctrine & Covenants Commentary

    Volume One - Sections 1 - 34
    Volume Two - Sections 35 - 57

Minute Musings: Spontaneous Combustions of Thought

    Volume One
    Volume Two
    Volume Three

Calendars:

    In His Own Words: Discovering William Tyndale
    As I Think About The Savior
    Scriptural Symbols

Children's Books

    Muddy, Muddy
    The Thirteen Articles of Faith
    Happy Birthday

Doctrinal Themes

    The House of the Lord

A Thought For Each Day of the Year

    Faith
    Repentance
    Baptism
    The Holy Ghost
    The Sacrament
    The House of the Lord
    The Plan of Salvation
    The Atonement
    Revelation

Professional Publications

    Diode Laser Soft Tissue Surgery Volume One
    Diode Laser Soft Tissue Surgery Volume Two
    Diode Laser Soft Tissue Surgery Volume Three

These, and other titles, are available from online retailers.

The ordinance that admits us into the fold of Christ must be carried out without ambiguity, for except we "be born of water and of the Spirit," declared the Savior, we "cannot enter into the kingdom of God." (John 3:5).

Quid magis possum dicere?

www.ingramcontent.com/pod-product-compliance
Lightning Source LLC
Chambersburg PA
CBHW060508240426
43661CB00007B/955